Fisheries By-Products
Technology

other AVI books on food science

Fishery By-Products
Technology

by JULIUS BRODY

Consulting Food Technologist,
Formerly Research Director on Fishery By-Products
Technology for Fishery Products Ltd., St. Johns,
Newfoundland, and Dehydrating Process Co., Woburn, Mass.

WESTPORT, CONNECTICUT

THE AVI PUBLISHING COMPANY, INC.

1965

Printed in the United States of America
BY MACK PRINTING COMPANY, EASTON, PENNSYLVANIA

Dedicated to

Professor Bernard Emerson Proctor

May 5, 1901 – September 24, 1959

A scholar and a gentleman who was endowed
with the rare ability of inspiring his students
and associates at the Massachusetts Institute of
Technology with an enthusiasm that enabled
them to attain loftier heights.

Foreword

The transformation of the processing of foodstuffs from an art to a science has been slowly evolving over the past 50 years. In the past decade, however, with the remarkable advances in the sister disciplines of microbiology, biochemistry, mathematics, and physics, an accelerated rate of progress has occurred and which now has resulted in the new discipline of "food science."

Throughout the civilized world today, the impact of food science is being felt in the form of better foods, more convenient foods, and better nutrition. This is not limited to the United States alone but may be seen in Europe and in Asia as well.

The sea food industry, up to approximately the beginning of World War II, was, in terms of industrial technology as well as in terms of marketing aspects, well behind other segments of the food industry. Science and technology, integrated in recent years with developments in refrigeration, thermal processing, packaging, and marketing, have brought into being a new type of sea food industry—a more dynamic one and one which, like other segments of the food industry, no longer sells raw products but rather converts these, in one form or another, into processed products and in so doing adds value to the products.

Each of these conversions, i.e., freezing, canning, or dehydration, as a modern processing procedure, involves a number of unit operations. In the course of these processing operations, by-products are created which must be either discarded or utilized.

As the population of the world increases at an explosive rate, scientists, economists, and humanists are concerning themselves, with an ever-increasing awareness, with man's ability to feed and clothe himself at the turn of the next century. It is, therefore, only natural that, since the seas cover some 70.8 per cent of the entire world surface, people interested in the problems of feeding our expanding population have turned to the marine products which is one of the sources as yet not completely exploited.

While several books have appeared recently dealing with the products of fisheries, most of these have been particularly pointed toward the technology of harvesting sea foods and the processing and preservation thereof. Relatively little space has been devoted to utilization of by-products. Those who have an understanding of the economics of food processing realize that economical and efficient utilization of foods and of food processing is possible only when one is able to utilize all parts of an animal. The meat industry, obviously, is the best example of this.

If meaningful advances are to be made in the utilization of the oceans for the feeding of man, if lowest costs of edible fishery products are to be achieved, attention must be paid to by-product utilization. Optimal utilization of by-products will not only result in better utilization of our resources but also in lower-cost foods.

The present volume is the only one which, to my knowledge, is devoted entirely to by-products of sea foods—their production and utilization. Mr. Brody, the author of the present volume, has had 30 years of close association with various phases of the food industry and has been particularly active in research in and production of fishery by-products. He holds several patents in by-product development and utilization. Thus, this book is one that fills a void in our literature in this most important field and which will help to solve some of mankind's present and future problems in feeding itself.

S. A. GOLDBLITH, Ph.D.

Professor of Food Science and
    Executive Officer
Department of Nutrition and Food Science
Massachusetts Institute of Technology
Cambridge, Mass.

Preface

The primary purpose of this book is to provide technical information and suggestions that may be useful in accomplishing a reduction of waste in perhaps the greatest of our natural resources, i.e., the fishery industry. Conservation of fish resources can best be carried out by better utilization of fishery by-products. These by-products are largely derived from the inedible portions that constitute approximately 50% of the fish carcass material of the catch. Neglect of up-grading the potential of fishery by-products utilization constitutes a serious waste in that, at present, minimum returns are obtained from the inedible portion of fish instead of maximum returns which could readily be obtained by the application of the principles and procedures outlined herein.

To illustrate this point further: to date (1965) the fishery by-products manufactured by fishery processors are limited largely to fish meal and fish oil. The entrails, a most valuable potential source of a large variety of biochemical, pharmaceutical, and nutritional products, are still being discarded by fishermen during the "gutting" operation which takes place aboard the ship right after the fish are caught.

The reason given for this wasteful act is that the fishing vessels are not equipped with proper refrigeration facilities to store the entrails, which are highly labile. Furthermore, the crew members do not possess the know-how for freezing fish viscera aboard the ship and subsequently thawing them out properly. Fortunately, a way to overcome this deficiency has been developed by the excellent research carried out on freezing and thawing fish "in the round," i.e., freezing and thawing the entire fish.

This thorough and exhaustive research which was carried out by the U. S. Fish and Wildlife Service Laboratory in East Boston, Mass., under the able leadership of Samuel R. Pottinger and Joseph F. Puncochar, has made possible the recovery of entrails from frozen fish without any sign of deterioration even after several weeks of storage aboard ship. Accordingly, anyone can now take advantage of this freezing and thawing process and recover valuable by-products from the entrails. With "shore" fishing, i.e., fishing that starts in the morning and ends at night, there is no problem in preserving entrails because of the relatively short time involved between catching and processing.

In pursuing his major objective of promoting the reduction of waste of valuable fishery raw materials by converting them into useful by-products, the author presents what, hopefully, is a comprehensive summary of the manufacture of practically all fishery by-products and of the industrial applications of the by-products.

The subject matter of the book is divided into three major parts: Part I describes the by-products obtained from the outer portion of fish, i.e., skins and scales, Part II discusses derivatives from entrails, and Part III deals with by-products obtained from fish scrap remaining after gutting and filleting, or by using the whole fish, e.g., trash fish. While most chapters fall sharply within this division, a few chapters have been placed arbitrarily in a major subdivision, because the product discussed could be produced from more than one part of the fish. For example, liquid fish glue could be made from skins and scales, and therefore it belongs in Part I, but it could also be produced from fish heads which would justify its classification in Part III. This chapter was put into Part I because most of the fish glues, at least the best grades of fish glues, are produced from fish skins.

Another objective in writing this book is to disseminate the valuable information on fishery by-products manufacture and utilization among the developing seacoast countries, making them more conscious of the great potential for industrial progress and development existing in their own "back yards." The adaptation of the principles and procedures outlined herein for producing a large variety of fishery by-products would also tend to stimulate interest in their fishery industries.

A combination of these two phases of such a vital industry would tend to advance the economic independence of the developing countries and would result in a general improvement in their standards of living. Because of the far reaching beneficial effects that the fishery industry, together with its by-products manufacture, could exert on developing seacoast countries, the less expensive and the less involved manufacturing procedures for fish meal and fish oil production are described along with some of the more advanced procedures, to serve as a starting point. For example, a modern plant for fish meal and fish oil production might cost from $25 to $50 thousand; yet a native in South America, Africa, or Asia can start producing fish meal, by using crude home-made equipment for as little as from $25 to $50 and applying that meal as a supplement to his poultry feed. To be sure, such fish meal will not have the same nutritional qualities as fish meal produced in a modern plant, but it could still serve a useful purpose in a limited way. "Half a loaf is better than none."

This strong desire of the author to serve the millions of people whose technology is less advanced than is that of the United States is responsible, on occasion, for the placing of a seemingly inordinate amount of attention on processes which are no longer generally used in the United States.

These older processes, it is believed, could occupy positions of great importance in the economies of developing countries.

A few topics in the text are perhaps inadequately covered. This is due to the paucity of basic information in the literature; not to a lack of diligence on the part of the author.

It is hoped that this book will arouse further interest in this vital field and will serve as a stimulus for further research by food technologists, food scientists and nutritionists, and others in the fishery industry.

Sincere thanks and appreciation are extended to Professor Samuel A. Goldblith, Department of Nutrition and Food Science, Massachusetts Institute of Technology, Cambridge, Mass., for his help in making a number of valuable corrections and suggestions on the Fish Protein Concentrate chapter, and for writing the Foreword.

The author also wishes to express his gratitude to Professor Philip M. Richardson for his generous help and encouragement. Professor Richardson applied to this text his broad knowledge of technical writing and experience that he gained during the years he was associated with the Food Technology Department at Massachusetts Institute of Technology.

Special thanks and appreciation are extended to:

The Fisheries Research Board of Canada, Ottawa, Canada and to Dr. J. C. Stevenson, Editor of the Board's publications, for granting permission to refer to many pertinent Canadian Government publications.

The many firms who generously furnished pictures of their equipment and flow charts.

The U. S. Fish and Wildlife Service, Washington, D. C. for furnishing the many reprints of their publications.

The author is very grateful to the following experts for reviewing various portions of the text and for their comments and helpful suggestions:

Robert S. Harris, M.I.T.

Cecil G. Dunn, M.I.T.

Sanford A. Miller, M.I.T.

R. E. Young, University of Mass., Waltham Field Station, Waltham, Mass.

Edward J. MacLeod, General Manager, Gloucester By-Products, Inc., Gloucester, Mass.

Earl P. McFee, Laboratory Director, Gorton's of Gloucester, Inc., Gloucester, Mass.

Mrs. H. B. Kenyon, President, Rogers Isinglass and Glue Co., Gloucester, Mass.

William L. Abramowitz, Chemist and Vice Chairman of the Board, Carlon Products Corp., Boston, Mass.

Richard Hands, Horticulturist, Mass.   Horticultural Society, Boston, Mass.

L. R. Moresi, Director, Shark Division.   Ocean Leather Corp., Newark, N. J.

William I. Gorfinkle, General Manager, J. O. Whitten Co., Winchester, Mass.

Ezra Levin, President, VioBin Corp., Monticello, Ill.

Irving B. Roberts, Field Editor, Boot and Shoe Recorder, Boston, Mass.

E. G. Reuter, President, Leys, Christie & Co., Inc. New York, N. Y.

Melvin Castleman, Chemical Engineer, Lloyd Laboratories, Peabody, Mass.

Edwin J. Kaine, Manager, John J. Riley Co., Woburn, Mass.

Samuel B. Beaser, Clinical Associate in Medicine, Harvard Medical School, Boston, Mass.

R. G. Ackman, Fisheries Research Board of Canada, Halifax, Nova Scotia.

Charles Best, College of Medicine, University of Toronto, Toronto, Canada.

Charles Butler, Bureau of Commercial Fisheries, Washington 25, D. C.

John Dassow, Bureau of Commercial Fisheries, Seattle, Washington

A. M. Fisher, Connaught Medical Research Laboratories, Toronto, Ont.

Hans Fisher, Dept. of Animal Science, Rutgers University, New Brunswick, N. J.

Herman S. Groninger, 'Jr., Bureau of Commercial Fisheries, Seattle, Wash.

William J. Hanna, Department of Soils, Rutgers University, New Brunswick, N. J.

Neva L. Karrick, Bureau of Commercial Fisheries, Seattle, Washington

L. Carlyle Morse, 75 Bond St., Gloucester, Mass.

Robert E. Norland, Norland Products, Inc., Cranbury, N. J.

Morris Omansky, Consulting Chemist and Rubber Technologist, Boston, Mass.

S. R. Pottinger, Bureau of Commercial Fisheries, Boston 10, Mass.

Lawrence R. Spiegel, 66 Summer St., Andover, Mass.

Maurice Stansby, Bureau of Commercial Fisheries, Seattle, Wash.

Mary Thompson, Bureau of Commercial Fisheries, Pascagoula, Miss.

Robert D. Usen, President, and General Manager, Usen Canning Co., Woburn, Mass.

C. Winchester, Bureau of Commercial Fisheries, Boston 10, Mass.

JULIUS BRODY

Boston, Massachusetts
September 1965

Contents

CHAPTER 1

Liquid Fish Glue

PLACE OF LIQUID FISH GLUE IN THE FOUR MAJOR CLASSIFICATIONS OF ADHESIVES

The various types of available adhesives are generally divided into four major classifications, each of which may be further subdivided with respect to type. The four major classifications are as follows: (A) adhesives derived from vegetables, (B) adhesives derived from animal proteins, (C) synthetic resin adhesives, and (D) inorganic cements.

A further subdivision of this classification is as follows: (**A**) **Adhesives Derived from Vegetables:** (1) starches, (2) dextrins, (3) cellulose adhesives, (4) natural gums, (5) soybean adhesives, (6) rubber latex, and (7) natural resins. (**B**) **Adhesives Derived from Animal Proteins:** (1) animal glues, (2) *liquid fish glue*, (3) blood albumin glues, (4) casein adhesives. (**C**) **Synthetic Resin Adhesives:** (1) urea-formaldehyde, (2) phenol-formaldehyde, (3) resorcinol-formaldehyde, (4) melamine-formaldehyde, (5) furan derivative resins, (6) polyurethans, (7) silicone resins, (8) acrylic resins, (9) vinyl resins, (10) allyl resins. (**D**) **Inorganic Cements:** (1) sodium silicate, (2) plaster of paris, (3) lime mortar, (4) sorel cement, (5) litharge, (6) iron cement, (7) sulfur cements, (8) dental cements.

Notwithstanding the extensive list of the various types of adhesives available, each one of these products has specific properties that produce optimum results under specified conditions. In some instances there are overlappings, yet fundamentally, each type is best suited for specific purposes under a definite set of conditions.

Similarly, liquid fish glue has its optimum usage and application as described in this chapter under the section entitled "Uses of Liquid Fish Glue."

PRESENT STATUS OF LIQUID FISH GLUE MANUFACTURE IN THE UNITED STATES

With the advent of the many new types of adhesives, some of which embody certain desirable characteristics that are lacking in liquid fish glue, the market for liquid fish glue in the United States has shrunk considerably. This critical situation could have been avoided to a large extent by a research program designed to impart to the glue some additional desirable properties to meet the demand for a more readily acceptable product. For example, a reduction in the hygroscopic property of liquid fish glue would constitute a useful modification and would upgrade its value as an adhesive.

Liquid fish glue as it is produced at present inherently possesses several useful adhesive properties that still render it a highly desirable product. These features are listed under the heading, "Advantages in Using Liquid Fish Glue" (see page 16).

Another cause for the decline of this industry in the United States is the shortage of the principal raw material, salted cod skins, used in the manufacture of liquid fish glue (Stansby 1963; Pottinger 1964). It is correct to state that salted cod skins are a rare commodity on the domestic market because of the drastic reduction in the salt cod industry in the United States. However, the fish skin shortage is not as serious as it appears to be. There is a considerable supply of cod skins in Nova Scotia, Newfoundland, and Iceland. After the proper washing and drying of the skins at their point of origin (Morse 1964), they can be imported economically to the United States and serve as an inexpensive raw material for liquid fish glue production.

Fish glue was considered a nearly universal adhesive until the wide variety of synthetic adhesives for special uses captured much of the market. According to Norland (1964), synthetic polyvinyl acetate emulsions are liquid and less expensive than liquid fish glue. Excellent fish glue, that might compete on the market as an adhesive, can still be made if sufficient research is carried out to attain this end.

The development of a nearly multipurpose adhesive would be most desirable in developing countries, in preference to the employment of many different kinds of adhesives.

HISTORY OF LIQUID FISH GLUE PRODUCTION

We are indebted to the inventive genius of John S. Rogers of Gloucester, Massachusetts, for developing the manufacture of liquid fish glue about 100 years ago.

Up to that time, liquid fish glue as we know it now, did not exist. Mr. Rogers, while engaged in farming activity, noticed the adhesive properties of fish skins while spreading them on his fields as fertilizer. They actually stuck to his shoes. Accordingly, he began to experiment with the fish skins that were so plentiful in his area, attempting to extract their adhesive substance.

Using simple home-made equipment, Rogers ingeniously assembled a system for the manufacture of liquid fish glue and patented the process. This marked the beginning of the Rogers Isinglass and Glue Co., Gloucester, Mass., which is still owned and controlled by the third generation of his descendants.

Rogers' invention is completely illustrated in one picture which still adorns the company stationery and represents, in miniature form, his process for liquid fish glue manufacture. It consists of a tea-kettle for producing steam, a tomato can for cooking fish skins, and shallow pans to hold the thin glue liquor directly under a couple of steam-heated rotating cylinders for concentrating the glue liquor. A small model of this device is located in the headquarters of the firm.

The principles involved in this simple invention were used to produce a full-sized plant, and for 100 years, the Rogers Isinglass and Glue Co.[1] produced several grades of top quality liquid fish glues (Kenyon 1963).

It should be noted that prior to 1960, the principal producer of liquid fish glue was the LePage Company, Gloucester, Mass.

SOURCES OF RAW MATERIAL

Two major sources of glue stock are available for the manufacture of liquid fish glue. They are: (1) fish skins, (2) fish heads.

The skins and heads of "ground-fish" such as cod, haddock, cusk, sole, pollack, and hake, whether salted or fresh, constitute the major sources of glue stock used in the manufacture of liquid fish glue. The skins originate from fish that contain less than one per cent oil. Accordingly, glue made from them is also very low in oil, which property is very desirable, since the presence of oil in a liquid fish glue reduces its adhesive strength.

The most valuable raw materials for the manufacture of liquid fish glue are the skins of cod and cusk, because their skins are thicker than those of any of the other fishes enumerated above; therefore, they furnish more collagen and yield more glue. Salted fish skins are preferred to fresh skins in the manufacture of liquid fish glue for the following reasons: first, from a production-scheduling standpoint, it is easier to handle salted skins without any undue hurry to prevent spoilage, since they are preserved; second, salted skins can be shipped to the liquid fish glue plant from a number of sources, increasing, thereby, the availability of the raw stock without lessening its quality.

Salting of fish skins is, however, only a stopgap procedure since it preserves the skins for only a relatively short time. For preservation in extended storage or for economical long distance transportation of fish skins, it is best to wash, dry, and bale the skins at or near the source. When salted cod skins are shipped, the freight cost on the salt and water is high enough to render their subsequent manufacture into liquid fish glue uneconomical.

---

[1] The Rogers Isinglass and Glue Co. is listed in the 1964 edition of "Directory of New England Manufacturers" as employing 13 people.

In the preservation of fish skins, it is best to wash the skins and dry them in air tunnel driers at low temperatures with rapid air circulation. In areas where sunlight is abundant and the relative humidities are low, the washed skins could be adequately dried by outdoor exposure.

Fish heads are used fresh. Liquid fish glue prepared from fish heads is inferior to that prepared from fish skins.

MANUFACTURING PROCEDURES

The manufacturing procedures for the production of liquid fish glue from (a) fish skins and (b) fish heads differ somewhat, although fundamentally they are similar. A detailed description of both methods follows:

Fish Skins

Washing of Stock.—The skins of cod and cusk or of the other groundfish, whether they are salted or not, must first be washed in cold running water to freshen them, as well as to remove foreign particles. If salted skins are used, considerably more time must be allotted to the washing to remove the salt.

The washing of salted skins to be used as glue stock may be carried out in any conveniently assembled contrivance that allows a thorough rinsing of the stock in running cold water for 12 hours or longer to remove all adhering foreign matter and to reduce its salt content to less than 0.1% chlorides in the wash water.

A convenient way of carrying out the washing operation consists of placing the stock in a roller mill washer, which consists of a cylindrical tank about 18 ft. in diameter and 5 ft. high. The stock is covered with water, and is agitated by means of a heavy wooden roller shaped like a truncated cone, which is shorter than the radius of the tank and which is attached at its smaller end to the center of the cylinder or tank.

Since the heavier section of the cone at its periphery is resting on the bottom of the tank, the cone simultaneously revolves and rotates in the washer, gently stirring the swelled-up stock. While this rotation is going on, the water inside the tank is gradually and continuously being changed by a small stream of water admitted at the top, while an equal amount of water flows out at the bottom.

The washing is continued until less than 0.1% of chlorides remains in the wash water. Reduction of the salt content to less than 0.1% is essential because a salt residual renders the finished glue hygroscopic. Whenever salt is present, the washing usually requires 15 to 18 hr. With fresh stock, 1 to 2 hrs. of washing is sufficient.

After the preliminary washing of the stock for salt removal, it is advisable to treat the washed stock by the following three steps in the order given (Smith 1943; Stansby 1963): (a) two-tenths of one per cent caustic soda or saturated lime, (b) two-tenths of one per cent hydrochloric acid. Use a sufficient amount of acid to wash out the alkali, and (c) final washing in cold running water.

Cooking of Washed Stock.—After the washing, the plumped-up raw stock is transferred to false-bottomed, rectangular, steam-jacketed "cookers." The false bottoms are covered with finely perforated screens. The stock is covered with approximately an equal weight of water, and steam is turned on. Johnston (1935) recommended adding $1/2$ gal. of glacial acetic acid per ton of washed skins prior to cooking to increase the clarity of the glue.

Cooking is continued for about eight hours. Subsequently, the dilute glue liquor is drawn off into a mixing tank and is simultaneously strained through the perforated screen during its passage, to remove suspended particles. This cooking constitutes the "first run."

Immediately after the "first run" extract of dilute glue liquor has been drawn off, the partially extracted stock is again covered with water and it is recooked at a somewhat higher temperature than in the previous "run." After the second cooking, the glue liquor is again drawn off into a mixing tank.

This cooking constitutes the "second run," which is weaker in adhesive strength than the "first run." Depending on the condition of the already twice extracted stock, frequently a "third run" is made. The strength of the glue decreases, however, with each successive run so that the "third run" product is considerably weaker than that of the previous two "runs."

Finally, the residue of the cooked stock is either dried and used as a supplement to poultry feed or to fertilizer (Tressler and Lemon 1951), or is added to the next freshened batch of stock.

This residue is particularly valuable as a poultry feed supplement since it contains at least 50% proteins in an easily digestible and assimilable form. Fish heads contain, in addition to protein, a high precentage of tricalcium phosphate, which is an essential ingredient in poultry feed formulations.

In the washing and cooking of skins, the principles of counter-current circulation should be followed.

Addition of Preservatives.—After all of the dilute glue liquor is in the mixing tanks, a suitable germicide is added to this highly perishable product and is thoroughly mixed with the liquor. This treatment is helpful in preventing microbial breakdown of the proteinaceous matter during delay in processing. Morse (1964) stated, however, that preservation of glue liquor for any considerable length of time is impractical because of its high water content. Clean apparatus and continuous methods could produce a very clean product, rendering the addition of preservatives unnecessary.

From this tank the liquor is pumped into a holding tank which is situated close to the evaporator. As it is fed into the evaporator, it is again strained through a fine wire screen to remove any residual particles, the presence of which could interfere with evaporation as well as with the use and application of the finished glue.

Evaporation.—Open pan evaporators that are exposed to atmospheric pressure are now outmoded and have given way to vacuum concentrators.

The type of vacuum evaporator particularly suited for concentrating dilute glue liquors is one that either reduces or eliminates foam formation during evaporation and subjects the glue liquor to a minimum processing temperature for the shortest possible time. These features and other desirable requirements are best met by using a processor such as the recently developed apparatus shown in Fig. 1, which is described as follows (Gerbasi 1964):

The dilute liquid fish glue is admitted into the feed section which is located above the thermal wall and is distributed in a thin uniform film by the centrifugal action of the rotor blades. Turbulence is imparted to the film as it spirals downward permitting a high rate of heat transfer into the film and in the formation of vapor. The concentrated material exits through the bottom discharge section while vapors rise upward through the separating section and out the vapor opening.

There is a number of advantages in using a processor of this type. They are as follows: (1) processing is completed in one pass, eliminating recirculation of the liquid, (2) localized overheating even with high heat flux is prevented by the action of the rotor blades, which maintain the thin film in continuous turbulent motion and insure continuous coverage of the heat transfer surface, (3) the time of product exposure to heat is extremely short because only a small amount of material is processed at one time; this feature renders the processor particularly suitable for concentrating heat sensitive products, (4) the processor is suitable for concentrating highly viscous or foamy materials, and (5) floor space requirement is small.

Improved Evaporator for Concentrating Glue Liquor (Fig. 1)

Operation of Evaporator.—(1) The drive unit provides the torque and speed for the rotor and blade system, (2) the rotor shaft thrust bearing supports the rotor and blade assembly, which bearing and seal are designed to facilitate cleaning and servicing of the unit, (3) the vapor outlet permits full exhausting of the vapor from the separator section, (4) the entrainment separator and vapor outlet section may be of several designs, the proper choice of design depends on degree of product foaming,

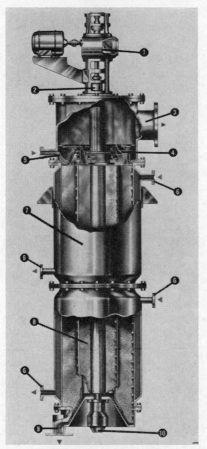

Courtesy of Rodney Hunt Machine Co.,
Orange, Mass.

FIG. 1. TURBA-FILM PROCESSOR

Improved evaporator for concentrating glue
liquor

characteristics of the vapor, etc., (5) the feed inlet at the top of the thermal section provides for uniform distribution of the feed material over the thermal wall, (6) heating medium inlets and outlets provide steam, Dowtherm, or other media for the compartments of the thermal section, (7) the thermal section consists of one or more jacketed units, (8) rotor and blade may vary to match design requirements, (9) product discharge head can be one of three types depending on the characteristics of the product as it reaches this point in the processor, and (10) the bottom bearing can be either external or internal.

The glue liquor is concentrated until it contains from 50 to 55% solids, which corresponds to a predetermined viscosity measured at a definite temperature. Temperature constancy during viscosity measurements is essential, since small temperature variations in the sample would markedly affect the results.

After the batch of glue has been concentrated to the proper consistency, small amounts of volatile essential oils, such as oil of sassafras or oil of wintergreen, are mixed with it. These essential oils are added primarily to mask the fishy odor of the glue, but simultaneously they enhance its keeping quality, supplementing the function of the preservatives. After the preparation of the batch is completed, it is drawn off into barrels or dispensed into jars.

Fish Heads

Fish heads, unlike fish skins, are usually obtained as fresh rather than salted stock. The procedure for extracting glue from heads differs somewhat from that of extracting glue from skins, as discussed in the immediately preceding sections.

Some of the differences are as follows: (1) some bleaching agents, such as sulfurous acid or sodium bisulfite, are added, (2) usually 1 to 2 gal. of glacial acetic acid are added per ton of stock during cooking to soften the bone and to aid in clarifying the glue, (3) still larger amounts of preservatives and essential oils are added than when processing fish skins.

The adhesive strength of this glue is considerably less than that of glue prepared from fish skins.

Morse (1964) stated that making glue from fish heads is mostly a matter of making fish meal. Due to the tonnage of the raw material extensive washing and cooking from the glue making standpoint alone does not seem to be practical. Accordingly, in practice, washing is skimpy and cooking is carried out primarily to reduce stickiness in the fish meal drier. The resulting glue may be of any grade and usually contains much salt.

TESTING OF LIQUID FISH GLUE

A number of tests can be applied to liquid glue in order to evaluate its usefulness and grade. These tests are the following: viscosity, gel point, moisture, speed of set, drying and hygroscopicity.[2] However, these determinations, which are relatively simple to perform, give at best only an indirect indication of the inherent value of the product.

The direct test that expresses the adhesive strength in concrete form, but is rather laborious and lengthy in performance, is the "shear test,"

---

[2] For detailed description of these tests, see Tressler and Lemon 1951, pp. 529–532.

which expresses the actual joint strength. This determination gives the force, in pounds per square inch, that is necessary to shear apart two blocks of wood glued together under strictly specified conditions. This test can be used to establish a correlation with the simpler tests that are being carried out daily in the laboratory, in order to evaluate their merits and to properly grade the glues.

The Shear Test

The shear test was developed by the U. S. Forest Products Laboratory, Madison, Wis., and is described on page 2 of the Federal Standard Stock Catalog C-G-463. It is essentially as follows:

Properly seasoned hardwood blocks such as maple or birch $7/8 \times 2^1/2 \times 12$ in. are used for the test. The wood should have a specific gravity of at least 0.65. The moisture content of the wood shall not be more than ten per cent. The glue is thinly but evenly spread with a brush on both sides of the contact surfaces. The blocks are joined at the treated surfaces and are placed under a 50 lb. pressure for 48 hr. at 70° to 80°F. and a relative humidity of 45 to 55%. After this period, each block is cut into smaller 2 in. units. Finally the smaller glued blocks are subjected to a shearing pressure using the Olsen Universal Testing Machine, which shears apart the two glued areas. The adhesive strength of the joints is obtained by dividing the total force applied to the total glued area and is expressed in pounds per square inch. When this test is carried out under uniform conditions of temperature, humidity, pressure, similarity of wood, thickness of glue applied, etc., it gives very accurate and consistent comparisons between various grades of glues evaluated.

Practical Plant Test

A practical test that can be used readily in production to determine the proper point of concentration is to weigh one gallon of concentrate. If it weighs $9^3/4$ lb. per gal. then it must have been concentrated to the proper point. However, this test is not fully reliable.

Viscosity Determinations Using the Brookfield Synchro-Lectric Viscometer

Introduction—The viscosities of liquid fish glues can best be determined by the up-to-date Synchro-Lectric Viscometer (Brookfield 1964), an instrument which embodies a considerable amount of skill and ingenuity and represents one of the nearest approaches to a universal type of viscometer ever devised. It measures readily, with accuracy and speed, the flow properties of liquids, covering a wide range of viscosities. For example, with two models of this instrument (Figs. 2 and 3), we can determine the flow characteristics of materials ranging from the thinnest pharmaceutical lotion to extremely viscous material such as molten glass, at elevated temperatures, by merely changing one simple basic part, i.e., the cylinder or disc spindle, and its rotational speed. The Brookfield Synchro-Lectric Viscometer is, therefore, especially valuable as a research and control instrument for the many industrial formulations and applications involving liquid fish glue as a basic ingredient.

Courtesy of Brookfield Engineering Laboratories,
Stoughton, Mass.

Fig. 2. Brookfield Synchro-Lectric Viscometer Model LV

With four spindles to measure fluids in low and medium viscosity regions

Principle of the Brookfield Synchro-Lectric Viscometer and Its Mode of Operation.—The Brookfield Synchro-Lectric Viscometer operates on a simple, time-proved principle. A synchronous (constant-speed) motor rotates a cylinder or disc spindle in the material under test.

The coupling between the driving motor and the driven spindle is a calibrated beryllium-copper spiral spring. The outer coil of the spring is attached to a dial which is driven at constant speed by the motor. The inner coil of the spring is secured to the spindle shaft which is supported by an almost-frictionless jewel bearing. A pointer is also attached solidly to the spindle shaft and is positioned just above the dial.

When the system is at rest the spring is completely relaxed and a "zero" relationship is established between the pointer and dial. When the motor is running and the spindle is immersed in the test material, the viscous drag causes the spindle (and thus the pointer) to "fall back" in relation to the dial to a point where the wound-up tension on the calibrated spring equals the viscous drag on the spindle.

Courtesy of Brookfield Engineering Laboratories,
Stoughton, Mass.

FIG. 3. BROOKFIELD SYNCHRO-
LECTRIC VISCOMETER MODEL RV

With seven spindles to measure
materials in medium and heavy
viscosity ranges

The resulting angular relationship of pointer and dial from "zero" position is a measure of viscosity when computed in terms of the particular spindle and speed used.

By utilizing a combination of speeds and spindles, many ranges and shear conditions can be covered by one instrument.

At a standard viscosity, low grade glue may contain 55% solids and weigh nearly 10 lb. per gal., while a high grade glue would contain closer to 40% solids, at the same viscosity and weigh around $9^1/_2$ lb., or less, per gal.

A ton of skins will produce about the same weight of dry glue regardless of whether it is of high or low grade; thus, the yield in gallons of high grade glue is greater than that of low grade glue because the former contains more water at the standard viscosity.

REDUCTION OF MINERAL CONTENT FROM STICKWATER
BY VARIOUS METHODS OF DIALYSIS

Introduction

Stickwater, or fish waste liquor, is the dilute liquid fish product obtained during fish meal production by cooking fish scrap or whole fish, followed by pressing the cooked material and centrifuging the press liquor. The aqueous effluent may contain from 20 to 65% (Ingvaldsen 1929) of the total nitrogenous content in dissolved or dispersed form.

Stickwater, as the name implies, has considerable "sticky" or adhesive value. When stickwater is concentrated and dried, however, it becomes very hygroscopic, which renders it practically worthless for use as an adhesive. Relatively high salt concentration in stickwater is a causative agent of hygroscopicity. Attempts have been made to reduce the salt content by dialysis. By the process of dialysis, salts diffuse or sieve through the pores of a semipermeable membrane which does not allow the passage of the colloidal particles of liquid fish glue.

Continuous Process With Membrane Dialyzer[3]

Viscose tubing ordinarily used as sausage casing, was applied by L. F. Smith (1932) for simple dialysis. Smith used a 150 ft. long viscose tube with a $^{15}/_{16}$ in. diameter coiled around a wooden frame and placed in a tank $2^1/_2 \times 3 \times 2^1/_2$ ft., filled with water (Fig. 4). Water varying from 151° to 160°F. circulated through the tank. Stickwater flowed through the

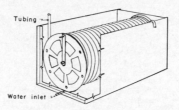

Courtesy of Fisheries Research Board
of Canada Pacific Experiment Station

FIG. 4.   APPARATUS FOR CONTINUOUS DIALYSIS

Membrane dialyzer

dialyzer at the rate of 4 gal. per hr., for about six hours, until 25 gal. were collected. The dialysis reduced the sodium chloride content of the stickwater from 3.4 to 0.3%. When another sample from the same stickwater batch was run through at 4 gal. per hr., but the temperature of the circulating wash water was held at 180°F., the dialyzate retained only 0.2% sodium chloride. The dialyzing membrane proved to be durable. It showed no signs of deterioration after it was used for a month, while the wash water was maintained at 131° to 140°F. Dialyzed stickwater proved superior in quality to some commercial glue samples, in that it showed a reduced tendency toward hygroscopicity.

The use of higher temperatures may well speed up dialysis, but it also tends to break down the adhesive strength of the glue. Furthermore, a reduction of salt content to 0.2%, while it may reduce the tendency toward hygroscopicity, makes the glue generally unacceptable.

[3] This process has been used, apparently, on a pilot plant scale only.

Demineralization of Liquid Fish Glue by Ionics' Electrodialyzer

General Principles.—Ionics, Incorporated, Cambridge, Mass., have proposed using an electrodialyzer selective membranes to carry out electrodialysis under suitable DC voltages. These membranes are thin sheets of specially prepared synthetic organic ion exchange or ion transfer resins. They have either a fixed positive charge or a fixed negative charge.

Anions penetrate through the fine capillary pores of an anion membrane, under the influence of a direct current, while the positive cations are repelled. At the same time, to maintain electrical neutrality, cations will go through the fine capillary pores of a cation membrane, under the influence of a direct current, while the negative anions are repelled.

De-Salting Procedure of Liquid Fish Glue by Ionics' Electrodialysis.—Electrodialysis as developed by Ionics, Incorporated, Cambridge, Mass., renders possible the desalting or the removal of electrolytes from a liquid fish glue dispersion. Preliminary, though inconclusive, indications are that electrodialysis improves the properties of the glue by reducing its mineral content drastically.

A schematic flow chart for an electrodialysis operation is shown in Fig. 5. A picture of an Ionics' electrodialysis unit is shown in Fig. 6.

Explanation of Schematic Flow Chart (Fig. 5).—The flow sheet shows three liquid streams being fed to the electrodialyzer (designated as stack). The product stream enters the stack, is partially demineralized, is recycled via a batch tank back to the stack for further demineralization, and is recycled again for additional demineralization, etc., until the required demineralization is achieved, as indicated by electrical-conductivity measurement. Then the demineralized-product stream is discharged automatically, as shown on the flow chart.

The water stream receives the salts as these are removed from the product stream. This water, or waste, stream also is recycled and is discharged with makeup water being fed on a feed-and-bleed basis.

A separate stream passes by the electrodes and picks up the electrode-reaction products such as gases. This stream subsequently is degasified. The rectifier and electrical wiring are not shown on the flow chart.

While the hydraulic capacity of a stack containing a given number of membranes of a given size can be varied over an approximately two-fold range, the output rate of a stack is quite variable and depends principally on the initial salt content of the solution to be demineralized and on the degree of demineralization desired. The greater the number of passes required, i.e., the more often a given product has to be recycled before being demineralized, the lower will be the output of the stack in terms of volume per unit time. To state it differently, the salt-removal capacity of

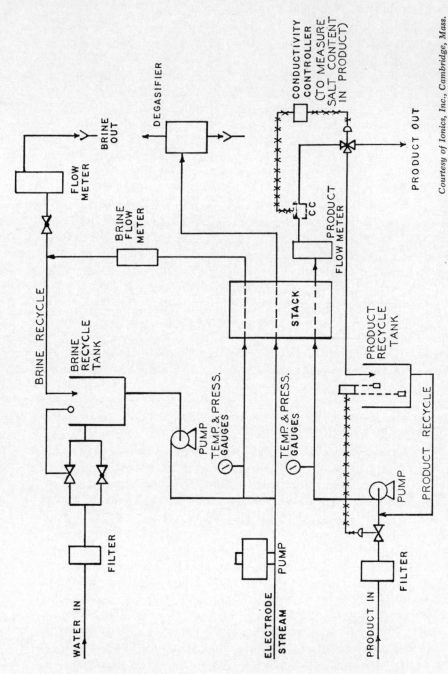

Fig. 5. Schematic Flow Sheet of Automatic Batch Type Electrodialysis Plant

Courtesy of Ionics Inc., Cambridge, Mass.

FIG. 6. ELECTRODIALYSIS UNIT

a stack is more or less constant so that the output of a stack depends on the amount of salt that has to be removed from a given feed.

PROCESS FOR INCREASING STRENGTH OR SPREADABILITY OF GLUE

A process for increasing the strength of animal and fish glues, or for increasing the spreadability of these glues without loss of strength is described in U. S. Patent 2,394,682 (Brody 1946). These tests for shear strength involved in this process were made using a Baldwin 60,000 lb. Hydraulic Testing Machine (Fig. 7).

Brody (1946) showed that adding a relatively small quantity of a hydrophilic colloidal clay, such as bentonite, to high-testing or intermediate-testing animal or fish glues resulted in a marked increase of strength; or, with greater dilution, these glues showed an increase in spreadability without loss of adhesive strength. The proportion of bentonite may range from about 2 to 15% of the amount of glue. Where increased strength without additional spreadability is desired, the percentage of bentonite to glue should not be over ten per cent. For increased spreadability without loss of strength, the amount of bentonite may be increased to 15%.

Courtesy of Wiedemann Machine Co., King of Prussia, Pa.

FIG. 7.   BALDWIN 60,000 LB. HYDRAULIC TESTING MACHINE

ADVANTAGES IN USING LIQUID FISH GLUE

Liquid fish glue possesses several distinct advantages over its nearest competitor—animal glue. These advantages are as follows:

It is the only liquid nonsynthetic glue produced that needs no further preparation and it is readily available for immediate application without any preliminary preparation. On the other hand, when dry animal glue is employed, the following operations must precede use: (1) a definite weight of dry glue and water must be weighed out in a fixed predetermined ratio for the ultimate adhesive strength required, (2) the mixture of glue and water must stay in a cool place for at least six hours, in order to allow the glue to soak up water and swell up, (3) the water-logged glue must be heated to approximately 140°F., in order to disperse the glue properly in the liquid, and (4) each time that the animal glue is applied, it must be heated to approximately 140°F., and it must remain hot while it is applied, or else it will gel and fail to penetrate the wood interstices.

Liquid fish glue sets slower than animal glues; this gives the operator ample time to adjust the joint properly, without forcing him to work with the speed and precision of a surgeon.

The slowness in the setting time of liquid fish glue enables the glue to penetrate the wood more deeply, resulting in better adhesion than when a fast-setting glue is used.

A jar of fish glue can be used day after day without any troublesome weighing, waiting, mixing, and heating.

USES OF LIQUID FISH GLUE

Liquid fish glue is used for the following purposes: (1) furniture making, (2) box making, (3) sizing, (4) in special cements, (5) for producing half-tone plates for photo-engraving, (6) in combination with hide glue in the production of belt-cement for leather belts, (7) repairing of musical instruments, toys, and crockery, (8) for small repair work and (9) bookbinding and labeling.

Norland (1964) pointed out the following additional uses: (1) in adhering push-outs for die cutting operations, (2) for reinforced gummed tapes where high initial tack and long open times are of advantage, (3) in shoe manufacturing, i.e., assembling wooden heels and temporary tacking of leather uppers, and (4) in the formulation of special printing inks.

BIBLIOGRAPHY

ALEXANDER, J. 1923. Glue and Gelatin. American Chemical Society Monograph Series. Chemical Catalog Co., New York.

BOGUE, R. H. 1922. Chemistry and Technology of Gelatin and Glue. 1st Edition. McGraw-Hill Book Co., New York.

BRADFIELD, R. 1928. An inexpensive cell for purification of colloids by electrodialysis. Ind. Eng. Chem. 20, 79–80.

BRAUDE, F. 1943. Modern Adhesives. 1st Edition. Chemical Publishing Co., New York.

BRODY, J. 1946. Glue. U. S. Pat. 2,394,682. Feb. 12.

BROOKFIELD, D. W. 1964. Personal communication. Stoughton, Mass.

DE BRUYNE, N. A. and HOUWINK, R. Editors. 1951. Adhesion and Adhesives. Elsevier Press, Houston, Texas.

DELMONTE, J. 1947. Technology of Adhesives. 1st Edition. Reinhold Publishing Corporation, New York, New York.

EKMAN, C. D. 1883. Extraction of glue from fish, hides, or bones. British Pat. 2680. Nov. 28.

FEDERAL STANDARD STOCK CATALOG. 1938. Catalog C-G-463. Shear test. Gov't. Printing Office, Washington, D. C.

GERBASI, E. C. 1964. Personal communication. Orange, Mass.

GROTH, L. A. 1882. Preparation of liquid glue from fish. British Pat. 5786. Dec. 5.

GUTTMAN, A. 1962. The utilization of fish skins for glue and other products. Progr. Rept. Atlantic Coast Sta. No. 73. Fisheries Res. Board Can., Ottawa.

HENDERSON, W. F. 1926. Cellulose sausage casings. U. S. Pat. 1,601,686. Sept. 28.

INGVALDSEN, T. 1929. Fish meals. Can. Chem. Metal. *13*, 129–131, 139.

IONICS INCORPORATED. 1963. Stackpack, a bench-scale, turn-key electrodialysis plant. Bull. L-2. 2nd Edition. Cambridge, Mass.

JOHNSTON, W. W. 1935. The manufacture of fish glue. Fisheries Res. Board Can., Atlantic Fisheries Exptl. Sta. Note No. 45. Halifax, N. S.

KENYON, H. B. R. 1964. Personal communication. Gloucester, Mass.

KERNOT, J. C., and SPEER, N. E. 1926. The production of glue and gelatin from fish. Rept. Adhesives Res. Com., *2* App. 3, Dept. Sci. Ind. Res. Great Britain.

KNIGHT, A. G. 1952. Adhesives for Wood. 1st Edition. Chemical Publishing Co., New York.

KNUDSON, E. 1920. Manufacture of fish glue. British Pat. 153,526. Nov. 11.

LOVERN, J. A. 1937. By-products of the fishing industry. Chem. and Ind. *56*, 75–81.

MASON, E. A., and Juda, W. 1959. Applications of ion exchange membranes in electrodialysis. Chem. Eng. Progr. *55*, No. 24, 155–162.

MORSE, L. C. 1964. Personal communication. Gloucester, Mass.

NORLAND, R. E. 1964. Personal communication. Cranbury, N. J.

PERRY, T. D. 1944. Modern Wood Adhesives. 1st Edition. Pitman Publishing Corp., New York, N. Y.

POTTINGER, S. R. 1964. Personal communication. Boston, Mass.

SMITH, L. F. 1929. The production of glue from fish waste. Fisheries Res. Board Can., Progr. Rept. Pacific Coast Sta. *3*, 5–8. Vancouver, B. C.

SMITH, L. F. 1930. Large scale production of fish glue. Fisheries Res. Board Can., Progr. Rept. Pacific Coast Sta. 7, 6–8. Vancouver, B. C.

SMITH, L. F. 1931. Fish glue and fish waste. Fisheries Res. Board Can., Progr. Rept., Pacific Coast Sta. 9, 23. Vancouver, B. C.

SMITH, L. F. 1932. Fish glue from fish waste I. Preparation by dialysis. Fisheries Exptl. Sta. Pacific. Contributions to Canadian Biology and Fisheries Vol VII, No. 14 (Series C, Industrial No. 6) Toronto.

SMITH, P. 1943. Glue and Gelatin. 1st Edition. Chemical Publishing Co., New York, N. Y.

STANSBY, M. E. 1963. *In* Industrial Fishery Technology, M. E. STANSBY, with editorial assistance of JOHN A. DASSOW. Reinhold Publishing Corp., New York, N. Y.

TRESSLER, D. K. 1921. Manufacture and properties of fish glue. Chem. Age 29, 173–175.

TRESSLER, D. K. 1923. Marine Products of Commerce. 1st Edition. Chapter 25. Fish Glue and Isinglass. Reinhold Publishing Corp., New York, N. Y.

TRESSLER, D. K., and LEMON, J. M. 1951. Marine Products of Commerce. 2nd Edition. Reinhold Publishing Corp., New York, N. Y.

WHITE, G. F. 1917. Fish isinglass and glue. U. S. Bur. Fisheries, Doc. 852, Washington, D. C.

CHAPTER 2

Gelatin and Isinglass Production

GELATIN

Introduction

Gelatin prepared from a by-product of the land animal industry has many useful applications in foods, pharmaceuticals, photographic and industrial products (Idson and Braswell 1957). It is used in the food industry in conjunction with other edible products, as a gelling, stabilizing, emulsifying, dispersing, or thickening agent (Selby 1951). For example, in the manufacture of gelatin desserts, gelatin is combined with sugar, acid, flavor, and color. The entire mixture is dissolved in warm water and allowed to set at refrigeration temperature. In this instance, gelatin serves as the gelling agent. In the production of ice cream, gelatin serves as the stabilizing agent.

From a nutritional standpoint, gelatin is an incomplete protein, since it lacks tryptophan, an essential amino acid (Dakin 1920). An animal or human being could not survive if it had to subsist on gelatin as its sole source of protein. However, gelatin is relatively high in lysine and methionine, whereas cereal grains such as wheat, rye, barley, and oats are deficient in these two essential amino acids.

Therefore, the daily consumption of as little as 15 gm. of gelatin could well serve as a supplement to the diet of low-income groups who subsist largely on a cereal and vegetable diet, and who suffer from the ill effects of a "hidden-hunger" for lack of a complete protein in their diets. Protein malnutrition affects two-thirds of the world's population or approximately two billion (two thousand million) people, who cannot afford to buy meat, eggs, or dairy products (see Chapter 18: Fish Protein Concentrate). This critical protein need could be remedied by supplementing their diets with gelatin, at a cost of 1 to 2¢ per day.

Furthermore, it would not be necessary to use the high testing grades of gelatin to satisfy this urgent nutritional need. The low testing grades of gelatin would do as well, since they contain the necessary lysine. This application of gelatin for cereal protein enrichment could be doubly beneficial: first, it would permit the many low-income people to thrive on their high cereal and vegetable diets; second, it could serve as a good outlet for the lower grades of gelatin.

Fish skins and fish bones could be used as a source of gelatin, although it is well known that gelatin from aquatic sources is not as good as gelatin

19

from animal sources insofar as its gelling properties are concerned. Limited as the physical properties of fish gelatin are, fish gelatin could be used advantageously in sea coast countries, which have a very small animal industry. In such countries a lower grade of gelatin obtained from fish skins would be better than no gelatin at all.

Distinction Between Gelatin and Glue

The difference between gelatin and glue is explained by Bogue (1922) in the following manner:

"In commercial parlance a gelatin differs from a glue only in that the former is a very high grade product, is of high jelly strength, is light in color, gives solutions that are reasonably clear, is sweet, and does not contain excessive impurities."

Preliminary Treatment of Raw Fish Stock for Gelatin Manufacture

In British Patent 235,635, granted to Joseph C. Kernot on June 18, 1925, a process is described for pretreating raw fish stock such as skins, in order to obtain a gelatin which is both deodorized and improved in its gel strength. Essentially, the process consists of washing the stock with water, treating it first with dilute base solutions, then following it with dilute acid solutions and rinsing the stock with water after the base and acid treatments. A more detailed description follows:

The raw fish skins are put in suitable vats and washed for 3 to 4 hours with running water. The water is then drained off and the skins are macerated for 6 to 8 hours with a dilute alkaline or alkali solution.

The solution should be very dilute, i.e., it should not exceed a 0.5% sodium hydroxide concentration. This low alkalinity is necessary in order to avoid too much swelling of the stock. The solution is drained off at the end of the first maceration period and a fresh basic solution is added. This treatment is repeated, at least, three times.

Subsequently, it is again washed thoroughly for 3 to 4 hours in running water. The water is drained off and the raw fish stock is macerated with a dilute weak acid, such as sulfurous acid, the same number of times as it was subjected to the alkaline or alkali treatment.

The acidity and alkalinity concentrations should be equivalent. After the acid treatments, the fish skins are thoroughly washed with water for the third time. The skins are now ready for the gelatin extraction.

The extracted liquors are concentrated and dried the usual way.

The mild alkaline treatment, according to Kernot, liberates all of the volatile bases which are the causative agents of the characteristic fish gelatin odors. The subsequent acid treatments remove the liberated bases. This process also imparts a stronger gel to the finished product since it removes albumins.

An Alternative Procedure for the Preliminary Treatment of Fish Skins for Gelatin Manufacture

Geiger *et al.* (1962) established experimentally the following conditions as being optimum for preparing dogfish gelatin: (1) wash skins in running tap-water at 45°F. for 24 hr., (2) treat skins at 68°F. for 24 hr. changing twice 0.2% sodium hydroxide solutions, followed by 15 min. of washing in running tap-water; subsequently, repeat the treatment twice with 0.2% of sulfurous acid solutions at 68°F. for 24 hr., and (3) wash skins for four hours in running tap-water.

Extraction of Gelatin from Treated Fish Skins

Add two parts of water for each part of pretreated material and extract gelatin at from 158 to 176°F. for two consecutive 30-min. periods.

Before arriving at the conclusion that the above described procedure produces gels with the highest melting point, Geiger *et al.*, evaluated extraction temperatures between 122° and 225°F., and extraction periods from 30 min. to 4 hours.

Bogue (1922) describes the manufacture of gelatin including isinglass.

Similarities Between Fish and Animal Gelatin[1]

Fish and animal gelatins have a number of similar properties. Either gelatin can be used as high-strength glue, and both make excellent bases for emulsions. Both products can be made sensitive to light by the addition of sensitizers, thereby they become useful in photographic processes.

Either chromic acid or chromium salts such as ammonium dichromate, potassium dichromate, or ammonium chromate can be added in varying proportions to make the gelatin sensitive to light. Exposure to light, especially actinic rays from an arc lamp or sunlight, insolubilizes the gelatin.

Uses of Fish Gelatin in Photographic Processes[1]

The uses of fish gelatin in photoengraving led to its adoption in other interesting photographic applications. A considerable amount is used in name plate manufacturing, where an image can be recessed by etching and then either filled in with lacquer or treated chemically to give a color that contrasts with the raised metal surface. This name plate is practically indestructible, since the recessed image can be read even though the lacquer has worn off.

---

[1] By permission from Norland. Norland Products, Incorporated, imports into the United States high grades of liquid fish glue and fish gelatin for which there is a continuing demand in the manufacture of photoengraving plates, as well as for other uses enumerated in the following paragraphs.

Fish gelatin has been used more recently in the chemical etching of metal parts. Here it is possible to duplicate photographically a complicated metal part on thin metal, and to chemically etch unwanted metal to make a precision part. The usual method is to coat and print both sides of the metal sheet, then etch from both sides, the printing on both sides being lined up very accurately. This process allows interesting metal fabrication which it would be impossible to do mechanically.

The optical industry has found an interesting application of fish gelatin in what is called a glue-silver process.

Another major application is in the formulation of coating for light-sensitive papers such as blueprint papers. Diazo-type materials are used as the light sensitizer with the addition of other chemicals that can be darkened with proper developing agents. The finished product gives a coated paper that can be exposed photographically, washed out with water to remove the soluble areas, and then developed to darken the insoluble areas.

In summary it may be stated that fish gelatin offers the unique properties of a liquid material which can be light sensitized and coated on almost any surface to give a photographically active coating.

ISINGLASS

Introduction

Isinglass is an excellent raw material for producing fish gelatin. The word "isinglass" is derived from a similarly sounding work in Dutch and German meaning sturgeon's air bladder or swimming bladder. It consists of collagen which can readily be hydrolyzed to a high-grade fish gelatin or adhesive, by heating the swimming bladder in water for a short period of time. The air bladders should be relatively large and easily detachable from the fish. Not all fish air bladders are suitable for isinglass production. In North America, air bladders obtained from large deep-water hake constitute the best raw material for isinglass production. One ton of hake yields about 45 lb. of dry isinglass containing approximately 85% gelatin while one ton of cod yields about 18 lb. of a poorer quality product, containing only 50% gelatin.

Structure and Function of the Fish Air Bladder

The fish air bladder, also known as fish sound or swimming bladder, is a compressible sac containing air. It is located in the abdominal cavity below the vertebral column, and consists of several external membraneous layers or coatings, the innermost layer being the thinnest. The layer adjacent to the innermost layer is thick and fibrous and is high in collagen.

In some fishes, such as hake, sturgeon, and carp, the swimming bladder is relatively large and well developed. Air bladders obtained from these fishes constitute, therefore, a good source of isinglass.

The function of the swimming bladder is to regulate the specific gravity of the fish, enabling it to maintain its position at any level in the water.

Production of Isinglass from Hake Swimming Bladders

Preliminary Treatment of Hake Swimming Bladders in Preparation for Isinglass Production.—Hake swimming bladders are readily detached from the backbone during the dressing operation aboard ship. They are usually scraped and washed, although the latter two operations could be omitted without materially affecting the quality of the isinglass. During transit, the air bladders are temporarily preserved by salting. After they are delivered ashore, they are slit open and thoroughly washed, and the black outer membrane is removed by scraping. The swimming bladders are then air-dried.

Manufacturing Procedure of Isinglass

The cleaned, desalted, air-dried, and hardened swimming bladders are softened by immersing them in water for several hours. The swimming bladders, or sounds, are then mechanically cut into small pieces and rolled or compressed between hollow iron rollers that are cooled by water and are provided with a scraper for the removal of any adhering dried material. This rolling process converts the isinglass into thin strips or sheets of from $1/8$ to $1/4$ in. in thickness.

The sheets are further compressed by ribbon rollers into ribbons about $1/64$ in. thick. These thin isinglass ribbons are easily dried while suspended in warm rooms for several hours. Finally the ribbons are rolled into coils.

Forms of Isinglass Produced

Isinglass is produced either as leaf- or book-isinglass. To prepare it in the former form, the swimming bladders are immersed in warm water to remove dirt and mucous membranes, and are then opened and air-dried.

Book-isinglass is similarly processed but the swimming bladders are folded and covered with a damp cloth. A two per cent hot water solution of either type of isinglass sets on cooling to a good firm gel.

Properties of Isinglass

Isinglass dissolves readily in most dilute acids or alkalis, but is insoluble in alcohol. In hot water, isinglass swells uniformly, producing an opalescent jelly with a characteristic fibrous structure which is absent in a gelatin sol. This characteristic behavior of isinglass in hot water serves as a method for differentiating it microscopically from a gelatin sol.

Uses of Isinglass

Isinglass is used as a clarifying agent for beverages such as cider, wine, beer, and vinegar by the enmeshing of suspended impurities in the fibrous structure of the swollen isinglass (Tressler and Lemon 1951).

Isinglass can also be used as an adhesive base. When dissolved in acetic acid, it forms a strong cement, especially useful for glass or pottery. Modified isinglass can be used for repairing leather belts, or as a size for textiles. It serves as an essential ingredient in the manufacture of India ink, and is used in the production of some confectionery products (Bogue 1922 and White 1917).

As an adhesive, or as a thickening, emulsifying, dispersing, or jelling agent, isinglass cannot compete with gelatin or liquid fish glue in the United States or in other technologically advanced countries. It could, nevertheless, be used in these ways advantageously in developing seacoast countries for their local consumption. This is particularly true in view of the fact that the plant setup for isinglass production is inexpensive and its manufacturing procedure is relatively simple as compared to the cost of large plants and up-to-date production methods for the manufacture of similar commodities in technologically advanced countries.

BIBLIOGRAPHY

ALEXANDER, J.   1923.   Glues and Gelatin.   1st Edition.   Chemical Catalog Co., New York.

AMES, W. M.   1947.   Heat degradation of gelatin.   J. Soc. Chem. Ind. 66, 279–284.

AMES, W. M.   1952.   The conversion of collagen to gelatin and their molecular structures.   J. Sci. Food Agr. 3, 454–463.

BECHER, C. Jr.   1950.   Isinglass and fish glue.   Seifen-Oele-Fette-Wachse 76, 391–392.

BELLO, J., and VINOGRAD, J.   1955.   Fundamental studies on gelatin.   U. S. Army Contract No. DA-49-007-MD-298.

BENDER, A. E., MILLER, D. S., and TUNNAH, E. J.   1953.   The biological value of gelatin.   Chem. and Ind. 799.

BOEDTKER, H., and DOTY, P. M.   1954.   A study of gelatin molecules, aggregates and gels.   J. Phys. Chem. 58, 968–983.

BOGUE, R. H.   1920.   Properties and constitution of glues and gelatin.   Chem. Met. Eng. 23, 154–158.

BOGUE, R. H.   1922.   Chemistry and Technology of Gelatin and Glue.   1st Edition.   McGraw-Hill Book Co., New York.

BOGUE, R. H.   1922.   Isinglass.   Chem. Age 30, 183–184.

BOWES, J. H.   1951.   Composition of skin-collagen and the effect of alkalis on collagen.   Research 4, 155–162.

CALWELL, J. R. 1952. Acid solutions of proteins. U. S. Pat. 2,592,120. April 8.

CASSEL, J. M., and KANAGY, J. R. 1949. The purification of collagen. J. Res. Natl. Bur. Std. 42, 557–565.

COHN, E. J., and EDSALL, J. T. 1943. Proteins, Amino Acids and Peptides. 1st Edition. Reinhold Publishing Corp., New York, N. Y.

CONRAD, L. J., and STILES, H. S. 1954. Improving the whipping properties of gelatin. U. S. Pat. 2,692,201. Oct. 19.

DAKIN, H. D. 1920. Amino acids of gelatin. J. Biol. Chem. 44, 524–525.

DECOUDON, C., and DECOUDON, R. G. H. 1951. Process for manufacture of gelatin and glue. French Pat. 992, 174. Oct. 15.

FERGUSON, C. S. 1950. Composition for preserving articles of food and the like. U. S. Pat. 2,532,489. Dec. 5.

GALLOP, P. M. 1955. Studies on a parent gelatin from ichthyocol. Arch. Biochem. and Biophys. 54, 501–512.

GEIGER, S. E., ROBERTS, E., and TOMLINSON, N. 1962. Dogfish gelatin. J. Fisheries Res. Board Can. 19, No. 2, 321–326. Vancouver, B. C.

GLASS, J. V. S. 1939. Manufacture of gelatin. U. S. Pat. 2,184,494. Dec. 26.

GRETTIE, D. P. 1950. Gelatin desserts. U. S. Pat. 2,519,961. Aug. 22.

GUSTAVSON, K. H. 1956. The Chemistry and Reactivity of Collagen. 1st Edition. Academic Press, New York.

HIGHBERGER, J. H. 1953. Methods of forming fibers from collagen. U. S. Pat. 2,631,942. Mar. 17.

IDSON, B., and BRASWELL, E. 1957. Gelatin, Advances in Food Research, 7, 235-338.

KANAGY, J. R. 1947 Chemistry of collagen. Natl. Bur. Stds. Circ. C458.

KERNOT, J. C. 1924. Improvements in and relating to the manufacture of glue, gelatin and meal from fish and other offal of marine origin. Brit. Pat. 235,-635. June 18.

LESPARRE, J. N. 1948. A coating composition for meat products. U. S. Pat. 2,-440,517. Apr. 27.

NEUMAN, R. E. 1949. Amino acid composition of gelatins, collagens and elastins from different sources. Arch. Biochem. 24, 289–298.

NEUMAN, R. E., and LOGAN, M. A. 1950. The determination of hydroxyproline. J. Biol. Chem. 184, 299–306.

NORLAND, R. E. 1964. Personal communication. Cranbury, N. J.

RANDALL, J. T. Editor. 1953. The Nature and Structure of Collagen. Academic Press, New York.

SELBY, J. W. 1951. Uses of gelatin in food. Food 20, 284.

SHEPPARD, S. E. and HOUCK, R. C. 1946. Methods of refining gelatin. U. S. Pat. 2,400,375. May 14.

SIFFERD, R. H. 1951. Preparation of gelatin. U. S. Pat. 2,580,049. Dec. 25.

SMITH, P. I. 1943. Glue and Gelatin. 1st Edition. Chemical Publishing Co., New York. Revised edition of a work published in London, 1929.

TRESSLER, D. K., and LEMON, J. M. 1951. Marine Products of Commerce. 2nd Edition. Reinhold Publishing Corp., New York, N. Y.

VEIS, A., and COHEN, J. 1955. The degradation of collagen. J. Am. Chem. Soc. 77, 2364–2368.

WALLERSTEIN, L., and PFANMULLER, J. 1942. Art of producing gelatin and glue. U.S. Pat. 2,290,081. July 14.

WHITE, G. F. 1917. Fish Isinglass and Glue. U. S. Bur. Fisheries Doc. 852. Washington, D. C.

CHAPTER 3

Pearl Essence

INTRODUCTION

An irridescent substance is deposited in the epidermal layer and on the scales of most pelagic fishes, i.e., fishes of the species which swim near the surface of the water, such as herring and mackerel. The lustrous effect of the irridescent material is produced by the organic compound guanin, a constituent of cell nuclei.

Only in its crystalline form does guanin reflect and refract light, serving as a camouflage for fish. The deposit on the belly side of the fish produces a bright silvery appearance which blends with the bright sky and helps it elude the larger fishes below.

Similarly, when viewed from above, the fish reflects a greenish gray light, which blends with the color of the water. This camouflage helps the fish to escape detection by the enemy from above.

Most of the crystalline guanin is deposited in the epidermis and it is not readily recoverable, but some of it is found adhering to the fish scales from which it is recovered by procedures which will be described.

The suspension of crystalline guanin particles in a suitable solvent is called "pearl essence." When the particles are deposited on the inside surfaces of hollow beads or on the outside of solid ones, they produce an optical effect very similar to that of genuine pearls.

Pearl essence is also used to impart irridescence to a large variety of articles such as ash trays, fishing rods, book covers, and finishes for textiles (Stansby 1963).

It is worthy of note that demersal fishes (species of fishes that live at the bottom of the ocean, such as cod, haddock, and flounder) have amorphous guanin deposited in their epidermal layer, apparently because they do not require lustrous crystal guanin for camouflage.

DIFFERENCES BETWEEN GENUINE PEARLS AND PEARL ESSENCE

Genuine pearls rank very high in value among commercial articles. They are of entirely different origin and chemical composition than pearl essence. Although the lustrous effects produced by the two substances are very similar, genuine pearls are valuable because of their luster. Whereas guanin is entirely organic in composition, the genuine pearl consists of layers of crystalline calcium carbonate alternating with layers of the horny organic substance called conchiolin, which binds the calcium carbonate layers.

A genuine pearl is elaborated inside the shell of a pearl-bearing mollusk, when some foreign substance is accidentally ingested. The pearl oyster, unable to rid itself of the irritant, coats it with calcium carbonate, presumably as a defense mechanism.

Numerous thin layers of the alternating organic and inorganic constituents are concentrically deposited on the initial irritating nucleus, resulting in a pearl which itself becomes an irritant. This process continues until the host dies. The pearl is found either in the mollusk or at the bottom of the ocean, remaining intact after the dead mollusk has decomposed.

Pearl essence and genuine pearls, are both produced as defense mechanisms, but they originate in entirely different parts of the body. In mollusks, the pearl is formed internally and serves a function which may be classified as a pseudo-defense mechanism, in view of the fact that it is finally responsible for the destruction of its host. In pelagic fishes, on the other hand, pearl essence is deposited in the integument and serves as an effective defense mechanism.

SOURCES OF PEARL ESSENCE

Guanin has a crystalline form and yields a silvery luster. It is deposited in the following pelagic fishes: herring, salmon, whitefish, sardines, menhaden, mackerel, butterfish, carp, barracuda, bonito, shad, mullet, and many others.

Sardine herring scales are the principal source of pearl essence in Maine. The scales that accumulate at the bottom of the boats constitute one source. Another source is the lustrous guanin sediment obtained from the water that is used to flush the fish in the canneries.

In California, the sardine or pilchard is a source of supply. Other American sources of pearl essence are silver carp of the Mississippi Valley, gizard shad of the fresh-water streams of Florida, whitefish and cisco of the Great Lakes, Pacific Coast salmon, Alaskan herring, southern mullet, and Atlantic menhaden.

An excellent summary of this subject was made by H. F. Taylor (1925). Tressler and Lemon (1951) also treat this subject extensively. This chapter is based largely on the publications of these authors. Brief reference is also made by Decker (1953) and Stansby (1963).

PROPERTIES OF PEARL ESSENCE

Pearl essence is either an aqueous or organic solvent suspension of the natural guanin crystals. To the aqueous suspension, ammonia is frequently added. The organic solvents used are amyl acetate, acetone, etc. The crystals are also prepared in a highly concentrated suspension in a thick lacquer of celluloid in amyl acetate.

Chemical Properties of Guanin

Guanin, a chemical composed of the purin base group, having the empirical formula, $C_5H_5N_5O$, is a 2-amino, 6-oxypurin, which is one of the constituents in the complex nucleo-proteins found in cell nuclei. The compound has the following structural formula:

$$
\begin{array}{c}
\text{HN—CO} \\
\text{H}_2\text{NC} \quad \text{C—NH} \\
\text{CH} \\
\text{N—C—N}
\end{array}
$$

Guanin is insoluble in water, ethyl alcohol, chloroform, ether, ethyl or amyl acetate, acetaldehyde, acetic anhydride, or in any neutral solvent. It is also insoluble in the following organic acids: dilute or glacial acetic, formic, lactic, salicylic, or citric. It dissolves to a limited extent in cold ammonium hydroxide solutions, to a greater extent in hot ammonia solutions, and to a still greater extent in hot supersaturated ammonia solutions. On evaporation from supersaturated ammonia solution, guanin crystallizes out in needles or plates.

Guanin is soluble in sodium and potassium hydroxide solutions and in dilute mineral acids. When acid solutions containing guanin crystals are neutralized with ammonia, the amorphous form is precipitated. It combines with many acids, acid radicals, organic groups, and inorganic salts. Strong oxidizing agents decompose it. Heating it to 480°F. does not change it. On ignition, it does not leave residue.

For guanin crystals to be suspended in a nonaqueous liquid, such as ether or amyl acetate, these solvents must be absolutely anhydrous. If any water is present in the solvent, the crystals will not settle in a compact silvery mass; instead, they will flocculate and the size of the floc will tend to increase with an increased concentration of water in the solvent.

Physical Properties of Guanin

The size of guanin crystals is, to a limited extent, proportional to the size of the fish from which it comes. For example, crystals from shad and whitefish are larger than those from sardines, herring, or alewives. However, the crystalline structure of guanin from different species of fish is similar.

The specific gravity of guanin crystals is approximately 1.6. The dimensions of shad guanin are $0.1 \times 0.02 \times 0.001$ mm. Accordingly, its volume would be 0.000,000,002 cc., its surface, 0.000,042,4 sq. cm., and its weight, 0.000,000,032 gm. One gram of crystals would contain about 312,-500,000 individual crystals, with an aggregate surface of more than 1 sq. yd.

Because of their large surface area, guanin crystals have adsorptive properties. They adsorb dispersed albumen particles and coloring matter from aqueous solutions. When suspended in fat soluble solvents, such as either or amyl alcohol, they adsorb the fat particles.

Guanin crystals resemble thin light blades and they owe their beauty in pearl essence to their continual whirling and turning in the suspended liquid, reflecting brilliant flashes of light in all directions. The light coming from the crystals is refracted and polarized and, as it passes successively two of these crystals, is broken into colors by a twisting of the polarized beam. The nearest analogy to their appearance is that of narrow strips of paper falling through air.

The crystals exhibit their maximum luster when they are lined up parallel to each other. Such an orientation takes place when a current is set up in the liquid containing them. In applying lacquers the maximum effect is obtained if the fluid flows.

Decker (1953) states that optimum irridescence of guanin crystals occurs when the crystals retain a hydrolyzed proteinaceous layer which enrobes them. When this layer is removed by proteolytic hydrolysis, the desirable optical effect of the guanin crystals is substantially reduced.

THE MANUFACTURE OF PEARL ESSENCE

Preservation of Scales

The scales are preserved by putting them into a brine of from 10 to 15% concentration and moving them around to wet all the scales. Then the brine is drained off and the scales are further freed from brine by squeezing them in muslin bags. Subsequently they are compressed tightly in metal cans or barrels. At no time must the scales be allowed to dry. If stored at 32°F. in this preserved condition, they will keep for several weeks.

Fundamental Considerations in Pearl Essence Production

Fish scales themselves do not enter into the manufacture of pearl essence. They are only the carriers of a relatively small portion of the lustrous guanin crystals because the crystals are largely deposited in the fish epidermis, only a small portion adhering to the scales.

Fundamentally, the process consists of collecting and washing the freshly removed scales. Subsequently the lustrous material is scrubbed from the scales, in a large agitator resembling a domestic washing machine, using as little water as possible. The lustrous sediment is next separated from the wash water by centrifugal force. The guanin crystals are then prepared (Taylor 1925) in either aqueous or nonaqueous pearl essence suspension.

Aqueous Suspensions.—The preparation of the aqueous type of pearl essence suspension requires, first, that the scales be well cleansed to remove adhering foreign particles. The scales from the belly side of the fish are preferred. The epidermis, if obtainable, is washed with the scales.

Agitating or scrubbing is done with water to which, preferably, some ammonia has been added, because an ammoniacal solution gradually dissolves the epidermis and leaves the crystals in suspension, sufficiently clean. The suspension is put through a strainer, not copper or brass, to remove the scales and trash. The pearly substance is further purified by allowing it to settle out in a cool place, then decanting off the supernatant liquid and replacing it with fresh ammoniated water. This cycle is repeated several times until the crystals are fairly well purified.

The ammonia exerts a doubly beneficial effect: first, it serves as a purifier, dissolving out the proteinaceous matter, and it also preserves the crystals indefinitely. Also, 0.3% salicylic acid might be used as a preservative of the aqueous suspension. Adhesives of animal or fish origin, such as fish glue or isinglass, may be dispersed in it.

Nonaqueous Suspensions and Lacquers.—Pearl essence may also be suspended in either organic solvents or acids, such as ethyl or amyl acetate, acetone, acetic anhydride, chloroform, carbon tetrachloride, acetic acid, etc. It is also presented to the market in the form of a thick paste of crystals, suspended in a viscous lacquer of celluloid in amyl acetate.

There are many variations in the manufacturing procedures of pearl essence—principally by the use of organic reagents. Taylor (1925) prepared a nonaqueous suspension of pearl essence by applying a modification of the flotation principle, usually applied to separate metallic compounds from low-grade ores. In this instance, the process depends on the property of guanin particles to become wetted by certain liquids, such as ether or any of the other fat-solvents, for example, chloroform, benzene, carbon tetrachloride or toluene, more readily than by water.

When an unstable ether emulsion of an aqueous guanin suspension is allowed to "break," or separate out, the guanin particles will be found in the supernatant ether layer. The other impurities will remain in the (submerged) aqueous layer. By utilizing the property of the fat-solvents for driving away water with its suspended impurities, from the surface of the crystals, a further purification of the guanin crystals is obtained.

In order to improve the efficiency of this flotation system, the albuminous proteins are removed by a proteolytic hydrolysis. The ether or other fat solvents cause all the undissolved organic matter to rise in the water and collect under the ether layer, while the guanin crystals remain suspended in the supernatant ether layer.

The lower aqueous layer is drawn off as completely as possible. The guanin particles in the ether layer are allowed to settle, the ether is drawn off and replaced by fresh, fat-free, anhydrous ether, and the particles are again allowed to settle. This procedure is repeated several times until the crystals are free from fat and water.

Finally, after sedimentation or centrifuging, the lustrous guanin crystals are transferred to acetone or amyl acetate, are concentrated, and the celluloid is added to produce a viscous paste. Dark-colored matter adhering to guanin may be precipitated from an acetone suspension.

The particle size of guanin crystals is very critical. The crystals should be neither too coarse nor too fine. Large crystals obtained from the larger species of fish produce a grainy coating, while minutely fragmented crystals, when separated from the coarser ones, appear chalky white or yellowish.

Intermediate sizes are desirable to produce the proper pearly effect. Larger particles can, of course, be fragmented in a pebble mill to smaller sizes, but this procedure should be carefully watched in order not to reduce them too finely.

ASSAYING OF PEARL ESSENCE

There are no standardized procedures for assaying pearl essence, nor are there any established standards for evaluating the finished product. However, an experienced worker should be able to distinguish fineness of grain, tint, luster, and concentration. With lacquers, viscosity must be taken into consideration. For practical testing of pearl essence, Taylor (1925) suggested microscopic examinations, which would give the shape and size of the particles, the color of the crystals, and the presence or absence of foreign matter.

BIBLIOGRAPHY

ANON. 1941. Pearls by diptank. Industrial Finishing and Painting News (Sherwin-Williams Co.) *1*, No. 2, 8. Cleveland, Ohio.

ANON. 1947. The silvery scales of the herring. Am. Fisheries *1*, No. 2, 17–18.

ANON. 1957. How pearl essence is made. Fisheries Newsletter *16*, No. 1, 21. Australia.

CARTER, N. M. 1943. Pearl essence from scales of British Columbia herring. Fisheries Res. Board Can., Progr. Rept. Pacific Coast Sta. *55*, 18–20.

DECKER, W. E.   1953.   Changing aspects of pearl essence technology.   Organic Finishing *14,* No. 7, 11.

ROBERTS, A. G.   1949.   Pearls without oysters.   Gemmologist *18,* 34–38.

STANSBY, M. E.   with the editorial assistance of J. A. DASSOW.   1963.   Industrial Fishery Technology.   Reinhold Publishing Corp., New York, N. Y.

TAYLOR, H. F.   1925.   Pearl essence; its history, chemistry and technology.   U. S. Bur. Fisheries.   Doc. 989.

TRESSLER, D. K., and LEMON, J. M.   1951.   Marine Products of Commerce.   2nd Edition.   Reinhold Publishing Corp., New York, N. Y.

CHAPTER 4

Leather Production from Fish Skins

INTRODUCTION

The skins of fishes and, especially, the hides of marine mammals have been converted into leather by methods that are essentially similar and generally applicable to leather production from land animals. This aquatic source of skins and hides would be a particularly desirable one for inhabitants of those global segments that are not blessed with the extensive green pastures and lush meadows necessary for grazing and maintaining large herds of cattle, or wherever extremes of climate and topography are unsuited for raising goats and sheep. Such countries include Japan, Indo-China, Thailand, Korea, the Philippines, Norway, the Arctic region, Sweden, Greece, Turkey, and a number of others where the shortages created by the undeveloped animal industry result in lack of sufficient leather for its people.

The shortage of leather from land animals is further intensified in some countries by religious restrictions. For example, Hindus regard cows as sacred. Mohammedans, Japanese, and the Semitic people are forbidden to eat pork. These dietary restrictions tend further to reduce the supply of animal hides and skins for the production of leather.

It is fortunate for most of the countries which cannot produce a sufficient number of land animals to supply needed protein that they are surrounded by large bodies of water which abound in fishes and marine mammals. This supply of oceanic life, if it were systematically tapped, could serve as a source of skins and hides that would supplement, and possibly even exceed, the supply of leather from land animals.

The fishes and aquatic mammals that could furnish hides are sharks, seals, walruses, porpoises, and dolphins. In fact, shark and seal skins have been used widely for many years. Ocean Leather Corp., Newark, N. J., has been converting shark skins into leather for shoes and other prestige leather goods since the year 1927, at which time shark leather joined the family of American leathers on a commercial basis. Also, "pin seal" has been produced on a commercial basis since before the turn of the century. These two exotic leathers may be classed, in production and use, with alligator skin leather, which is the best known of the three to the general public (Moresi 1964).

Other fishes that could supply skins on a large scale are salmon, skates, rays, and the "ground-fish," i.e., cod, haddock, cusk, pollock, and hake.

The skins of salmon have been utilized to some extent but those of the "ground-fish" have been neglected, even though they could produce beautiful and useful leather, particularly suitable for the manufacture of small novelties.

Even in countries where there are abundant supplies of land animal skins, such as in the United States, leather from aquatic sources could supplement or replace many types of leather from land animals, provided the economics of the process would permit such a substitution. A recently developed process has produced salmon skin leather which might well replace the customary animal skin leather that has been used for shoe uppers. This development was pioneered by the late John Metz, a seasoned veteran of the leather industry.

The story of this accomplishment is graphically related in two publications namely, the *New England Homestead* and *Leather and Shoes*. By combining considerable effort with technological know-how and with the cooperation of Ocean Leather Corp., Metz (1953) succeeded, after a number of years of patient experimentation, in producing leather from salmon skins for shoe uppers. In fact, this new salmon skin leather has many advantages for use in footwear over leather produced from land animal skins.

The story of Metz's developments may serve to illustrate the potentialities of fish skin leathers. It is particularly noteworthy that this new type of salmon skin leather has been developed in Boston which is the center of the land animal leather industry in the United States.

Furthermore, it could be stated, in a general way, that the large scale conversion of salmon skins to leather could apply, with modifications, to skins and hides from other aquatic sources. Such developments could be useful in the United States and more so in countries that are in dire need of leather if these countries could exert the necessary effort in the exploitation and development of this almost inexhaustible source of raw material in their own "back-yards."

HISTORICAL BACKGROUND OF THE LEATHER INDUSTRY

Leather making is regarded as the world's oldest industry, dating back to prehistoric times. Archaeological records indicate that crude leather was "manufactured" more than 20,000 years B.C. (Anon. 1963). It even preceded the housing and food industries, since early man lived in caves and had no facilities for fire making and cooking, he was accustomed to eating his food raw but he needed a protective covering for his body. Accordingly, he made leather in a crude way from animal hides, by simply drying the hides first and pounding them against rocks to soften them.

According to the biblical account of approximately 5700 years ago, Adam and Eve used skin clothes, for we read:

"Unto Adam and unto his wife did the Lord God make clothes of skin and clothe them" (Genesis, III:21).

The ancient Arabs are credited with having devised a unique vegetable tanning process. The Hebrews discovered oak-bark tanning which was used for many centuries and was still about the only tanning material used in medieval times. Throughout ancient history of China, Persia, Egypt, Greece, and Rome, there are references to leather-making and to its many uses, including those for military purposes.

The Dead Sea scrolls that were recently discovered were made from tanned skins of sheep and goats. The tanning of these skins was so skillfully carried out that the scrolls have withstood the elements for over 2000 years and are still intact.

The first major problem confronting the early leather producers was the adequate preservation or curing of perishable skins and hides. Sundrying constituted the earliest method for their preservation. Later, skins and hides were treated with oils to prevent their deterioration. Subsequently, skins and hides were preserved by vegetable tanning, which was carried out with the aid of aqueous extracts of twigs, leaves, pods, fruits, shrubs, plants, barks, and roots.

Up to the turn of the twentieth century, progress in leather manufacturing was slight, being based primarily on trial and error discoveries. Development of the chrome tanning process early in the twentieth century marks the greatest advance in this industry (Roberts 1964). It has greatly accelerated the tanning operation, reducing it from four months required for vegetable tanning to one month for chrome tanning. It has also increased the strength of the leather. About 20% of leather is still manufactured by the old vegetable tanning technique, which is particularly applicable to heavy leather, such as sole leather or leather belting (Kaine 1964).

DEFINITIONS:

It seems essential to define a few terms that will be used here over and over again:

Leather is the skin or hide of an animal chemically processed to prevent its deterioration by microbes.

The term skin refers to the outer coating of small land animals, such as sheep, goats, or calves, or of fishes, such as salmon or cod.

The term hide refers to the external covering of large land animals, e.g., cattle or horses or of marine mammals, such as porpoises or walruses.

FUNDAMENTAL PRINCIPLES AND PROCEDURES
OF LEATHER MANUFACTURE

The fundamental principles involved in the production of leather from hides and skins of land animals are applicable, with modifications, to similar raw material from aquatic sources. Since each type of skin or hide requires special procedures best suited to its characteristics, manufacturing details differ in the production of the many different types of leather (Moresi 1964). Nevertheless, regardless of the origin of the raw material, the production procedures are all governed by the same basic rules, which are applicable to the entire industry.

The similarity in properties, characteristics, and composition of the two kinds of raw material seems to justify the above indicated analogy in respect to their processing. The similarity in composition of skins can be seen from the fact that every skin or hide is divided into three distinct layers as follows: (1) "epidermis" is the outer thin layer of epithelial tissue, (2) "derma" or "corium" is a much thicker layer of connective and other tissues referred to as the "true skin." Its principal constituent is collagen, which is present in the largest amount in the skins and is the chief component responsible for the formation of leather by combining with tanning agents after the epidermis and flesh have been removed, and (3) "flesh" contains fatty tissue, loose connective tissue, and some muscle tissue.

The major operations in the manufacture of leather (Moresi 1964; Kaine 1964) are as follows:

Curing of Hides and Skins

As soon as the skins are removed from the animal or fish and adhering flesh is trimmed off, preservatives are added, otherwise incipient decomposition would set in, which would have a deleterious effect on the properties of the finished leather. When salt is used as the preservative, it is usually spread over the flesh side and the skin is stored in such a way as to allow the brine to drain. In tropical countries, such as India and Java, skins are usually preserved by dehydration.

The tanning operations required to convert hides and skins into leather depend upon a number of variable factors such as the kind of raw stock being treated, the ultimate use of the leather, and many others. Fundamentally, according to Moresi (1964), the following operations are involved: (1) beam house, (2) tanning, (3) fat-liquoring and dyeing, (4) drying, (5) finishing, and (6) measuring and shipping.

A brief description of each of these operations follows:

Beam house operations involve the preparation of the raw stock for tanning. It consists of (1) washing and soaking, (2) liming and sulfiding, and (3) splitting and bating.

Washing and Soaking.—The hides and skins are washed and soaked with water by the method of drum washing, paddle washing, or soaking in vats. The washing and soaking operation plumps up the skins and hides, restoring them thereby to their original state of texture and consistency.

Liming and Sulfiding.—Before skins and hides are converted into leather, all hair and epidermis, which are composed chiefly of the protein keratin, must be removed. A saturated solution of calcium hydroxide, which has a maximum pH of 12.5 is most suitable for liming because this attacks the keratin almost exclusively. Thus, the hair and epidermis are softened and loosened. Collagen, which is the principal constituent of leather, is not appreciably damaged at pH 12.5 (Wilson 1948).

Courtesy of John J. Riley Co., Woburn, Mass.

FIG. 8.   LIMING VAT

Liming Procedure.—The liming vats (Fig. 8), which are either wooden or concrete, contain water, to which is added lime in amount equal to ten per cent of the weight of hides. Two per cent of the lime weight is sodium sulfide which is used to accelerate the reaction for the removal of hair and epidermis.

The washed and rehydrated skins or hides are then transferred to the liming vats. The hides are subjected to several fresh limings during the first few days. Fresh lime is used for each batch (Moresi 1964).

After the lime treatment, the skins are placed in a vat of warm water to facilitate the removal of the hair.

Splitting and Bating.—Adhering flesh is "split" or trimmed off. Next, bating hydrolyzes the elastin fibers in the skin, which, before the hydrolysis, interfere with the proper swelling of the skins (Fig. 9). Bating is carried out with the aid of proteolytic enzymes, particularly trypsin (Wilson 1948).

Oropon, a product of Rohm and Haas, is one of the principal enzymes (bates) now in use (Moresi 1964). Since the enzyme acts best at pH 8.5,

Courtesy of John J. Riley Co., Woburn, Mass.

FIG. 9.   BATING, PICKLING, AND TANNING DRUMS

the bating solution is acidified to that pH with lactic acid. This operation also delimes the solution. Elimination of the elastin fibers and lime softens the skin, preparatory to tanning (Kaine 1964).

Tanning preserves hides and skins, rendering them resistant to deterioration. The two principal types of *tannages* are *vegetable,* which is an extract from either bark or whole trees, such as oak, hemlock, chestnut, quebraco, or sumac, and *mineral,* the principal example of which is chromium. There is also an alum tannage and a raw hide tannage.

Fundamentally, vegetable tanning is applied principally to heavy leathers used for luggage, wallets, belts, fine leather goods, soles, and belting, while chrome tanning is used for uppers of shoes (Moresi 1964).

Tanning operations are carried out in drums or paddles, into which tan liquors and skins are placed. The strength or concentration of the tanning solutions is gradually increased in order to prevent plugging of the surface pores which, in turn, would interfere with the tanning efficiency.

At present, tanning may require from 1 to 4 weeks, depending upon the types of hides or skins being tanned, thickness of skins, and other factors.

The chrome tanning process and the properties of the finished leather may be affected by a large number of variables, such as temperature, time, basic chromium sulfate concentration, and degree of agitation.

Fat-Liquoring and Dyeing are carried out in drums. During the fat-liquoring operation, the leather is lubricated with oils and greases. de-

Courtesy of John J. Riley Co., Woburn, Mass.

Fig. 10. Splitting Machine to Even Out Thickness of Leather

signed to replace the natural oil which has been removed during the beam house operations. The strength and mellowness of the leather are improved by fat-liquoring. Aniline dye stuffs are used for coloring the skins.

During or after these operations, the hides and skins are shaved, or "split" to the desired thickness on automatic shaving machines (Fig. 10) and are put through wringers, or setting-out machines. These machines remove surplus water, smooth out wrinkles in the leather, and prepare the leather for drying.

Drying is done on tacking boards, toggle machines, or pasting units. The leather is pasted on large glass frames which automatically go through a tunnel drier.

Finishing operations are done either by hand or by machine (Fig. 11). The finishing colors are applied by hand swabbing, by spraying in booths, or by spray machines attached to a tunnel drier. Dry splitting machines level the leather to the desired thickness. Machines are used also for ironing, glazing, and staking. Machine equipment includes large plating and embossing presses.

Courtesy of John J. Riley Co., Woburn, Mass.

FIG. 11.   FINISHING MACHINE

Courtesy of Ocean Leather Corp., Newark, N. J.

FIG. 12.   THREE TANNING DRUMS AND A BATE PADDLE

Measuring machines are designed to measure the square footage, irrespective of the shape and size of the leather.

Fig. 12 shows three tanning drums and a bate paddle.

GENERAL REMARKS ON LEATHER PRODUCTION

The converting of hides and skins into leather is a broad subject. It is impossible to specify in this summary the tanning materials and chemicals used, the time schedules of the operations, testing, temperatures, etc.

There is substantial variance, depending upon the nature of the raw stock and upon the end uses of the leather (Moresi 1964).

For detailed information concerning tanning, coloring, and finishing processes, the reader is referred to O'Flaherty *et al.* (1956–1963).

EXAMPLES OF LEATHER PRODUCTION FROM THREE AQUATIC SOURCES

The application of the above principles, with modifications, to three following types of skins from aquatic origin will be briefly described here: (1) salmon skins, (2) sharkskins, and (3) ground-fish skins.

Principal Differences Between Tanning Fish Skins and Land Animal Skins

The tanning of fish skins varies principally from that of land animal skins in the following respects:

Scale, or shagreen, is removed from the former while hair is removed from the latter. The scale, in the case of shark hides, is removed by chemical processes—not by scraping. It is carried out in paddles or drums. It is a delicate operation and no attempt is made herein to specify the chemicals used or the heat and time elements involved.

Vegetable tannages are generally used on shark and other fish skins, such, for example, as salmon, and on reptiles. Other types of tannage could be used for shark hides if the shagreen could be removed from the hides at the fishing stations or in the beam house. So far, a satisfactory process to do this has not been developed (Moresi 1964).

Salmon Skins

One of the difficulties experienced with earlier aquatic leathers was that, during the removal of scales and skins, its surface would be scratched and torn, rendering it unsuited for leather production. The Pacific American Fisheries, Inc., Bellingham, Wash., a large canning company of the Pacific Northwest, has remedied this drawback with salmon skins. By their patented process the skin and backbone can be removed from salmon undamaged.

In 1948, about three million pounds, or over 60,000 cases, of skinless and boneless salmon were produced (Anon. 1949). This pack could produce several hundred thousand skins.

Tanned salmon skins could be converted into a smooth, flexible leather of fine texture and durability, retaining its natural and variable pattern. This tends to give an "exclusive individuality" to each processed skin.

Notwithstanding the soft and pliable texture of salmon skins, they are, nevertheless, quite strong and durable. This is another asset in their application to footwear. Salmon skins are of medium to light weight and can be shaved to required thickness. The skins are irregular in shape, and run, on the average, about 6 in. in width and 15 in. in length (Metz 1953).

In the United States and similar countries, no salmon leather is being produced. It was never used to any large extent. The failure to exploit salmon leather is not due to difficulty in processing the skin but to economic impracticability. In the United States, salmon leather cannot compete with synthetics and leather from land animals (Butler 1964).

General Manufacturing Procedure.—The skins are soaked and the scales are removed mechanically leaving only the "scale pattern." The scales are cut off at the "roots," thereby eliminating the raspy surface condition which is prevalent in most aquatic type skins. The mechanical descaling process, resulting in a smooth finish, is necessary because so far there has been found no way to chemically de-scale salmon skins.

It is possible to dye salmon skins to give a wide variety of colors. The surface of the skin exhibits a two-tone effect, due to the fact that the skin surface and scale follicles take on different depths of color in the dyeing process.

Salmon skins are aniline-dyed. Skins are first drum-dyed in suitable dye baths, then hung to dry to allow the dye to set completely. After the dye has set, the skins are wetted back, pasted out, seasoned, glazed, and finished in the usual way.

As to porosity and comfort against the foot, salmon skin compares favorably with the best leather in this respect. The leather can be cleaned with any good leather polish and the original colors hold well (Metz 1953).

It is possible that, after a number of problems will have been overcome, such as that of determining the suitability of the skin, producing a skinning apparatus, and determining the effects of size, texture, tanning, and other similar considerations, salmon skin leather will show the way to the production of leather from other aquatic sources.

Sharkskin

The protective coating of sharkskin which corresponds to scales of other fishes consists of a calcareous deposit known as shagreen. The shagreen must be removed to render the sharkskin suitable for leather manufacture. Earlier scraping methods proved very uneconomical because they damaged most skins.

Progress in sharkskin leather production was stepped up with the appearance of the patented processes of Kohler (1925) and Rogers (1920–1922). The process for the removal of shagreen from sharkskins was developed for the Ocean Leather Co.

Between 1920 and 1927, within which period L. R. Moresi became President and General Manager of Ocean Leather Co., many changes were made to improve the process.   It was not until about 1925 that shark leather became suitable for use in shoes and fine leather goods.   Moresi gives the following account of the history of the utilization of sharkskin leather:

One of the first uses on a volume basis resulted from the introduction of sharkskin leather for the tips of the famous *shark tip shoes* for boys, misses, and children.   These shoes were widely publicized by most of the best manufacturers of children's shoes and by leading retailers throughout the country. Sharkskin tips replaced metal tips and, because of their long-wearing and non-scuffing qualities, they proved ideal for this purpose.   In the early thirties, shark tips were considered to be the most important development in shoes for boys, misses, and children.   The production of the leather was limited but sufficient quantities were produced to interest a few high-grade shoe manufacturers. Today, although the quantity of leather available is still comparatively small, practically all of the high grade men's shoe manufacturers have sharkshin shoes in their "line."   Also, sharkskin leather is used by prestige manufacturers of belts, watch bands, wallets, and fine leather goods of other kinds.

The identification and evaluation of the various types of sharks and the methods of catching them, removing the skins, and preserving them, are adequately discussed in a U.S. Government publication (Anon. 1945).

The Ocean Leather Corp., exclusive tanners of shark leather in the United States since 1925, has published the Fourth Edition of its booklet titled, "*The Shark Fishing Industry.*"   It lists ten species of sharks, which are commercially valuable for their hides and by-products.   The procedures for skinning the sharks and for fleshing, curing, packing, and shipping the hides, as well as the defects in shark hides, are adequately described in this booklet.

Tanning Operations.—The preliminary preparation of sharkskins for tannage is similar to that of animal skins.   First, the skins are freshened with water to wash out the salt and to soften them.   Subsequently, the skins are limed, fleshed on a machine, and bated.   The skins then are ready for tanning.

The procedure for removing the skin covering is the principal difference in the operation of tanning between shark leather and other leathers.   Because of the procedure practiced in the removal of the shagreen, chrome tannage cannot be used on sharkskin.   The hair on the hides of bovine animals is removed in the beam house with lime and sulfide.

Ground-Fish Skins

The tanning of ground-fish skins such as skins of cod, haddock, cusk, and pollock is somewhat simpler than that of sharkskin.   The sequence of operations is as follows: removing scales, leaching out salt, and treating skins with sodium carbonate to saponify small amounts of oil present. Bating is carried out as described before. Tanning is accomplished by either the vegetable or chrome method. Generally for this type of skins, chrome tanning is used since it produces soft and pliable leather.

The follicles remaining after removal of scales from the fish skins affect the thickness of the skins which in turn affects the depth of color that the dyed skins take on. This difference in color depth results in attractive color designs.

Up to the present time (1965), no leather from ground-fish skins is being produced in the United States—primarily because it cannot compete with leather produced from land animal skins or with synthetic leather. In seacoast countries, however, in which the livestock industry is not as highly developed as it is in the United States, the production of leather from ground-fish skins appears to be feasible.

SUMMARY OF LEATHER MANUFACTURE FROM FISH SKINS

The three examples described above for producing leather from aquatic sources serve to illustrate the parallelism existing between the general principles of leather production outlined earlier and their application to processing fish skins. The great many types of leather produced result principally from the wide variety of possibilities involved in manufacturing, namely: types of skins used; kinds of tanning, coloring, and finishing chemical reagents applied; concentration of chemical reagents; time and temperature of skin exposure to the chemical reagents; and type and degree of mechanical processing employed. All these variables revolve around the main "guiding posts" of leather manufacture, which are liming, bating, vegetable or chrome tanning, dyeing, and finishing.

BIBLIOGRAPHY

Anon. 1945. Guide to Commercial Shark Fishing in the Caribbean Area. Fishery Leaflet No. 135. U. S. Fish and Wildlife Service, Washington, D. C.

Anon. 1949. Leather from salmon skins. Pacific Fisherman 47, No. 3, 57–60.

Anon. 1951. Salmon skin leather shoes. Leather and Shoes 122, No. 6, 31–32.

Anon. 1957. The Shark Fishing Industry. Ocean Leather Corp. Newark, N. J.

Anon. 1963. The wondrous world of American leathers. Boot and Shoe Recorder. 164, No. 2, 69–93.

Blackadder, T. 1934. Method of chrome tanning of leather. U. S. Pat. 1,-985,439. Dec. 25.

Butler, C. 1964. Personal communication. Washington, D. C.

Harvey, N. D. Jr. 1932. Unhairing bath and process of treating hides. U. S. Pat. 1,844,160. Feb. 9.

Joy, A. F. 1953. Case of the tanned leather. New England Homestead. *126*, No. 9, 28–30.

Kaine, E. J. 1964. Personal communication. Woburn, Mass.

Kates, H. G. 1948. Luggage and Leather Goods Manual. Luggage and Leather Goods Mfgrs. of America, New York.

Kohler, T. H. 1925. Tanning and "dearmoring" fish skins. U. S. Pat. 1,524,-039. Jan. 27.

Lamb, M. C. 1923. The Manufacture of Chrome Leather. Anglo-American Technical Co., London.

Lamb, M. C. 1925. Leather Dressing. 3rd Edition. Anglo-American Technical Co., London.

Marriott, R. H. 1931. Principles of the liming process. Leather World *22*, 303–305.

McLaughlin, G. D., and Theis, E. R. 1925. Some principles of depilation. J. Am. Leather Chemists' Assoc. *20*, 246–276.

McLaughlin, G. D., and Theis, E. R. 1945. The Chemistry of Leather Manufacture. Reinhold Publishing Corp., New York, N. Y.

Metz, J. 1953. Personal communication. Boston, Mass.

Moresi, L. R. 1964. Personal communication. Newark, N. J.

O'Flaherty, F., Roddy, W. T., and Lollar, R. M. 1956–1963, Editors. The Chemistry and Technology of Leather. Volumes 1 to 4. Reinhold Publishing Corp., New York, N. Y.

Orthman, A. C., Surak, J. and Koch, J. R. 1936. Gelatin as substrate for measuring enzyme activity of commercial bating preparations. J. Am. Leather Chemists' Assoc. *31*, 484–515.

Orthman, A. C. 1937. Chemistry in chrome tanning. J. Am. Leather Chemists' Assoc. *32*, 459–567.

Orthman, A. C. 1945. Tanning Process. Hide and Leather Publishing Co., New York.

Pound, T. I., and Quinn, F. H. 1939. Evaluation of tanning materials. J. Intern. Soc. Leather Trades Chem. *23*, 94–105.

Proctor, H. R. 1922. The Principles of Leather Manufacture. 2nd Edition. D. Van Nostrand Co., New York.

Roberts, I. B. 1964. Personal communication. Boston, Mass.

Rogers, A. 1920. Sharkskins preparatory to tanning. U. S. Pat. 1,338,531. Apr. 27.

Rogers, A. 1921. Preserving sharkskins and the like. U. S. Pat. 1,395,773. Nov. 1.

Rogers, A. 1922. Treating sharkskins and the like. U. S. Pat. 1,412,968. Apr. 18.

Rogers, A. 1931. Industrial Chemistry. 5th Edition. D. Van Nostrand Co., Inc., New York.

Shreve, R. N. 1956. The Chemical Process Industries. 2nd Edition. McGraw-Hill Book Co., New York.

Smith, P. I. 1942. Principles and Processes of Light Leather Manufacture. Chemical Publishing Co., Inc., New York.

Smith, P. I. 1949. Standard Handbook of Industrial Leathers. David Woodroffe, Editor, Nat'l Trade Press Ltd., London.

Theis, E. R., Serfass, E. J., and Weidner, C. L. 1937. Properties of chrome tanning extracts. J. Am. Leather Chemists' Assoc. *32*, 166–180.

TRESSLER, D. K., and LEMON, J. M.   1951.   Marine Products of Commerce. 2nd Edition.   Reinhold Publishing Corp., New York, N. Y.

TURLEY, H. G.   1935.   Unhairing hides and skins.   U. S. Pat. 2,016,260.   Oct. 1.

WILSON, J. A. and MERRILL, H. B.   1926.   Methods for measuring the enzyme activities of bating materials.   J. Am. Leather Chemists' Assoc. 21, 2–18.

WILSON, J. A., and MERRILL, H. B.   1931.   Analysis of Leather and Materials Used In Making It.   McGraw-Hill Book Co., New York.

WILSON, J. A.   1936.   Comparative values of tanning extracts.   Hide and Leather 80, No. 13, 10–11.

WILSON, J. A.   1948.   Modern Practice in Leather Manufacture.   Second Printing.   Reinhold Publishing Corp., New York, N. Y.

CHAPTER 5

Fish Liver Oils

INTRODUCTION

Fish liver oils were used in the treatment of rickets as early as the Middle Ages. About 300 years ago certain fish liver oils were prescribed as a cure for night-blindness. Early in the twentieth century, with the development of vitamin chemistry, it was definitely established that night-blindness and rickets are largely caused by a dietary deficiency in vitamins A and D respectively.

Both vitamins A and D are found in certain fish liver oils in various proportions.

CURRENT IMPORTANCE OF THE FISH LIVER OIL INDUSTRY

The fish liver oil industry is at present (1965) particularly valuable to the many developing countries that cannot afford to produce vitamin A synthetically. Furthermore, by utilizing fish livers for the production of oil to supply vitamins A and D, it is possible to obtain simultaneously a vitamin B complex concentrate from the fish liver residue (see Chapter 7) plus a protein of good quality.

In the United States, there has been a decline in the fish liver oil industry since 1950 because of the advent of synthetic vitamin A which can be produced at a lower cost than the natural vitamin. According to Lee (1963), however, there has been a recent revival of interest in natural vitamin sources and in improvements in processing which may lead to some degree of recovery of vitamin oil processing in the United States.

CLASSIFICATION OF VARIOUS TYPES OF LIVERS

Butler (1955) arbitrarily classified fish livers on the bases of oil content and vitamin A potency as follows: (1) high oil content-low vitamin A potency, (2) low oil content-high vitamin A potency, and (3) high oil content-high vitamin A potency.

Reasons for Classification of Livers

Special processing is required for the extraction and separation of the vitamin-bearing material from the proteinaceous liver tissue, especially in low oil content-high vitamin A potency livers, where the oil and vitamin A are held closely connected to the protein and lack the advantage that a large volume of oil possesses by exerting a solvent effect on the oil soluble vitamins.

The process that applies to Class A livers is not suitable for processing Class B livers. Therefore, this arbitrary classification of fish liver oils is made to facilitate the subsequent description of the most suitable extraction procedure for each class of oils.

High Oil Content—Low Vitamin A Potency Liver Oil

This group includes livers of cod, haddock, hake, grayfish, and other similar fish livers. Such livers contain from 50 to 75% of oil by weight, and they range in vitamin A potency from 500 to 20,000 U.S.P. units.

Since such livers have a high oil content of relatively low vitamin A potency, they do not justify a costly extraction procedure. Furthermore, the large volume of oil present acts as a solvent for the vitamin A and thereby facilitates its extraction.

Direct Steaming of Cod Livers.—This procedure is the simplest one for the extraction of oil from cod livers. Essentially, it involves the direct heating of livers with steam, at low pressure, piped into the cookers.

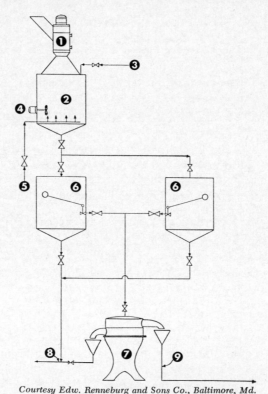

Courtesy Edw. Renneburg and Sons Co., Baltimore, Md.

Fig. 13. Flow Diagram for Fish Liver Oil Recovery

The "cooking" results in the thermal rupture of the liver cells which releases the oil. The oil rises to the surface and it is either dipped off manually or it overflows into an adjacent storage tank.

Another, and, more popular, procedure for oil extraction by steam is, first, to place the livers in a large tank into which steam is injected. Norwegian regulations require that the livers be heated to 185°–192°F. Heating is continued until the livers disintegrate and release the oil. The supernatant oil is either skimmed off, filtered and transferred into a settling tank, or, preferably, it is centrifuged to remove suspended solids and moisture (Fig. 13).

If the livers are heated in a steam-jacketed kettle, instead of by direct-steam, they should be mechanically stirred to facilitate disintegration and the livers are heated only to 158°–167°F. The liberated oil is separated as described in the immediately preceding paragraphs.

A flow diagram for fish liver oil recovery is shown in Fig. 13.

Small Scale Extractor of Cod Liver Oil.—An inexpensive percolator method of cod liver oil extraction has been suggested by Labrie and Fougere (1937), which is applicable to small-scale operations on shore. A diagram of this apparatus is shown in Fig. 14. A description of the apparatus and its mode of operation as given by Bailey (1952), follows:

The principle of this apparatus, a diagram of which is shown in Fig. 14, is that of a percolator in which the extracting agent is steam, instead of boiling water. The whole is constructed from galvanized sheet iron, and can be heated on an ordinary stove or over a fire. The lower reservoir is filled with three quarts of water.

On boiling, the steam formed reaches the livers, which are in the upper perforated reservoir through the pipe, entering Z through the holes X, and entering the upper reservoir through the holes Y. As it is rendered, the oil flows through the perforations C in the outside of the upper reservoir, down the annular space, and out through the opening at B.

The outer cylinder is insulated with a layer of asbestos. The galvanized-iron cylinder in which the livers are placed is pierced with holes $1/_{12}$ in. in diameter and spaced $1/_2$ in. apart. This cylinder is supported in the apparatus by the steam pipe and turns on ball bearings. The steam pipe is also fixed solidly to the two ends of the apparatus. Thus the cylinder which contains the livers can be turned easily around the steam pipe which acts as an axis.

A simple arrangement, consisting of a sleeve which fits over the steam pipe, permits shutting of the holes Y during filling of the cylinder with livers. The sleeve is lowered by means of an iron wire handle until it shuts off the holes. A rubber or cork stopper at the top of the steampipe acts as a safety valve.

To operate the apparatus, water is placed in the lower reservoir and the whole unit placed on a stove. When the water in the lower reservoir begins to boil, livers are placed in the upper cylinder, the sleeve is raised, and the top of the steam pipe is closed with the stopper D. Boiling is continued for about five hours during which time fresh lots of livers are added.

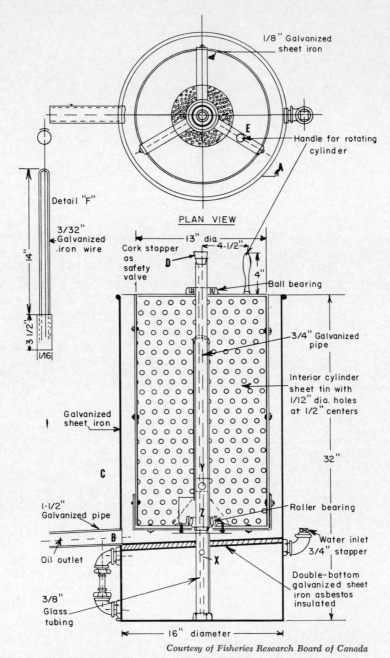

1/8" Galvanized sheet iron

Handle for rotating cylinder

PLAN VIEW

Detail "F"

3/32" Galvanized iron wire

14"

3 1/2"

1/16

13" dia.

4-1/2"

Cork stopper as safety valve

D

E

A

4"

Ball bearing

3/4" Galvanized pipe

Interior cylinder sheet tin with 1/12" dia. holes at 1/2" centers

Galvanized sheet iron

C

32"

1-1/2" Galvanized pipe

Roller bearing

B

Water inlet 3/4" stopper

Oil outlet

X

Double-bottom galvanized sheet iron asbestos insulated

3/8" Glass tubing

16" diameter

Courtesy of Fisheries Research Board of Canada

Fig. 14.   Small-Scale Extractor of Cod Liver Oil

It is necessary to agitate the livers from time to time with a stick, to ensure that all the livers come in contact with the steam. Toward the end of the operation, the cylinder can be turned easily by the handle E. Boiling is continued for as long as oil flows from the cylinder. It is possible to obtain 80% of the oil contained in cod or similar livers with this apparatus without having to press the residue.

From the oil outlet, the oil flows through a cloth bag strainer into a separator, which consists simply of a galvanized iron box fitted with two outlets, one at the bottom, and one halfway up the side. After separation, the oil is run off through the side outlet, a suitable oil level being maintained by adjustment of the water level in the tanks by means of the bottom outlet.

The chief advantage of this extractor is the fact that good commercial oil can be produced by it without the necessity of a steam boiler. An apparatus with external dimensions of 32×16 in., having a cylinder 24×13 in., should have a capacity of 25 gal. of livers every six hours. The apparatus is simple and easy to construct; it could be built readily by almost any sheet-metal shop.

Modifications of the Steaming Method for Oil Extraction

Other procedures have been proposed for the extraction of vitamin A from fish livers but they are not widely used. However, they will be briefly described here to illustrate the general principles involved.

Harrison and Hamm Process.—The Harrison and Hamm process (1941) for oil extraction from grayfish livers involves grinding of the raw livers and removing the freed oil by means of a basket centrifuge. It is claimed that 80% of the assayed oil content of the livers can be removed by this "cold" extraction method.

Oil Flotation Process.—Another method for the extraction of cod liver oil without steaming of the livers, which is supposed to give a very good recovery of oil and vitamins A and B is known as the "Flotation Process." Such a plant operates at Rimouski, Quebec by the Canadian Cod Liver Oil Co., Ltd. This process is described in *"Canadian Chemistry and Process Industries,"* Vol. 27, p. 555 (October, 1943). It is essentially as follows:

As soon as the livers are removed from the entrails, they are treated with Hopkinson's (1938) preservative (see p. 64). It is stated that this compound performs several functions: it preserves the livers, it coagulates the liver proteins, and it inactivates the enzymes.

When the preserved livers are brought to the plant, they are first dumped into a hopper and then are passed on a conveyor belt, to drain off most of the preservative. The livers are then very finely ground and mixed with water at the proper temperature in tall, cylindrical, open-top flotation tanks.

A supernatant oily layer is soon formed containing about 0.5% protein and water. The supernatant oil is drained off. The aqueous suspension of proteins also contains the residual water soluble preservative all of which is removed during the subsequent dehydration and filtration steps. Oxidation of the crude oil during storage and subsequent refining is prevented by keeping it under an atmosphere of nitrogen.

To refine the oil further, it is heated in a vacuum drier for about seven seconds to dehydrate it and to coagulate the residual proteins which are next removed from the oil together with the residual water soluble preservative, by very fine filtration. Finally the oil is destearinated by chilling it to about 32°F. and filtering out the stearine from the oil. The refined oil is stored under a nitrogen atmosphere, to exclude air and to prevent oxidation.

The B. E. Bailey Procedure.—Another approach to the same problem was reported by Bailey (1941). He states that the addition of certain chemicals, such as calcium chloride, results in a coagulation of the liver protein tissue. The contracted tissue, in turn, releases about 50% of a low potency oil. The remaining higher potency oil must be released by other methods such as steaming or solvent extraction.

Reduced Pressure or Vacuum Cooking.—In some plants the cooking is performed under a partial vacuum, thereby enabling the process to proceed at a reduced temperature. This process is designed primarily to obtain a higher yield of oil and, incidentally, it shortens the time of treatment, although, as far as vitamin A yield is concerned, it matters very little which procedure is used. The benefits derived are doubtful, and frequently do not warrant the extra expenditure necessary for this type of plant.

There are two types of such plants: vertical and horizontal. The Scott Patent vacuum unit consists of a vertical jacketed vacuum boiler, equipped with stirring paddles. The supernatant oil is decanted and the remaining liver tissue is drawn off through a bottom drain and subjected to solvent extraction for the recovery of the residual oil. The O. Wilhelm cooker is of horizontal, low-pressure type.

Extraction Without Heat.—Johnson (1924) describes a method for producing destearinated medicinal cod liver oil in the absence of any added heat. The procedure is essentially as follows:

Fresh livers are cooled to several degrees below the freezing point and they are transferred to a jacketed glass-lined tank wherein a freezing mixture is circulated through the jacket to freeze the livers. The frozen livers are, then, pressed in the frozen state, to extract the oil. It is asserted that this process results in a higher yield of a first grade medicinal oil. While the yield of oil is higher, by this method, yet, the vitamin A content remains the same.

The Wentworth Method.—Wentworth (1938) described another method for oil extraction from cod without the use of heat. It is essentially a forced dehydration method. After a mechanical disintegration of the livers, either dry beet pulp or dehydrated cereal grain pulp is admixed with the disintegrated livers. The dehydrating agent extracts water from the liver protein tissues with the simultaneous coagulation of the liver proteins and, as a result, the oil is released. The residual oil is removed by cold pressing.

The drawback with the cold extraction procedures is that the lipolytic enzymes are not entirely inactivated, and would tend to resume their activities if the moisture content in the oil is in excess of 0.3%. It is, therefore, advisable to pasteurize the cold extracted oils promptly in order to inactive the enzymes.

Low Oil Content-High Vitamin A Potency Liver Oil

This group includes livers of halibut, tuna, rockfish, lingcod, and sablefish. These livers contain 4 to 28% oil, by weight, and range in vitamin A potency from 25,000 to 600,000 U.S.P. units per gram of oil. In this class of fish, the liver oil is more closely held by the proteinaceous liver tissues.

Simple steaming methods, such as are applied to high oil content livers, are not sufficient. The oil and vitamin A extraction, therefore, depends first upon the successful digestion or solubilization of the protein, which, in turn, would release the enclosed oil and vitamin A.

Digestion Procdeure.—There are four digestion methods that are applicable to the extraction of vitamin-bearing oils from livers of low oil content-high vitamin A potency. They are (Butler 1955) as follows: (1) alkali digestion process, (2) enzyme and alkali digestion process, (3) acid digestion method, and (4) solvent extraction of oils.

A detailed description follows:

Alkali Digestion Process.—The livers are first ground through a hammer-mill or food-chopper to reduce their particle size. Comminution might be omitted if the livers can be sufficiently stirred during the subsequent processing to facilitate digestion.

A mild alkali digestion is the easiest method for releasing vitamin-bearing oils from livers that are high in vitamin A potency but low in oil content. This process involves the addition of from 1 to 2 per cent, by weight, of sodium hydroxide, or from 2 to 5 per cent, by weight, of a weak alkali such as sodium carbonate, and it is accompanied by stirring, while cooking with live steam at 180°–190°F. The liquefaction releases the maximum amount of oil. The liquefied livers are immediately subjected to centrifuging.

It is essential to have a complete digestion, since the vitamin A yield is directly proportional to the degree of digestion, which, in turn, is dependent on the length of processing time. The length of time required for processing depends upon the pH, temperature, particle size or degree of comminution, and amount of agitation of the digestion mixture. Too much alkali would cause excessive soap formation and emulsification, as well as adsorption of vitamin A by the soap.

It is advisable to add first a sufficient amount of alkali to neutralize the free-fatty acids, and then add a small excess of alkali for the digestion. Obviously, the greater the degree of decomposition, the larger the amount of alkali needed for this dual purpose.

At this point the mixture exists in three phases: oil, water, and dispersed particles. Such a mixture can best be separated in a three-phase separator.

The equipment used for preparing livers for digestion, such as holding tanks, pumps, pipes, and grinders should be flushed with water in the minimum amount required to transfer any oil and liver particles into the digestion tank. The amount of water used should not exceed one-half to one part to one part of liver, in addition to the water formed by direct steam condensation. This precaution is designed to prevent or reduce the amount of emulsification and adsorption of vitamin A on soaps, and also to compensate for the alternative advantages gained by using an excess amount of water, such as better heat transfer, mobility, and better contact of livers with the digestive agents, i.e., alkalies or enzymes.

The optimum digestion time depends upon a number of factors such as pH, degree of agitation, and the temperature of the mixture, size of particles, and types of livers used. For example, grayfish livers ground through a $1/8$ to $1/4$ in. mesh disintegrator screen require approximately one hour for digestion at a pH of from 8 to 9 and at a temperature of 180–190°F.

Usually, the free-fatty acid content is first determined, then, a sufficient amount of alkali is added to neutralize the acidity, leaving a slight excess of alkali for digestion. Too much alkali should be avoided since excessive alkalinity causes soap and emulsion formation.

Two patents on alkali digestion processes will be briefly summarized.

"Process of Obtaining Vitamin-Containing Oil." Young *et al.* (1938).— The procedure consists of immersing the fish livers in a tank of water held at 180°F. Sodium hydroxide is added to neutralize the free-fatty acids. The amount of alkali added depends on the degree of decomposition of the livers.

The livers are digested at 194°F., for one hour, with constant stirring. Within two hours after the agitation is stopped, the digested liver mass is separated into two layers, consisting of a bottom aqueous layer and a supernatant oily layer in the form of a semiemulsion. The bottom layer is drained off.

The oil is separated from the emulsion by adding to the latter three volumes of a five per cent saline solution and stirring the mixture for about 15 min. This treatment partially breaks the emulsion and it washes out the free alkali. After two hours of settling, the bottom aqueous layer is again drained off, and washing of the supernatant oily layer is repeated. Finally, the washed oily emulsion is heated to 167°F., and immediately centrifuged.

To remove traces of moisture remaining in the centrifuged oil, it is agitated in the presence of a dehydrating agent, e.g., anhydrous sodium sulfate. To protect the oil against oxidation, carbon dioxide gas is admitted at the bottom of the tank. The gas also brings about the desired agitation.

"**Method of Treating Fish Livers.**" Hempel (1939).—The procedure consists of grinding the livers to a smooth, fluid consistency and digesting them at a pH of from 8.5 to 12.5, using the weaker type of alkalies, such as borax, ammonium hydroxide, or trisodium phosphate. Alkalies that have a buffering action are particularly desirable, so as to facilitate the maintenance of the most desirable pH. The pH values recommended are designed to promote two functions, namely: (1) to neutralize the free-fatty acids and (2) to peptize the proteins without bringing about a saponification of the oil.

In this process, one part of from 26° to 28° Bé. solution of ammonium hydroxide to three parts of livers is recommended. To the mixture, enough water is added to make its volume double that of the livers used. The alkali, presumably, penetrates the livers and accelerates the digestion.

Digestion takes place at 170°–175°F., for from 15 to 20 min., which is sufficient to liquefy the livers. The oil is released from the tissues and is separated by centrifuging. The oil is washed and dried by a method similar to that described in the preceding patent.

Enzyme and Alkali Digestion Process.—A modification of the alkali digestion process has been suggested by Brocklesby and Green (1937). They precede the alkali digestion with an enzymatic hydrolysis. Their process is as follows.

The livers are ground and diluted with an equal volume of water. The pH is adjusted to from 1.2 to 1.5, using a 25% hydrochloric acid solution; then 0.05% commercial pepsin, based on the weight of livers, is added to the livers in the form of an aqueous suspension.

The enzymatic hydrolysis is maintained, with constant stirring, for from 35 to 48 hr., at a temperature of 110°–120°F. Upon completion of the peptic hydrolysis, the mixture is adjusted to pH of approximately 9 through the cautious addition of a saturated solution of sodium carbonate. The mixture is then subjected to the alkali digestion for about one hour at 175°F. Subsequently, the oil is separated by centrifuging.

Since the alkali digestion forms soaps to which vitamin A often adheres and is carried into the water phase, Brocklesby and Green suggest the following procedure for the ultimate recovery of vitamin A. The aqueous soapy discharge is mixed with a vitamin-poor, edible oil, heated to 175°F., and stirred to allow the added oil to extract the oil soluble vitamins from the aqueous soap solution. The added oil is then centrifuged off. This process is repeated if a further vitamin A recovery is feasible.

Similarly, the vitamin A concentration of a low vitamin A potency oil can be built up by the application of the counter-current system of wash oils. When such oil washings are applied a sufficient number of times, they can reduce the vitamin A in the liver mass to practically zero. However, it is a rather laborious procedure.

Advantages of the Enzymatic Hydrolysis.—The two advantages of the enzymatic hydrolysis are: (1) it tends to minimize the difficulty encountered in separating the oil from the emulsion formed by the alkali digestion, and (2) the addition of a mineral acid stops the action of lipases, thereby preventing the formation of free-fatty acids, although the cessation of the lipolytic action is only of a temporary nature.

Disadvantages of the Enzymatic Hydrolysis.—According to Butler (1955), the disadvantages of enzymatic hydrolysis lie in the requirement that the processing tank be constructed of acid-resistant material. The steam-jacketed tank must be equipped with a slow-speed stirrer and should be fairly tightly covered. The temperature should be automatically controlled.

The prolonged period required for the enzymatic hydrolysis, involves a much larger investment in equipment and in cost of processing than is necessary for the alkali digestion method. Also, considerable difficulty is encountered in controlling the excessive foaming resulting from the carbon dioxide evolution when sodium carbonate is added to the acidified mixture.

Acid Digestion Method.—Van Deurs (1931) describes a process for extracting animal or vegetable oils by macerating the material and changing the pH of the ground product to approximately 1.5, after which the material is cooked, agitated, and centrifuged. It is claimed that this treatment alters the surface tension of the product and releases the oil.

Solvent Extraction of Oils—Principles.—In the successful extraction of oil from fish offal or fish livers by means of a solvent, it is advisable, first, to disintegrate the product, and, second, to remove as much moisture as possible. Oftentimes, these two steps could be accomplished simultaneously by autoclaving the material which would tend to break it up, as well as to reduce its moisture content, followed by a drying of the material.

The disintegrated and desiccated product allows a better penetration and wetting by the solvents. It also allows, subsequently, a better recovery of the solvent from the solid particles. For economic reasons, the solvent and oil solution should be as concentrated as possible before it is subjected to distillation.

Requirements of Solvents for Oil Extraction.—The solvents for oil extraction should possess certain desirable properties which would render them particularly suitable for that purpose. Such oils should be (1) nontoxic, (2) noninflammable, (3) inexpensive, (4) noncorrosive, (5) available in large quantities, (6) easily purified, (7) only slightly soluble in water, (8) stable, (9) low in specific heat, (10) low in latent heat of evaporation, (11) good in solvent power for oils, and (12) low in boiling point (Brocklesby 1941). These properties prevent the meal and oil from being adversely affected during distillation and oil recovery. Vitamins should remain stable in the solvent and during distillation.

Some of the earlier oil solvents suggested were ethyl ether, acetone, dioxane, benzene, petroleum ether, trichlorethylene, carbon disulfide, carbon tetrachloride, and ethylene dichloride. Trichlorethylene is regarded as the most important solvent for fat extraction.

Although solvent extraction methods for fish liver oil recovery preceded the development of alkali digestion methods, the solvents have, to a considerable extent, been superseded by the alkalis, primarily because it has been practically impossible to find a solvent that would fulfill all of the above specifications. Recently, with the advent of new and more suitable solvents that are used in the vegetable oil industry, the solvent extraction process is regaining popularity and added interest.

Procedures for the Solvent Extraction of Oils.—There are many variations of the general procedure for the solvent extraction of oils. The optimum conditions for each type of product should, therefore, be experimentally ascertained. The process described by Nielson (1937) is an illustration of this process.

Nielson recommends the steaming of livers such as those of halibut at from 158 to 167°F., for from 30 to 45 min., with suitable stirring. After cooking, the livers are drained free of the aqueous material, while hot. Then they are placed in tight containers, and covered with a layer of paraffin, or carbon dioxide gas to protect the oil against oxidation.

The livers are rapidly cooled to —10°F., and are extracted with peroxide-free diethyl ether or a similar solvent. Subsequently the extract is filtered and subjected to vacuum distillation to separate the oil from the solvent, which is re-used in another extraction.

There are two more patents for solvent extraction. Buxton (1944) developed a procedure in which the livers are warmed with acetic acid and are then extracted with an organic solvent such as ethylene dichloride.

The extract is filtered, the acetic acid is washed out with water, and the solvent is distilled off.   It is claimed that the acetic acid penetrates the liver cells and thereby effectively releases the oil.

In the method of Nitardy and Jones (1937), the oil is extracted by any one of the three solvents: ethylene dichloride, dichlorethyl ether, or tri-chlorethylene.   Before the livers are subjected to the solvent extraction, the liver proteins are coagulated by heating in a manner which does not re-duce the vitamin A and D potencies.

Advantages of the Solvent Extraction Methods.—When solvent extrac-tion methods are used, the liver tissues tend to disintegrate and to coagu-late uniformly, resulting in a larger recovery of oil.

Disadvantages of the Solvent Extraction Methods.—The disadvantages of all solvent extraction methods (Butler 1955) are principally as follows: (1) the solvents impart to the extracted oils dark reddish colors, increased viscosities, as well as foreign odors, (2) free-fatty acids in the oils remain untouched and require subsequent alkali refining treatment, (3) solvents must be free from peroxides, as impurities, which tend to accelerate the oxidation of the oils, and, thereby, impair their keeping qualities, and (4) the elevated temperatures for the prolonged periods necessary for com-plete removal of solvents contribute to oxidation and loss of vitamin A.

Extraction Procedure for Livers Very Low in Oil Content.—Brocklesby and Green (1938) describe a procedure for the recovery of the oil soluble vitamins from livers that do not yield their oil directly, e.g., salmon livers. Their process consists of covering the minced livers with any suitable oil, such as grayfish liver oil or pilchard oil, and heating it at 212°F., for from 30 to 60 min. with stirring.

The solvent action of the added oil removes some of the liver oil and vi-tamins from the liver tissue.   The composite of released oil and added oil is removed either by centrifuging or by settling, but preferably the former. This procedure might be repeated several times for the further recovery of oil and vitamins.

The vitamin A and D content of oils for animal feed, such as pilchard body oil, could be enriched by using them as wash oils in the extraction of oil from salmon livers.

High Oil Content—High Vitamin A Potency Liver Oil

Livers which do not come under either of the two headings, class A or class B, have been put into a third class of "high oil content-high vitamin A potency livers."   This class of livers is subdivided into two groups as fol-lows:

(a) Livers containing from 30 to 75% oil by weight, with a vitamin A potency of from 0 to 340,000 U.S.P. units per gram. Livers from basking sharks typify the low-potency oils, whereas, livers from hammer-head sharks have been reported to contain as much as 340,000 U.S.P. units of vitamin A per gram.

(b) Livers containing from 45 to 75% oil by weight, with a vitamin A potency of 20,000 to 200,000 U.S.P. units per gram, such as livers from soup-fin sharks, where females have livers containing 20,000 units while males have livers containing 200,000 units. For distribution of oil and vitamin A in a soupfin shark, see Fig. 15 and 16.

TYPES OF COD LIVER OIL MANUFACTURED

The three types of cod liver oils produced are:

(a) No. 1 oil, (b) No. 2 oil, and (c) cod oil.

A detailed description of these three types of oils follows:

No. 1 Oil

No. 1 oil or the medicinal grade of cod liver oil is produced by processes described above. It is used exclusively for pharmaceutical purposes. Only oils which ooze out from the livers in a natural way and simply by the thermal rupture of the cells, at a relatively low temperature, e.g., 180°–190°F., may be used for medicinal purposes.

For the production of the medicinal or No. 1 grade of cod liver oil, only fresh livers are used. They are first rinsed in cold water and freed from dirt, blood, and gall-bladders. Inferior livers are thrown out. Similarly, slink livers which are the green ones that are low in oil, are also discarded.

No. 2 Oil

No. 2 oil is produced by further processing the residue of the first extraction. Thus, after No. 1 oil has been skimmed off the residue is subjected to additional steaming, followed by pressing. The expressed oil constitutes No. 2 oil.

No. 1 oil is superior in quality to No. 2 oil. These two grades of oil differ markedly in color; the No. 1 oil has a light straw color, whereas No. 2 oil has a reddish orange color, imparted to it as a result of a partial oxidation of the oil, which is accompanied by a loss in vitamin A potency. No. 1 oil has a considerably higher vitamin A potency than No. 2 oil. The latter oil is used as a stock feed oil. It can also be applied for industrial purposes such as for the softening of leather prior to tanning.

Since synthetic vitamin A has largely replaced the natural vitamin A, the demand for No. 1 medicinal oil has decreased very markedly, and the price has dropped accordingly. However, No. 1 oil is still in demand to a limited extent, for domestic use and to a much larger degree, for export trade. Recently, the demand for natural vitamin A has increased.

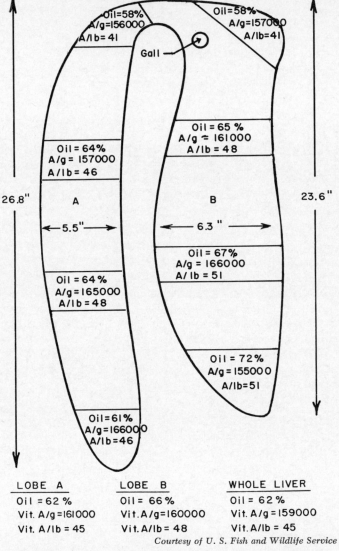

A/g - USP units of Vit. A
per gram of oil.

A/lb-Millions of USP units
of Vit. A per lb. of liver.

Oil=58%
A/g=156000
A/lb=41

Oil=58%
A/g=157000
A/lb=41

Gall

Oil = 65 %
A/g ≒ 161000
A/lb = 48

Oil = 64%
A/g = 157000
A/lb = 46

A

26.8"   ←5.5"→   B   23.6"

←6.3"→

Oil = 67%
A/g = 166000
A/lb = 51

Oil = 64%
A/g=165000
A/lb = 48

Oil = 72%
A/g = 155000
A/lb=51

Oil=61%
A/g=166000
A/lb=46

LOBE A	LOBE B	WHOLE LIVER
Oil = 62 %	Oil = 66 %	Oil = 62 %
Vit. A/g =161000	Vit. A/g =160000	Vit. A/g =159000
Vit. A/lb = 45	Vit. A/lb = 48	Vit. A/lb = 45

Courtesy of U. S. Fish and Wildlife Service

Fig. 15. Distribution of Oil and Vitamin A in a Soupfin
Shark Liver (Liver No. 1)

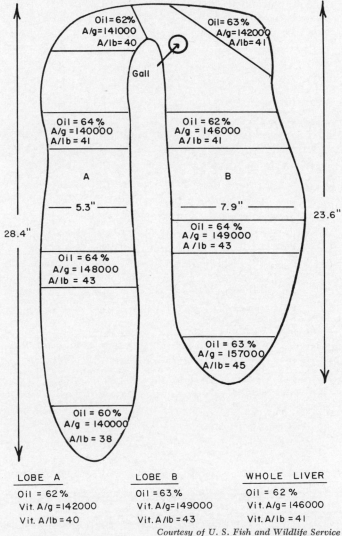

A/g –USP units of Vit. A
per gram of oil.

A/lb– Millions of USP units
of Vit. A per lb. of liver.

Oil= 62%
A/g= 141000
A/lb= 40

Oil= 63%
A/g=142000
A/lb= 41

Gall

Oil = 64%
A/g =140000
A/lb = 41

Oil = 62%
A/g = 146000
A/lb = 41

A

B

— 5.3" —

— 7.9" —

28.4"

23.6"

Oil = 64 %
A/g = 149000
A/lb = 43

Oil = 64 %
A/g = 148000
A/lb = 43

Oil = 63 %
A/g = 157000
A/lb = 45

Oil = 60%
A/g = 140000
A/lb = 38

LOBE A	LOBE B	WHOLE LIVER
Oil = 62%	Oil =63%	Oil = 62 %
Vit. A/g =142000	Vit. A/g=149000	Vit. A/g=146000
Vit. A/lb=40	Vit. A/lb =43	Vit. A/lb = 41

Courtesy of U. S. Fish and Wildlife Service

Fig. 16. Distribution of Oil and Vitamin A in a Soupfin
Shark Liver (Liver No. 2)

Cod Oil

Cod oil is prepared from livers that have partially decomposed and which yield an oil that is dark in color and high in free-fatty acids. It competes in the market with the various fish body oils and it finds similar outlets. The oil is often sulfonated and used in the leather-tanning industry. Its function is to soften and lubricate the leather fibers. Its other industrial uses are in the production of printing inks, oil-cloth, linoleum, paints, varnishes, and for tempering steel articles such as steel springs.

TYPES OF SPOILAGE OF COD LIVERS

The spoilage of cod livers may be anyone of several types or may be a combination of forms. They are: (1) chemical spoilage caused by rancidity, (2) biochemical spoilage caused by enzymes, or (3) microbial spoilage caused by fermentation or putrefaction of the liver tissue proteins.

METHODS OF COD LIVER SPOILAGE PREVENTION

Cod liver spoilage prevention involves the application of a number of precautions. They include the use of clean, air-tight containers which should be filled close to the top to minimize air space. The viscera should be separated from the livers, otherwise the enzymes of the digestive tract will also decompose the livers.

The use of ice is of very short duration. Freezing affords a much better degree of retardation.

CHOICE OF PROCESSING METHODS GOVERNED
BY CONDITION OF LIVERS

Vitamin bearing fish livers might reach the plant either fresh or preserved in several ways. Butler (1955) discusses the relative advantages and disadvantages of the various procedures as applied to each type of raw material which might appear in any one of the following five ways: (1) fresh livers and viscera, (2) frozen livers and viscera, (3) salted livers and viscera, (4) formalin-preserved livers, or (5) Hopkinson's (1938) method for preserving livers. Further explanations follow:

Fresh Livers and Viscera

"Fresh Livers" are referred to as livers which have not been frozen or to which no preservative has been added. Such livers are very vulnerable to microbial action, so that their extent of decomposition is an essential consideration in choosing a processing method. If the steaming method is applied to a low vitamin A potency but high oil content liver, then, it might, very likely, happen that the relatively large amount of free-fatty acids formed by lipolytic action would be imparted to the finished oil. Similarly, oils treated in this fashion might retain odoriferous protein degradation products.

If these decomposed livers were treated by the alkali digestion procedure, a portion of the added alkali would be removed in converting the free-fatty acids to soaps. The soaps would tend to form a stable protein-oil-water emulsion during the digestion and this would adsorb some of the vitamin A. The emulsion might be broken to free the oil, but the vitamin bearing oil adsorbed in the soap is not easily recovered, even if wash oils are added to the aqueous portion for subsequent oil-solvent extraction purposes. The resulting product obtained from the wash oil, which has been fortified with the oil and vitamin A from the soap, is actually a diluted oil with lower vitamin potency than that from the original fresh livers.

The vitamin oils recovered by solvent-extraction retain all the free fatty acids, and, as a result of the solvent treatment, are usually darker in color than oils extracted by the alkali method.

Frozen Livers and Viscera

Cold storage at 0°F. or lower, with air exclusion, is sufficient to withstand spoilage at least for several months. This method for the preservation of livers is ideal. After thawing the frozen livers, their softened tissues are much more vulnerable to microbial, biochemical, and chemical changes than they were before freezing.

Freezing to 0°F. definitely ruptures the cells which release a considerable portion of the oil upon thawing but a proportional amount of the vitamin A content of the entire liver is not necessarily released because this preliminary oil run is lower in vitamin potency than the residual oil that adheres to the proteinaceous tissues. Hence, sampling such oil for vitamin potency by the usual "core method" would give erroneous results.

The use of frozen livers requires rigid plant operating technique, with plans in advance to thaw definite amounts daily. Any mechanical failure would disrupt the processing operations, leaving a highly perishable product exposed to decomposition.

A satisfactory arrangement would be to keep the frozen livers in reserve, where fresh livers are processed quite steadily, so that any excess of livers, for daily production, is frozen and subsequently processed at a time when there is a shortage of fresh livers. Thus, a steady rate of production and a constant utilization of plant facilities are maintained.

Salted Livers and Viscera

In areas where there is no means of refrigeration or processing available, e.g., the shark fishing area of Lower California, livers are usually salted with 10% by weight of a good grade of salt. Salting is carried out on fresh livers after the gall-bladder, blood, and slime have been removed. The livers are cut 2 to 3 in. thick and, after salting, they are packed in air-free containers. Such preserved livers keep for several months.

Improperly preserved livers result from insufficient washing, the use of insufficient salt, spreading the salt unevenly on the livers, or partial decomposition of the livers before salting. Salt coagulates the tissues, rendering them more difficult to process than fresh or frozen livers.

Formalin-Preserved Livers

Formalin, in as little as 0.25% by weight (Brocklesby and Green 1938) while it is an excellent preservative, also coagulates protein. If the livers are preserved whole, the outer layer becomes case hardened; if the livers are ground first, they coagulate. An excess of formalin (2.5 to 5%) also coagulates the liver tissue, rendering subsequent digestion difficult.

Hopkinson's Method for Preserving Livers

Hopkinson (1938) found that the combined action of a germicide and a base adequately preserves livers. The procedure is as follows:

Livers are removed from viscera promptly after the fish are caught and they are placed in an aqueous solution of a germicide and a base. The best bases for the purpose are those having a pH of 9 or more, such as the hydrate of sodium carbonate ($Na_2CO_3 \cdot 10H_2O$). The germicides which can be used are formaldehyde, phenol, resorcinol, cresol, or alcohol. Two per cent by weight of each will be found satisfactory for fresh fish livers and most other material.

At port, the material is rendered in the conventional way, which consists of cooking the material and then pressing it to extract oil. The residue liver press cake is dried for sale as poultry feed.

Preservative for Thoroughly Ground Livers

A satisfactory preservative for livers can be prepared as follows: mix nine parts of soda ash with one part of sodium nitrate. Dissolve the two powders in an equal volume of water. Treat livers that have been washed and thoroughly ground, with five per cent, by volume, of the preservative (Anon. 1945).

VARIABLES AFFECTING THE QUALITY OF THE FINAL OIL PRODUCED

According to Butler (1955), the quality of the oil produced is affected by the following variable characteristics: (1) condition of livers, (2) process employed, and (3) optimum storage and shipment conditions for livers and oil. A discussion of each phase of the problem follows.

Condition of Livers

When the cod liver oil is to be marketed as the medicinal grade, it is of primary importance to start the extraction of fish liver oil from fresh livers. The Norwegian Government specifies that the livers must be fresh and free from blood and gall-bladders. They also give the optimum time and temperature for processing.

It has been pointed out earlier that No. 1 oil is light yellow in color. On the other hand, No. 2 oil is inferior in quality. It has a reddish color, indicating partial oxidation of the oil, which is accompanied by a loss in vitamin A potency.

Process Employed

The processing procedures of the fish livers which affect the quality of the finished product, may be summarized as follows: (1) steaming, (2) solvent extraction, and (3) alkali digestion.

Steaming.—Steaming releases the oil by means of the thermal rupture and agitation of the liver tissues. It is the simplest and most economical method. With fresh livers, the extracted oil is of good quality but with stale livers, the free fatty acids present might remain in the oil and necessitate an alkali refining. Furthermore, the yield by this method is not complete because the heating and the pressure applied is not sufficient to release all the oil. Frequently, from 25 to 30% of oil remains in the cod liver pressings.

Solvent Extraction.—In using solvents for extracting cod liver oil, care must be taken that the solvents are free from impurities that might affect the quality of the oil; e.g., the presence of peroxides tend to accelerate the oxidation of the oil during extraction. Oxidation imparts a reddish color to the oil and simultaneously reduces its vitamin A potency. Either prolonged heating or heating at elevated temperatures in this process accentuates these disadvantages.

Alkali Digestion.—In using the alkali digestion process in one of its modifications, great care should be exercised in using the proper amount of alkali; otherwise, saponification and vitamin A adsorption on the formed soaps would take place. If these difficulties can be properly circumvented, alkali digestion is most acceptable for the recovery of vitamin oils.

Optimum Storage and Shipment Conditions for Livers and Oils

Besides maintaining the vitamin potency of the oil during the processing stage, it is equally important to protect the quality of the oil during storage and shipment. Generally, oils and livers may be affected by: (1) storage temperature, (2) type of container, (3) moisture or foreign matter, and (4) sunlight and air.

Storage Temperature.—It is imperative to store oils or livers in a cool place, since oxidation is accelerated by an increase in temperature.

Type of Container.—Vitamin oils or livers may be shipped in rust-free drums of 5, 15, 30, or 55 gal. size after they have been thoroughly cleaned and dried. They should be filled to capacity, with a minimum of headspace remaining which is usually filled with an inert gas such as nitrogen or carbon dioxide to displace the air. In the absence of this precaution the residual air might oxidize the oil and reduce the vitamin A potency. Airtightness is obtained by sealing the bungs with sheet metal or wire.

Some producers tin coat their drums, others use the more recently developed enamels in order to prevent any reaction between the container and the vitamin or oil. Before adopting either practice, its merits should be ascertained, particularly regarding the possibility of causing any deleterious effect on the oil or vitamins.

Low-potency oils that are used for animal or poultry feed are usually pumped directly from storage tanks in the plant into tank cars or boat tanks, which are thoroughly cleaned and filled to maximum capacity leaving only a minimum of air space.

Moisture or Foreign Matter.—Oil should contain less than 0.3% of moisture or sediment, other than stearine or waxes. It should also be free from proteins which are usually dispersed or suspended in the moisture and eventually produce obnoxious odors.

Tanks should be thoroughly cleaned after use in order to avoid leaving a thin oil film on the sides and bottom of the containers. The presence of peroxides in this thin film would tend to reduce the vitamin A potency in any oil placed subsequently in such unclean tanks.

Sunlight and Air.—Oil exposed to air and sunlight would tend to undergo undesirable changes reducing thereby its vitamin A potency. These two drawbacks might be considerably reduced or overcome, first, by arranging or placing the tank in such a position that no light reaches the oil; second, by displacing the overhead air with an inert gas, such as nitrogen or carbon dioxide.

EXTRACTION OF FISH VISCERA OIL

The oil content of the viscera of certain fish, such as swordfish, halibut, lingcod, black cod, and rock-fish is very low, thus, their oil extraction is somewhat difficult. However, the viscera of these fish are relatively high in vitamin A content. The process for the simultaneous extraction of the small amount of oil and the vitamin A from the viscera is similar to the treatment of livers with a low oil content. The procedure (Bailey 1952) is essentially as follows: the viscera are ground up and alkali digested. A "pickup oil," such as herring oil, which is low in vitamin A content, is thoroughly admixed with the alkali digested viscera and the entire mixture is centrifuged. Extraction with fresh "pickup oil" or "wash oil" is repeated as often as necessary in order to obtain the entire vitamin A content from the viscera. This method for extracting vitamin oils from viscera is applicable only in the absence of the stomach, the liver, the milt, or the roe.

Solvent-extraction methods could be used to obtain a better yield of oil with a higher vitamin A potency.

BIBLIOGRAPHY

Anon. 1944. Atlantic coast dogfish livers. Can. Fisherman 3, No. 4, 6.

Anon. 1945. Guide to Commercial Shark Fishing in the Caribbean. U. S. Fish and Wildlife Service. Fishery Leaflet 135.

Bailey A. E. 1951. Industrial Oil and Fat Products. 2nd Edition. Interscience Publishers, New York.

Bailey, B. E. 1941. Preparation of vitamin A oils from dogfish livers. Fisheries Res. Board Can., Progr. Rept. Bull. 50, 10–12.

Bailey, B. E. 1943. Stability during household storage of vitamin A. Fisheries Res. Board Can., Progr. Rept. Bull. 54, 15–17.

Bailey, B. E. 1952. Editor. Marine Oils, with Particular Reference to Those of Canada. Bull. 89. Fisheries Res. Board Can., Ottawa.

Baird, F. D., Ringrose, A. T., and Macmillan, M. J. 1939. Stability of vitamin A in mixed feeds. Poultry Sci. 18, 441–448.

Brocklesby, H. N., and Green, K. 1934. Methods for production of fish liver oils from livers of low oil content. Fisheries Res. Board Can., Progr. Rept. Bull. 22, 18.

Brocklesby, H. N., and Green, K. 1937. Variations in vitamin A content of liver oils in the grayfish. Fisheries Res. Board Can., Ottawa.

Brocklesby, H. N., and Green K. 1938. The preservation of halibut livers and intestines. Fisheries Res. Board Can., Progr. Rept. Bull. 36, 7–9.

Brocklesby, H. N. Editor. 1941. The chemistry and technology of marine animal oils with particular reference to those of Canada. Fisheries Research Board Can. Bull. 59. Ottawa.

Bucher, G. C., Clegg, W., and Sanford, F. B. 1948. Distribution of oil and vitamin A in fish livers. U. S. Fish and Wildlife Service. Fishery Leaflet 290.

Butler, Charles. 1955. The fish liver oil industry. U. S. Fish and Wildlife Service. Fishery Leaflet 233.

Buxton, L. O. 1942. Effect of carbon treatment on fish liver oils, vitamin A destruction and peroxide formation. Ind. Eng. Chem. 34, 1486–1489.

Buxton L. O. 1944. Treating fish livers. U. S. Pat. 2,345,099. Mar. 28.

Crowther, H. E. 1947. Oil separation method for vitaminiferous protein material and the like. U. S. Pat. 2,413,692. Jan. 7.

Ewe, G. E. 1934. Stability of cod liver oil under commercial distribution conditions. J. Am. Pharm. Assoc. 22, 1085–1086.

Guttman, A. 1950. The value of cod liver residue. Fisheries Res. Board Can., Progr. Rept. Atlantic Station 49, 5.

HARRISON, R. W., and HAMM, W. S. 1941. Extraction of vitamin A from dog-fish livers. Pacific Fisherman *39*, 9, 37–39.

HEMPEL, H. 1939. Method of treating fish livers. U. S. Pat. 2,156,985. May 2.

HOLMES, A. D., and PIGOTT, M. G. 1942. Comparative stability of vitamin A in cod liver oil. J. Am. Pharm. Assoc. *31*, 521–523.

HOPKINSON, L. T. 1938. Method of producing oil from oil-containing protein material. U. S. Pat. 2,107,245. Feb. 1.

JOHNSON, E. M. Jr. 1924. Process of producing cod-liver oil. U. S. Pat. 1,519,-779. Dec. 16.

LABRIE, H., and FOUGERE, H. 1937. New cod liver oil extractor. Fisheries Res. Board Can., Progr. Rept. Gaspe Exptl. Sta. Bull. *21*, 6–8.

LEE, C. F. 1963. Processing fish meal and oil. *In* Industrial Fishery Technology, M. E. Stansby, Editor, with the editorial assistance of J. A. DASSOW, Reinhold Publishing Corp., New York, N. Y.

NIELSON, C. 1937. Method of extracting liver oil. U. S. Pat. 2,078,404. Apr. 27.

NITARDY, F. W., and JONES, W. S. 1937. Extraction of vitaminiferous oils. U. S. Pat. 2,067,279. Jan. 12.

PARFENTJEV, I. A. 1946. Recovery of fatty substances. U. S. Pat. 2,395,790. Feb 26.

POWER, H. E., and VAN DEN HEUVEL, F. A. 1950. A new method of processing cod livers. Fisheries Res. Board Can., Progr. Rept. Atlantic Coast Sta. Note No. 114.

PUGSLEY, L. I. 1937. Variations in vitamin A content of liver oils in the grayfish. Fisheries Res. Board Can., Progr. Rept. Pacific Coast Sta. *33*, 3–5.

RAPSON, W. S., and SCHWARTZ, H. M. 1944. South African fish products. J. Soc. Chem. Ind. *63*, 18–21.

SANFORD, F. B., and JONES, G. I. 1946. Liquid gold. International Fisherman and Allied Worker *6*, No. 4,5.

TANIKAWA, E. 1965. Marine Products in Japan. Published by the author who is Professor of Marine Food Technology, Faculty of Fisheries, Hokkaido University, Hakodate, Hokkaido, Japan.

TRESSLER, D. K., and LEMON, J. M. 1951. Marine Products of Commerce. 2nd Edition. Reinhold Publishing Corp., New York, N. Y.

VAN DEURS, J. A. S. 1931. Process for treating fatty raw materials. U. S. Pat. 1,833,061. Nov. 24.

WALFORD, L. A. 1944. Observations on the shark fishery in the central part of the Gulf of California with records of vitamin potency of liver oils and with keys to identification of commercially important sharks. U. S. Fish and Wildlife Service, Fishery News *6*, No. 6, 3.

WENTWORTH, H. A. 1938. Method of preparing fish liver oils. U. S. Pat. 2,-134,163. Oct. 25.

WOOD, B. A., and FERGUSON, E. J. 1941. Commercial production of fish-liver oils. J. Council Sci. and Ind. Res. *14*, No. 4, 311–314.

YOUNG, F. H., and ROBINSON, H. D. 1938. Process of obtaining vitamin containing oils. U. S. Pat. 2,136,481. Nov. 15.

CHAPTER 6

Non-Fat Components of Fish Oils

INTRODUCTION

Fish oils consist principally of long chain fatty acid triglycerides. In addition, fish oils contain a number of nonfat constituents, also known as unsaponifiable substances, which are oil soluble and which occur in varying amounts depending on the source from which the oil is obtained. While the unsaponifiables are usually present in fish oils, they may also be extracted from the fish organs with the oils during production of fish body oils or fish liver oils. These non-fat components consist of the following (1) vitamin A, (2) vitamin D, (3) cholesterol, (4) lecithin, (5) pigments of fish oils, (6) glyceryl ethers, and (7) hydrocarbons.

A brief description of these substances (Bailey 1952) follows:

VITAMINS

Vitamin A

Physiological Properties of Vitamin A.—The fat-soluble vitamin A is found in high concentrations in liver oils of certain fish species. It is also found, to a lesser degree, in fish body oils and fish organ oils of other fish species. The vitamin A potency present in a species of fish, whether in livers or in organs, constitutes a distinguishing characteristic of the species (Table 1).

An adequate supply of vitamin A in the diet is essential to life, growth, reproduction and lactation. Vitamin A deficiency in the diet of animals renders most of their epithelial tissues susceptible to infection. In humans, vitamin A deficiency may lead to colds, diseases of the respiratory tract, infections of the eyes accompanied by exudations at the corners of the eyes, a decrease in the capacity of the eyes to accommodate themselves to proper vision in dim light, diarrhea, skin disturbances, and/or a degenerative nervous system. On the other hand, excessive amounts of vitamin A are harmful.

The precursor of vitamin A is synthesized in plants as the pigment carotene, along with several other closely related pigments. Carotene occurs not only in carrots from which it was first isolated, but also in green plants, where its characteristic golden yellow color is masked by the more abundant green chlorophyll. Mammals convert carotene to vitamin A.

Neilands (1947) showed that, under specified conditions, fish are also able to convert carotene slowly to vitamin A. However, the occurrence of

69

TABLE 1

VITAMIN A CONTENT OF OILS FROM FISHERY SOURCES HAVING COMMERCIAL IMPORTANCE IN THE UNITED STATES & ALASKA (BUTLER 1955)[1]

Common Name	Area in Which Fish Are Caught	Source of Oil	Per Cent of Round Weight[2]	Oil Content, %	Vitamin A Content in U.S.P. Units Per Gram of Oil	
					Range	Average
Soupfin shark	Pacific (male)	Liver	10	55–68	45,000–200,000	120,000
"	" (female)	"	10	65–72	15,000–40,000	32,000
Grayfish (dogfish)	" -Alaska	"	10	67–72	2,000–20,000	5,000
" "	" -Hecate Strait	"	10	65–70	7,000–15,000	10,000
" "	" -Wash.-Ore.	"	10	50–70	8,000–25,000	14,000
" "	" -N. Calif.	"	10	62–68	12,000–20,000	15,000
Halibut	Pacific-area 3[3]	Liver	1.5–3	8–21	40,000–160,000	87,000
"	" - " 2[4]	"	1–1.75	17–27	20,000–65,000	40,000
"		Viscera[5]	2.5–5	2–5	70,000–700,000	200,000
Sablefish	Pacific	Liver	2–2.5	10–26	50,000–190,000	90,000
"		Viscera	3–4	5–12	90,000–250,000	125,000
Lingcod	Pacific	Liver	1–1.5	8–20	40,000–550,000	175,000
"		Viscera	1.8–3	4–15	10,000–175,000	40,000
Sleeper shark	Pacific	Liver	10–15	40–55	5,000–15,000	7,000
Mud shark	"	"	10–15	60–65	5,000–7,000	5,500
Great blue shark	"	"	[6]	30–45	7,000–27,000	20,000
Hammerhead shark	" -Atlantic	"	"	30–40	30,000–120,000	50,000
" "	"	"	"	55–75	20,000–150,000	60,000
" "	Atlantic	"	"	[6]	5,000–140,000	40,000
Little black tip	Florida	"	"	[6]	10,000–125,000	50,000
Tiger shark	Florida	"	"	40–60	5,000–25,000	5,000
Sand-bar shark	"	"	"	45–60	2,000–5,000	3,000
Nurse shark	"	"	"	[6]	3,000–15,000	8,000
Dusky shark	"	"	"	[6]	1,000–10,000	3,000
Leopard shark	Pacific	"	"	40–50	5,000–60,000	25,000
Bay shark	"	"	"	60–75	2,000–20,000	10,000

Species	Region	Part				
Thresher shark	"	"	"	45–55	1,000–5,000	3,000
Mexican shark	"	"	"	40–50	20,000–80,000	40,000
Gray smooth hound	Argentina-Brazil	"	"	50–60	10,000–25,000	20,000
Cazon shark	Pacific	"	7–10	30–45	10,000–200,000	50,000
Albacore tuna	"	"	1.5–2	7–20	10,000–60,000	25,000
Bluefin tuna	"	"	[6]	4–6	25,000–100,000	75,000
Yellowfin tuna	"	"	"	3–5	35,000–90,000	50,000
Skipjack tuna	"	"	"	4–6	30,000–60,000	40,000
Bonito	"	"	"	4–12	15,000–60,000	35,000
Swordfish	Pacific-Atlantic	Viscera	1.4–2.6	8–35	20,000–400,000	250,000
	"	Liver	3–6	6–12	2,000–30,000	10,000
Black sea bass	Pacific	Liver	[6]	13–20	100,000–1,000,000	300,000
Totuava	Pacific	Liver	[6]	15–25	40,000–400,000	[6]
Cod	Atlantic		3–5	20–60	1,000–6,000	2,000
Rosefish		Waste[7]	[6]	2–4	3,000–5,000	[6]
Halibut	Pacific	Liver	1.5–2.5	15–25	40,000	"
Rockfish	"	"	1–1.5	5–25	14,000–300,000	"
	"	Viscera	1.5–2.5	2–15	15,000–125,000	"
Petrale sole	Pacific	Liver	1–1.5	6–25	4,000–175,000	
Herring		Body	[6]	5–25	50–300	90
Pilchard			[6]	5–25	50–800	100
Menhaden	Atlantic		[6]	5–20	500	[6]

[1] These data compiled from reports of research at the laboratories of the Fish and Wildlife Service and of the Fisheries Research Board of Canada, and from articles published by representatives of commercial processors of fish livers and viscera. For the most part, the data are based on large lots of material or on samples taken over the normal season for the species. Vitamin D data for some of these species are included in Table 3.

[2] Per cent of round weight means the proportion of liver weight to the weight of the entire fish (undressed) expressed as per cent.

[3] Area 3 is defined by the International Halibut Commission regulations as follows: "Area 3 shall include all the convention waters off the coast of Alaska that are between Area 2 and a straight line running south from the southwestern extremity of Cape Sagak on Unmak Island, at a point approximately latitude 52°49'30" N., longitude 169°07'00" W., according to Chart 8802, published January, 1942, by the United States Coast and Geodetic Survey, and that are south of the Alaska Peninsula and of the Aleutian Islands and shall also include the intervening straits or passes of the Aleutian Islands."

[4] Area 2 includes: "all convention waters off the coasts of the United States of America and of Alaska and of the Dominion of Canada between Area 1B and a line running through the most westerly point of Glacier Bay, Alaska, to Cape Spenser Light as shown on Chart 8304, published in June, 1940, by the United States Coast and Geodetic Survey, which light is approximately latitude 58°11'57" N., longitude 136°38'18" W., thence south one-quarter east and is exclusive of the areas closed to all halibut fishing in Section 9 of these regulations."

[5] Viscera, unless otherwise designated, means the contents of the body cavity minus the liver, stomach, and gonads.

[6] The source from which information listed here was obtained did not supply data under this heading.

[7] Waste is the entire body of the rosefish minus the fillet or edible portion. It includes head, backbone, skin, and viscera.

vitamin A in fish oils follows this generally accepted cycle: the phyto-plankton, i.e., the minute floating plants that contain carotene and other vitamin A precursors, are consumed by the zooplankton, which are the minute animal organisms living in the sea. The zooplankton assimilate carotene and convert it into astacin, another carotenoid pigment. Fish eat the zooplankton and convert the astacin into vitamin A.

Hickman *et al.* (1944) and Quackenbush *et al.* (1942) showed that supplementing vitamin A in the diet with vitamin E (tocopherol) in-creases the effectiveness of the former. Hickman *et al.* (1944) referred to this phenomenon as a "sparing" action.

Pure vitamin A, extracted from fish, has a biological activity of about 4,-000,000 U.S.P. units per gram.

Chemical and Physical Properties of Vitamin A.—Vitamin A occurs in several forms: vitamin A_1 and vitamin A_2.

Vitamin A_1.—Vitamin A_1 is the same as vitamin A. It is the predominant form occurring in fish, particularly, in fish livers. It has five conjugated double bonds.

Structural Formula for Vitamin A:

$$
\begin{array}{c}
CH_3 \quad CH_3 \\
\diagdown \diagup \\
C \\
\diagup \quad \diagdown \\
H_2C \quad\quad C-CH{=}CH-\overset{\overset{\displaystyle CH_3}{|}}{C}{=}CH-CH{=}CH-\overset{\overset{\displaystyle CH_3}{|}}{C}{=}CH-CH_2OH \\
| \quad\quad\quad \| \\
H_2C \quad\quad C-CH_3 \\
\diagdown \quad \diagup \\
CH_2
\end{array}
$$

Vitamin A_2.—Vitamin A_2 is found in livers and some tissues of fresh-water fish. The biological activity of vitamin A_2 is approximately 1,300,-000 U.S.P. units per gram (Shantz 1948). It has six conjugated double bonds. Vitamins A_1 and A_2 have different absorption spectra; similarly, they differ in the absorption spectra of their reaction products with anti-mony chloride.

Most of the vitamin A in fish liver oil occurs in the form of esters which are far more resistant to oxidation than the free-alcohol form of the vita-min. However, only a portion of the vitamin A is in the alcohol form. Complete saponification converts the vitamin A ester form to the free-alcohol form.

Vitamin A is inactivated by light, and more powerfully by oxidation, which can act directly on either the pure vitamin or on the vitamin in the presence of oxidized oils. Heating a vitamin A bearing oil at a relatively high temperature in the presence of air or oxygen will cause a very rapid diminution in most of its vitamin A potency; but heating the oil in the absence of air or oxygen results in considerably less deterioration of vitamin A potency.

When an oil is oxidized at room temperature, its vitamin A potency changes very little at first, i.e., during the induction period, while the peroxides in the oil form slowly. Subsequently, the peroxides increase very rapidly, and this is accompanied by a rapid decrease in vitamin A potency (Lowen *et al.* 1937) see Table 2.

TABLE 2

STABILITY OF VITAMIN A IN HALIBUT LIVER OIL STORED AT ROOM TEMPERATURE IN OPEN
FLASKS, EXPOSED TO DIFFUSED LIGHT (LOWEN ET AL. 1937)

Time In Days	Peroxide Value	Vitamin A Value (U.S.P. Units Per Gram)
0	9.1	. . .
1	. . .	78,000
7	38.1	79,500
17	80.5	79,500
21	135.0	46,500
24	194.0	16,500
26	263.0	9,450
31	381.0	2,850

Table Courtesy of Industrial and Engineering Chemistry. Copyrighted by the American Chemical Society and reprinted by permission of David E. Gushee, Editor.

Rancid fats, containing a high peroxide content, can, in the absence of air, destroy vitamin A (Smith 1939). However, vitamin A is not destroyed by a high free-fatty acid content in the fish oil (Swain 1948).

Some antioxidants prevent deterioration of vitamin A. The four isomeric forms of tocopherol are good antioxidants for vitamin A in fish liver oils. When lecithin is added to tocopherol it acts as a synergist and increases the effectiveness of the tocopherol. Slanetz and Scharf (1945) stated that the beneficial effect may not be due to the lecithin itself but to impurities in the lecithin.

Dassow and Stansby (1949) reported that the antioxidant nordihydroguaiaretic acid (N.D.G.A.) stabilizes vitamin A in oil. The effectiveness of the antioxidant was improved when 0.1% citric acid was added to 0.1% N.D.G.A. Simons and Buxton (1943) were granted a patent on a method of stabilizing vitamin oils and concentrates with 0.1% acetyl methyl carbinol. Musher (1946) received a patent on a procedure for preventing deterioration of vitamin A by emulsifying an oil with from 3 to 20 parts of blackstrap molasses.

Vitamin A is very rapidly destroyed by traces of cobalt and copper compounds, when present in vitamin bearing oils. Lead, iron, manganese, nickel, aluminum, zinc, and tin also have a deleterious effect on vitamin A, but to a lesser degree. Treating oils with activated carbon or fuller's earth may indirectly accelerate the oxidation of vitamin A by eliminating the naturally occurring antioxidants in the oil.

Vitamin A bearing oils may be hydrogenated at low temperatures with only a small loss in potency. Drummond (1919) hydrogenated oil at 482°F., for four hours and thereby completely destroying its vitamin A potency.

Diller (1938) found that chlorinating cod liver oil with more than 0.1% chlorine reduced extensively its vitamin A potency. Cady and Luck (1930) found that bubbling sulfur dioxide through the oil for 15 min. at 68°F., reduced considerably the potency of vitamin A. Treating the oil with solid sodium bisulfite at 212°F., in a stoppered bottle for 24 hr. destroyed vitamin A; but when it was subjected to the same conditions for only four hours, there was no apparent loss in potency. Bubbling hydrogen sulfide through the oil at 212°F., for six hours caused substantial loss in vitamin A. Ammonia gas bubbled through for 25 hr., or dry formaldehyde for one hour at 212°F., did not affect the vitamin, but chlorine gas destroyed it in 15 min. at 212°F.

The vitamin A of an oil prepared from fresh livers is much more stable than the vitamin prepared from stale livers, because in the latter, peroxides are elaborated by the lipoxidases of the stale livers.

Vitamin D

Physiological Properties of Vitamin D.—Vitamin D occurs naturally in at least two major forms that show antirachitic activity: (1) vitamin D_2 also known as "calciferol," or activated ergosterol and (2) vitamin D_3 also known as "activated 7-dehydrol cholesterol." They differ in their physiological activity.

Vitamin D_2 can also be produced by ultraviolet irradiation of ergosterol (Steenbock and Black 1924), imparting to it antirachitic activity which is of equal value to both man and four-footed mammals; but it is useless in poultry rations. A good method for producing vitamin D_2 is by irradiating ergosterol in a slurry of yeast and water with ultraviolet light. Fish oil, especially cod liver oil, is the best natural source of vitamin D_2.

Vitamin D_3 can also be produced by irradiating the pro-vitamin 7-dehydro cholesterol, or it can be obtained directly from cod liver oil, where it occurs as the chief natural form of vitamin D. Its antirachitic activity is of equal value to humans, animals, birds, rats, and chicks.

A deficiency of vitamin D, in its various forms, in the diets of growing animals causes rickets, which manifests itself in the formation of soft teeth and soft bones that fracture easily.

The synthesis of vitamin D is technically much simpler to carry out than the synthesis of vitamin A. Vitamin D, like A, occurs in fish oils largely as esters, with some of it in the free form. Bailey (1943) showed that the potency of the free vitamin D is greater than that of vitamin D esters.

Stott and Harris (1945) have shown a marked increase in potency of natural vitamin D on fortifying it with synthetic vitamin D_3.

Chemical and Physical Properties of Vitamin D.—All vitamins D, like the vitamins A, are soluble in oils and in the common oil solvents, such as ether, chloroform, and benzene. In pure form the vitamins D are white, odorless crystals. All vitamins D are sterols. The stability of natural vitamins D to heat, light, and oxidation is greater than that of vitamin A.

Cod and halibut liver oils stored for 16 months, whether exposed to light or in the dark, in either completely or partially filled drums, show a very slight loss in antirachitic potency. Fish livers and viscera are the best sources for natural vitamin D (Table 3).

Heating oil to 392°F., even in the absence of oxygen, destroys its vitamin D potency slowly and at 842°F., its potency is rapidly destroyed. The vitamin D potency is only slightly affected by either saponification of the oil with boiling 20% alcoholic potassium hydroxide, or hydrogenation at 131°F., for 36 hr., using a colloidal platinum catalyst.

Free-fatty acids in cod liver oil have very little effect on vitamin D. Bills (1925) found that the vitamin in a sample of crude Newfoundland cod liver oil was not affected by hydrogen peroxides, hydrogen sulfide, sulfur dioxide, or formaldehyde, but it was slowly destroyed by direct steam or by contact with mineral acids, and it was rapidly destroyed by nitrous fumes.

OTHER COMPONENTS

Cholesterol

Cholesterol and its esters are the only sterols that occur in fish oils. A few typical examples of the range of the cholesterol content in per cent, found in the following sources, are (Bailey 1952): (1) halibut liver oil, 7.0; (2) Atlantic cod liver oil, 0.3; (3) salmon egg oil, 3.0; (4) commercial pilchard oil, 0.7; and (5) oil from shrimp waste, 19.0.

Kimizuka (1938) showed that the consumption of cholesterol or its esters through the use of medicinal fish liver oils or fish body oils, has no untoward effect on the organism. Cholesterol is present in substantial amounts in wool fat, egg yolk, and milk. Cholesterol occurs in all cells of the animal body either by ingesting animal foods or through biosynthesis from small molecules. The average adult person carries approximately 200 gm. of it in his tissues. Cholesterol does not occur in the plant kingdom. The level of cholesterol present in blood is clinically important. Cholesterol is present in bile.

Cholesterol is a monatomic alcohol, with one double bond, occurring

TABLE 3

VITAMIN D CONTENT OF OILS FROM FISHERY SOURCES (BUTLER 1955)

Common Name	Area in Which Fish are Caught	Source of Oil	Vitamin D Content in International Units Per Gram of Oil
Albacore tuna	Pacific	Liver	25,000–250,000
Bluefin "	"	"	20,000–70,000
Yellowfin "	"	"	10,000–45,000
Skipjack "	"	"	25,000–250,000
Bonito	"	"	50,000
Swordfish	" -Atlantic	"	2,000–25,000
Mackerel, Pacific	Pacific	"	1,400
Albacore tuna	"	Waste[2]	67
Halibut	"	Liver	1,000–5,000
"	"	Viscera[3]	100–500
Sablefish	"	Liver	600–1,000
"	"	Viscera	100
Lingcod	"	Liver	1,000–6,000
"	"	Viscera	100–200
Rockfish	"	Liver	300–5,000
Cod	"	"	85–500
Ishinagi	"	"	3,800
Barracuda	"	"	2,000
Black sea bass	"	"	5,000
Beluga whale	"	"	50–100
Grayfish (dogfish)	"	"	5–25
" "	"	Body[4]	29
Ratfish	"	Liver	2–5
Soupfin shark	"	"	5–25
Herring	"	Body[5]	25–160
"	"	Liver	250
Pilchard	"	Body[5]	20–100
King salmon	"	Liver	100–500
" "	"	Offal[6]	50–150
Sockeye "	'	Liver	200–600
" "	"	Offal	100–300
Silver "	"	Liver	100–500
" "	"	Offal	100–200
Pink "	"	Liver	100–600
" "	"	Offal	100–300
Chum "	"	Liver	100–500
" "	"	Offal	50–100
Starry flounder	"	Liver	1,000
Rex sole	"	"	150
Skate	"	"	25
Mud shark	"	"	20
Snoek	South Africa	"	500–6,000
"	" "	Viscera	85
Stonebass	" "	Liver	700–1,300
Stockfish	" "	"	50–380
"	" "	Viscera	3
Kingklip	" "	Liver	85–600
Halibut	" "	"	1,000–2,000
Cod	" "	"	100
Ling	New Zealand	"	500
Yellowtail	Australia	"	9,000–17,000
Halibut	Atlantic	"	2,000
Mackerel, common	"	"	750
Rosefish	"	Waste[7]	50
Dogfish	"	Liver	3

Table Courtesy of U. S. Fish and Wildlife Service.
[1] Data on vitamin A content of most of these fish are to be found in Tables 1 and 2.
[2] Waste indicates offal from the cannery fish cleaning tables. The raw eviscerated fish is pre-cooked prior to this cleaning operation, hence some of the tuna body oil has been lost from this waste before it is made into meal and oil.
[3] Viscera indicates the contents of the body cavity minus the liver, stomach, and gonads.
[4] Body indicates the entire body of the fish minus the liver.
[5] Body indicates the entire body of the fish including the liver and viscera.
[6] Offal indicates the cannery trimmings, including heads, livers, and viscera but not eggs.
[7] Waste indicates the entire body of the rosefish minus the fillet or edible portion. It includes head, backbone, skin, and viscera.

with higher fatty acids, partly as an alcohol and partly as an ester. Cholesterol is soluble at room temperature in ether, benzene, chloroform, and other organic solvents; but in cold water, it is sparingly soluble, i.e., 100 parts of water will dissolve only 0.25 part of cholesterol. Notwithstanding its low solubility in water, it, nevertheless, forms aqueous dispersions and emulsified suspensions.

Cholesterol is derived from the unsaponifiable portion of fish liver oils during the production of vitamin A concentrate by saponifying the oils. The unsaponifiable fraction is dissolved in approximately equal parts of hot methyl alcohol, cooled to within the range of from $+5°F.$ to $-4°F.$, and stored overnight at that temperature. The crystalline cholesterol precipitate is filtered off and washed with cold absolute methyl alcohol.

Kraybill et al. (1940) described a commercial method for the production of sterols, which could apply to fish oil. It involves the direct adsorption of the sterols from the oil by aluminum silicate, extraction from the oil-saturated adsorbent with acetone, distillation of acetone, and extraction of sterols with methanol. O'Leary (1947) found that fish meal produced in Nova Scotia ranged in cholesterol content from 6 to 10 lb. per ton.

Cholesterol is used to manufacture 7-dehydro cholesterol which is converted into vitamin D_3 by irradiation with ultraviolet light. It is also used in the production of leather dressing, waterproofing material, cosmetics, ointments, and hormones.

Lecithin

Lecithin belongs to a group of fat-like compounds called phospholipides or phosphatides. A phospholipide consists of glycerol with one of its alcoholic groups esterified with phosphoric acid which is further partially esterified with an organic base. The other two alcoholic groups are esterified with fatty acids. The phospholipides can occur in two forms depending on whether the phosphoric acid-base radical group is attached to the alpha (terminal) carbon or to the beta (central) carbon in glycerol. The general structure of phospholipides is as follows:

```
        Alpha form                          Beta form
CH2—O—fatty acid radical            CH2—O—fatty acid radical
 |                                   |
 |                                   |        O—base radical
 |                                   |       /
CH—O—fatty acid radical             CH—O—P=O
 |                                   |       \
 |                                   |        OH
 |              O—base radical       |
 |             /                     |
CH2—O—P=O                           CH2—O—fatty acid radical
        \
         OH
```

Lecithin, the most important member of the phospholipides, consists of glycerol with two of its alcoholic groups esterified with a saturated and an unsaturated fatty acid; the third alcoholic group is esterified with phosphoric acid which is further partially esterified with the organic base choline: a nitrogen containing alcohol.

Lecithin is found in almost all animal and vegetable tissues where oil is present. It is the only phosphatide that is found in fish oils in limited but noticeable amounts. It dissolves readily in alcohol, ether, chloroform, benzene, or carbon disulfide. Acetone can precipitate lecithin from an alcohol-ether solution or from chloroform. Lecithin is insoluble in water, but when mixed with a small amount of water, it hydrates and swells, resulting in a thick emulsion or colloidal dispersion. Further dilution with water, and agitation, tends to thin out the aqueous emulsion or colloidal dispersion. It can combine with acids, bases, and certain salts such as cadmium chloride.

Lecithin is both a wetting and an emulsifying agent. These unique properties are imparted to it because the choline-phosphoric acid portion of the lecithin molecule is highly water-soluble and the fatty acid portion of the molecule is insoluble in water, but soluble in fats. It also has antioxidant as well as nutritional or pharmaceutical value because of its choline and inositol content. It is also a good dispersant. Consequently, lecithin has many applications in the manufacture of food, pharmaceutical, and industrial products.

The following are examples of typical uses of lecithin:

(1) As an emulsifier in the production of margarine.

(2) In chocolate manufacture, the addition of about 0.5% lecithin to chocolate liquor reduces its viscosity considerably, thereby saving on the use of cocoabutter, which would be more costly to use in order to obtain the same viscosity. Lecithin also serves as an emulsifier and wetting agent and it improves substantially the quality of the treated product.

(3) As an antioxidant in edible oils and fats.

(4) As a dietary supplement because it introduces choline and inositol.

(5) In cosmetics, as an emulsifying, penetrating and emollient agent.

(6) In paints, lacquers and printing inks, as an effective interfacial agent and dispersing agent.

(7) In rubber manufacturing, to promote curing and vulcanization.

(8) In petroleum products, as an antioxidant and dispersant.

(9) For fat liquoring, in leather production and textile finishing.

(10) To promote efficient utilization by the body of vitamins A and D.

(11) To improve the quality of bakery products.

(12) To form coacervates with proteins, carbohydrates, salts, alkaloids, dyes, etc., rendering them oil soluble.

A fluid lecithin is preferred to any other consistency because of ease in handling and in dissolving it. Fluidity is imparted to lecithin by adding to it about three per cent of high fatty acids such as stearic acid or soybean oil fatty acids.

Most of the commercially available lecithin is derived from soybeans, and some from egg yolks; nevertheless salmon roe could serve as a good source of lecithin after the fish odor has been removed from it. Hall (1929) stated that lecithin can be deodorized by treatment with either steam or an inert gas under vacuum.

Pigments of Fish Oils

Pigments occurring in fish oils (Bailey 1952) may principally be due to the following two causes: (1) natural oil-soluble pigments found in fish and (2) color changes occurring in fish oils either before, during or after processing, resulting in various pigment formations.

A further discussion of these causes follows:

Natural Oil-Soluble Pigments Found in Fish Oils.—The carotenoids, embracing the red, orange, and yellow oil-soluble pigments occur naturally in a number of different plant and animal fats. Moore (1929), and others have shown that some carotenoid pigments formed in plants are vitamin A precursors, or provitamins, i.e., they are converted by animals and fish from the active carotenoid form into vitamin A. Fish obtain vitamin A principally by ingesting smaller aquatic animal forms that already have vitamin A, or to a smaller extent, by converting the active carotenoid pigments into vitamin A.

Various carotenoid pigments found in fish are (1) astacin—principal red color in salmon oil (Sorensen 1935); also in livers, roes, and flesh of various other fishes, (2) fucoxanthin—principal yellow pigment in pilchard oil, (3) xanthophylls—pilchard oil, (4) carotene—pilchard oil, (5) taraxanthin and zeaxanthin—in the skins of a large variety of fishes.

Fucoxanthin and the xanthophylls, although similar to carotene, are "inactive" pigments, i.e., they do not act as precursors of vitamin A, in animal nutrition.

Chlorophyll (Tompkins 1930) occurs in pilchard oils only when pilchard feeds on microscopic green plants. Chlorophyll is probably the only naturally occurring noncarotenoid pigment in fish oils. The greenish color disappears when the oil is exposed to sunlight for as little as one day.

Color Changes Occurring in Fish Oils Either Before, During or After Processing, Resulting in Various Pigment Formations.—Color changes occurring in fish oils and fish liver oils before, during, or after processing, resulting in various pigment formations, may be due to several causes: (1) spoilage of fish during transportation, (2) temperature and time of processing, and (3) rancidification.

Further explanations follow:

Spoilage of Fish During Transport.—The raw stock should be as fresh as possible in order to yield light oil. Oil extracted from deteriorated stock yields darker oil.

Temperature and Time of Processing.—It is well established that excessive heat applied to raw fish stock for a prolonged period of time would result in darkening of the oil.

Rancidification.—Protein breakdown products developing in stale fish act as catalysts to accelerate rancidification of the darkened oil. Improperly cleaned containers may contaminate the oil. The oxides of metals such as iron, lead, and copper, when dissolved in oil that contains moisture and free fatty acids, can accelerate the rancidification and darkening of fish oils. Briod and Christiansen (1930) showed that cod liver oil stored for three months in contact with iron became darker and increased in iron content.

Glyceryl Ethers

In glyceryl ethers, which are obtained after hydrolysis, only one of the three hydroxyl groups in glycerol is tied up with fatty alcohols in an ether linkage. The other two hydroxyls retain their alcohol function. The molecular structure and melting points of the three commonest glyceryl ethers are as follows:

$$CH_2OH$$
$$|$$
$$CHOH$$
$$|$$
$$CH_2-O-C_{16}H_{33}$$
Chimyl alcohol
m.p. 142–144 °F.

$$CH_2OH$$
$$|$$
$$CHOH$$
$$|$$
$$CH_2-O-C_{18}H_{37}$$
Batyl alcohol
m.p. 158–160 °F.

$$CH_2OH$$
$$|$$
$$CHOH$$
$$|$$
$$CH_2-O-C_{18}H_{35}$$
Selachyl alcohol
m.p. 63–68 °F.

Several patents have been issued covering various applications: Baldwin and Bunbury (1933) described the use of sulfonated glyceryl ethers for cutting, cleaning, and dispersing agents. Baldwin, *et al.* (1936) stated that glyceryl ethers are useful as ingredients for textile treatment media, and as perfume fixatives. Baldwin and Bunbury (1937) covered the production of glyceryl ethers from selachyl alcohol as useful in sizing, flax-ratting, bleaching, mordanting, mercerizing baths, and as a special type of detergent.

Hydrocarbons

Several hydrocarbons have been found in fish oils. Certain shark liver oils may contain about 85% of hydrocarbons in their unsaponifiable portion. Squalene ($C_{30}H_{50}$) a highly unsaturated hydrocarbon containing six unsaturated bonds per molecule, is the main hydrocarbon found in certain shark liver oils. Its structural formula is as follows:

$$CH_3$$
$$C=CH(CH_2)_2C-CH(CH_2)_2C=CH(CH_2)_2$$
$$CH_3 \qquad CH_3 \qquad CH_3$$

$$CH_3$$
$$CH=C(CH_2)_2CH=C(CH_2)_2CH=C$$
$$CH_3 \qquad CH_3 \qquad CH_3$$

Squalene

A very small amount of squalene has been found in Newfoundland cod liver oil (Drummond and Baker 1929). Generally, fish liver oils with a high content of unsaponifiable matter may contain squalene. Tsujimoto (1932) found, in his investigations on liver oils from various sources, that the lower the specific gravity of the oil, commencing with 0.9000, the higher the squalene content. This observation checks with the fact that squalene, by itself, has a specific gravity of 0.8559 at 68°F.

Squalene has very little nutritive value. It is worthy of note that the presence of squalene in fish renders it free from parasites. Squalene imparts a brilliant sheen to natural and artificial silks, when it is incorporated in their finishing operations. Other suggested used are as a lubricant, as a carrier of perfumes, and for filling thermometers.

Some of the patents that have been granted for the various uses of squalene are as follows: (1) Bunbury and Sexton (1935) mentioned the use of squalene hexahydrobromide as an intermediate in the production of retarding agents for rubber manufacture. (2) Bunbury, et al. (1934) described a treatment of squalene-containing oils which converts them into emulsifying agents for the textile, rubber, and other industries.

BIBLIOGRAPHY

ANON. 1946. Vitamin Production in Argentina. Norsk Medicinal Union, Bergen, Norway.

BAILEY, B. E. 1941. Preparation of vitamin A oils from dogfish livers. Fisheries Res. Board Can., Progr. Rept. Pacific Coast Sta. 50, 10–12.

BAILEY, B. E. 1943. Stability during household storage of vitamin A. Fisheries Res. Board Can., Progr. Rept. Pacific Coast Sta. 54, 15–17.

BAILEY, B. E. Editor. 1952. Marine Oils with Particular Reference to Those of Canada. Bull. 89. Fisheries Res. Board Can., Ottawa.

BAIRD, F. D., RINGROSE, A. T., and MACMILLAN, M. J. 1939. Stability of vitamin A in mixed feeds. Poultry Sci. 18, 441–448.

BALDWIN, A. W., and BUNBURY, H. M. 1933. Detergent agents. Brit. Pat. 398,818. Sept. 11.

BALDWIN, A. W., and BUNBURY, H. M. 1937. Sulphated selachyl alcohol. U. S. Pat. 2,101,831. Dec. 14.

BALDWIN, A. W., HEILBRON, I. M., and JONES, W. E. 1936. Ethers of polyhydric alcohols. U. S. Pat. 2,038,705. Apr. 28.

BAXTER, J. G. 1939. Hydrocarbons and vitamins from animal oils by vacuum distillation. U. S. Pat. 2,169,192. Aug. 8.

BETHKE, R. M., RECORD, P. R., and WILDER, O. H. M. 1939. Stability of carotene and vitamin A in mixed rations. Poultry Sci. *18*, 179–187.

BILLS, C. E. 1925. The resistance of the antirachitic substance in cod-liver oil to reagents. J. Biol. Chem. *64*, 1–9.

BILLS, C. E. 1937. New forms and sources of vitamin D. J. Am. Med. Assoc. *108*, 13–15.

BILLS, C. E., MASSENGALE, O. N., and IMBODEN, M. 1934. Demonstration of the existence of two forms of vitamin D in fish-liver oils. Science, *80*, 596.

BOSE, S. M. 1947. Effect of storage and acidity on the protection of vitamin A in shark-liver oil by antioxidants. Current Sci. *16*, 119–120. India.

BRIOD, A. E., and CHRISTIANSEN, W. G. 1930. A study of the darkening of cod liver oil in the presence of iron. J. Am. Pharm. Assoc. *19*, 1308–1309.

BROCKLESBY, H. N. 1941. Editor. The Chemistry and Technology of Marine Animal Oils with Particular Reference to Those of Canada. Bull. 59. Fisheries Res. Board Can., Ottawa.

BUNBURY, H. M., SEXTON, W. A., and STEWART, A. 1934. Sulphonation of squalene and oil containing squalene. U.S. Pat. 1,961,683. June 5.

BUNBURY, H. M., and SEXTON, W. A. 1935. Squalene derivative and making the same. U. S. Pat. 1,991,999. Feb. 19.

BURKHARDT, G. H., et al. 1934. Pigmented marine animal oils. I. Pigments from the angler fish, the prawn and the whale. Biochem. J. 28, 1698–1701.

BUTLER, C. 1955. The fish liver oil industry. U. S. Fish and Wildlife Service, Fishery Leaflet 233.

BUXTON, L. O. 1942. Effect of carbon treatment on fish-liver oils, vitamin A destruction and peroxide formation. Ind. Eng. Chem. *34*, 1486–1489.

CADY, O. H., and LUCK, J. M. 1930. Chemistry of vitamin A. J. Biol. Chem. *86*, 743–754.

CAWLEY, J. D., ROBESON, C. D., WEISLER, L., SHANTZ, N. D. and BAXTER, J. G. 1951. Synthesis of vitamin A active compounds containing repeated isoprene units. U. S. Pat. 2,576,103. Nov. 27.

CHALMERS, W., and BIELY, J. 1940. Pilchard oil as a source of vitamins A and D. Proc. Roy. Soc. Can. *145*, 1940.

CHANNON, H. J. 1928. The biological significance of the unsaponifiable matter of oils. III. Fish-liver oils. Biochem. J. *22*, 51–59.

DANIELLI, J. F., and FOX, D. L. 1941. Surface chemistry of carotenoids. I. Astacene. Biochem. J. *35*, 1388–1395.

DASSOW, J. A., and STANSBY, M. E. 1949. Stabilization of vitamin A in halibut liver oil with nordihydroguaiaretic acid (NDGA). J. Am. Oil Chemists' Soc. *26*, No. 9, 475–479.

DILLER. 1938. Vitamin A investigations. Deut. Apoth. Ztg. *53*, 869–874.

DRUMMOND, J. C. 1919. Research on the fat-soluble accessory substance. I. Observation upon its nature and properties. Biochem. J. *13*, 81–94.

DRUMMOND, J. C., and BAKER, L. C. 1929. Further studies of the chemical nature of vitamin A. Biochem J. *23*, 274–291.

DRUMMOND, J. C., and HILDITCH, T. P. 1931. The Relative Values of Cod Liver Oils from Various Sources. H. M. Stationery Office. London.

EMBREE, N. D. 1946. Report of the vitamin committee 1945–46. Oil and Soap *23*, No. 9, 275–276.

EULER, B. V., EULER, H. V., and HELLSTROM, H. 1928. The relation of antimony chloride reaction to vitamin A and carotin. (In German). Svensk Kem. Tid. 40, 256–262.

HALL, H. 1929. Method of purification of lecithin and other phosphatides, as well as similar substances. German Pat. 487,335. Nov. 21.

HARRISON, R. W., and HAMM, W. S. 1941. Extraction of vitamin A from dogfish livers. Pacific Fisherman, 39, No. 9, 37–39.

HICKMAN, K. C. D. 1944. Adventures in vacuum chemistry. Am. Scientist 33, 205–231.

HICKMAN, K. C. D., KALEY, M. R. W., and HARRIS, P. L. 1944. Sparing action of natural tocopherol concentrates on vitamin A. J. Biol. Chem. 152, 303–311.

HOWAT, D. D. 1942. Applications of molecular distillation. I. Commercial production of vitamin A. II. Vitamins D and E. Chem. Age 46, 41–43.

JONES, G. I., CARRIGAN, E. J., and DASSOW, J. A. 1948. Utilization of Alaskan Salmon Cannery Waste. U. S. Dept. of Commerce, Office of Technical Services, Rept. No. 2. Section 2.

KASCHER, H. M., and BAXTER, J. G. 1945. Vitamin A in fish liver oil. Ind. Eng. Chem., Anal. Ed. 17, 499–503.

KIMIZUKA, T. 1938. Biochemical studies of unsaponifiable substances. J. Biochem. 469–488.

KRAYBILL, H. R., THORNTON, M. H., and ELDRIDGE, K. E. 1940. Sterols from crude soybean oils. Ind. Eng. Chem. 32, 1138–1139.

KRISTJANSON, S. 1951. Separation of cholesterol from halibut-liver oil. Fisheries Res. Board Can., Progr. Rept. Pacific Coast Sta. 88, 51–52.

KUHN, R., and MORRIS, C. J. O. R. 1941. Synthesis of vitamin A. U. S. Pat. 2,-233,375. Feb. 25.

LOWEN, L., ANDERSON, L., and HARRISON, R. W. 1937. Cereal flours as antioxidants for fishery products. Halibut liver and salmon oils. Ind. Eng. Chem. 29, 151–156.

MATTILL, H. A. 1927. Oxidative destruction of vitamins A and E, and protective action of certain vegetable oils. J. Am. Med. Assoc. 89, 1505–1508.

MILLER, W., and JONKOVSKY, V. 1942. Effect of manganese sulfate on the stability of vitamins A and D of cod liver oil when stored in mixed feeds. Poultry Sci. 21, 200–202.

MOORE, T. 1929. Carotene and vitamin A. Lancet I, 499–500.

MORTON, B. H. 1944. Examination of the unsaponifiable material of fish-liver oils. Fisheries Res. Board Can., Progr. Rept. Pacific Coast Sta. No. 58, 13–16.

MOSHER, W. A., DANIELS, W. H., CELESTE, J. R., and KELLEY, W. H. 1958. The unsaponifiable fraction of menhaden oil. Com. Fisheries Rev. 20, No. 11 a (supplement), 1–6.

MUSHER, S. 1946. Preserving vitamin containing oils. U. S. Pat. 2,410,455. Nov. 5.

NEILANDS, J. B. 1947. Conversion of carotene to vitamin A in fish. Arch. Biochem. and Biophys. 13, 415–419.

O'LEARY, J. S. 1947. Cholesterol content of fish meal. Atlantic Fish Exp. Sta. Mimeo. Ann. Rept. for 1947. Appendix No. 34.

PUGSLEY, L. I. 1937. Variations in vitamin A content of liver oils in the grayfish. Fisheries Res. Board Can., Progr. Rept. Pacific Coast Sta. 33, 3–5.

PUGSLEY, L. I., MORRELL, C. A., and KELLEY, J. T. 1945. A survey of the vitamin A and D potencies of the liver oil of Atlantic cod. Can. J. Res. 23F, 243–252.

QUACKENBUSH, F. W., COX, R. P., and STEENBOCK, H. 1942. Tocopherol and the stability of carotene. J. Biol. Chem. 145, 169–177.

ROBESON, C. D., and BAXTER, J. G. 1943. Alpha-tocopherol, a natural antioxidant in a fish-liver oil. J. Am. Chem. Soc. 65, 940–943.

ROBENSON, C. D., and BAXTER, J. G. 1945. Vitamin A. Nature 155, 300.

ROBINSON, F. A. 1938. Stability of vitamin A and D to oxidation. Biochem. J. 32, 807–814.

ROSENBERG, H. R. 1942. Chemistry and Physiology of the Vitamins. Interscience Publishers, Inc., New York.

SANFORD, F. B. 1945. A rapid method for determining the vitamin A potency of fish livers. Fishery Market News 7, No. 4, 7–8.

SEBRELL, W. H. JR., and HARRIS, R. S. 1954. The Vitamins, Chemistry, Physiology, Pathology. Three volumes. Academic Press, New York.

SHANTZ, E. M., CAWLEY, J. D., and EMBREE, N. D. 1943. Anhydro vitamin A. J. Am. Chem. Soc. 65, 901–906.

SHANTZ, E. M. 1948. Isolation of pure vitamin A_2. Science 108, 417–419.

SIMONS, E. J., BUXTON, L. O., and COLMAN, H. B. 1940. Relation of peroxide formation to destruction of vitamin A in fish-liver oils. Ind. Eng. Chem. 32, 706–708.

SIMONS, E. J., and BUXTON, L. O. 1943. Stabilization of fat-soluble vitamins. U. S. Pat. 2,331,432. Oct. 12.

SINNHUBER, R. O., and LAW, D. K. 1947. Vitamin A and oil content of fish livers and viscera. Fishes of the Oregon Coast. Ind. Eng. Chem. 39, 1309–1310.

SLANETZ, C. A., and SCHARF, A. 1945. Effect of soybean phosphatides on vitamin A metabolism. J. Nutr. 30, 239–243.

SMITH, E. L. 1939. Action of peroxides on vitamin A. Biochem. J. 33, 201–206.

SOBOTKA, H., KANN, S., and LOEWENSTEIN, E. 1943. The fluorescence of vitamin A. J. Am. Chem. Soc. 65, 1959–1961.

SORENSEN, N. A. 1935. Red color in salmon oil. (In German). Z. Physiol. Chem. 235, 8–11.

STANSBY, M. E. 1953. Composition of fish. U. S. Fish and Wildlife Service. Fishery Leaflet 116.

STEENBOCK, H., and BLACK, A. 1924. Fat soluble vitamins XVII. The induction of growth promoting and calcifying properties in a ration exposed to ultraviolet light. J. Biol. Chem. 61, 405–422.

STOTT, W., and HARRIS, C. C. 1945. Synergistic effect of cod-liver vitamin D on synthetic vitamin D_3. Nature 155, 267.

STRAIN, H. H., and MANNING, W. 1942. Occurrence and interconversions of various fucoxanthins. J. Am. Chem. Soc. 64, 1235.

SWAIN, L. A. 1942. Adsorption of vitamin A from treated dogfish-liver oil. J. Fisheries Res. Board Can., Progr. Rept. Pacific Coast Sta. 53, 7–9.

SWAIN, L. A., and MCKERCHER, B. H. 1945. Examination of the unsaponifiable matter of marine oils. III. Fisheries Res. Board Can., Progr. Rept. Pacific Coast Sta. 65, 67–69.

SWAIN, L. A. 1948. Chromatographic analysis of the unsaponifiable matter of marine animal oils. J. Fisheries Res. Board Can. 7, 389–402.

SWAIN, L. A. 1948. Chromatographic analysis of the unsaponifiable matter of marine animal oils. Can. Chem. Process. Ind. 32, 553–554.

TANIKAWA, E. 1965. Marine Products in Japan. Published by the author who is Professor of Marine Food Technology, Faculty of Fisheries, Hokkaido Univ., Hakodate, Hokkaido, Japan.

TOMPKINS, P. W. 1930. Sardine oil color standards. Oil and Fat Ind. 7, 55–58.

TRESSLER, D. K., and LEMON, J. M. 1951. Marine Products of Commerce. 2nd Edition. Reinhold Publishing Corp., New York, N. Y.

TSUJIMOTO, M. 1932. Liver oils of elasmobranch fish. J. Soc. Chem. Ind. 51, 317–323T. Japan.

WALFORD, L. A., 1944. Observations on the shark fishery in the central part of the Gulf of California with records of vitamin potency of liver oils and with keys to identification of commercially important sharks. U. S. Fish and Wildlife Service, Fishery Market News 6, 3.

CHAPTER 7

Production of Vitamin Concentrates

PRODUCTION OF VITAMIN A AND D CONCENTRATES

Several methods for concentrating vitamins A and D from fish oils are described by Bailey (1952). They are (1) saponification, (2) short-path distillation, and (3) adsorption.

Saponification

The first and most popular method used for preparing vitamin A and D concentrates is by saponification. This involves saponifying the oil, i.e., splitting the triglycerides of oil into glycerol and fatty acids with the formation of soaps, but leaving some unsaponified oil, because the presence of some unsaponified oil renders the process more efficient. Subsequently, the soaps are diluted with water and the vitamins are extracted with a water-immiscible solvent such as ethyl ether, or ethylene dichloride.

The solvent layer is separated from the aqueous portion and it is distilled off. In the saponification process both vitamins A and D are extracted simultaneously. Oils that are high in unsaponifiable matter content and low in vitamin A potency, such as shark liver oil, cannot be concentrated above 50,000 units of vitamin A per gram.

This potency is far short of the U.S.P. requirement, which states that a vitamin A concentrate should have 200,000 units per gram. Other methods, such as short-path distillation, are therefore used for concentrating these types of oils.

Short-Path Distillation

The short-path distillation method has recently replaced the saponification process to a considerable degree. The efficiency of the apparatus used in this method has been largely improved with the development of the high vacuum pump operating in the region of one micron (0.001 mm. mercury) pressure.

A thin film of oil is distributed on a heated surface, under high vacuum; the vitamin concentrate distills off and condenses on a nearby cooled surface. In the short-path distillation process, vitamins A and D can be separately removed from the oil.

Adsorption

Swain (1948) concentrated vitamin A of fish oils by first converting the vitamin A in an oil to the alcohol form by methanolysis of the oil, then separating it from the fatty-acid methyl esters by adsorption on alumina or silicic acid. Similarly, Karnovsky *et al.* (1948) obtained a vitamin A concentrate from fish liver oils by alcoholysis followed by adsorption on alumina. Brocklesby and Kuchel (1938) concentrated vitamin A by its adsorption on soaps formed *in situ*, and simultaneously refined the oil by this process. This method is relatively simple.

Patents.—There is a number of patents describing various techniques and modifications for concentrating vitamins A and D. They are, Buxton, 2 (1946), Dryden and Buxton (1946), Hoffman-LaRoche and Co. (1933), and Van Orden (1946).

Recent Developments in Vitamin A Concentrate Research

Recently several investigations have been made in the Tokai Regional Fisheries Research Laboratory, Tokyo, Japan on the economical manufacture of vitamin A concentrates from fish liver oil. Shimma and Tanaka (1959) have analyzed molecular distillates of vitamin A concentrates chromatographically. They ascertained that molecular distillation was very useful for refining vitamin A concentrates and for removing non-vitamin materials that have conjugated double bonds.

Higashi *et al.* (1959A) have purified vitamin A concentrates with methanol. Higashi *et al.* (1959B) found that by treating an acid clay with an aqueous solution of ammonia, urea or caustic soda and subsequently drying, pulverizing and heating it, such a weakened acid clay could be used for adsorbing impurities from a vitamin A concentrate.

PRODUCTION OF VITAMIN B COMPLEX CONCENTRATES

Water-soluble B complex vitamins can be concentrated in two fishery by-products, viz., fish press-liquor and proteinaceous residue of fish livers, after oil extraction. With further processing, these vitamins can also be extracted from their carriers.

A description of the procedures applied to each of these processes follows.

Production of B Complex Vitamin Concentrates in Fish Press-Liquor

The production of water-soluble B complex vitamin concentrates in press-liquor obtained during the manufacture of fish-meal from whole fish may be illustrated by Lassen's (1940) processes. Lassen described the manufacture of vitamin preparations consisting of fish concentrates as well as pure crystalline B complex vitamins. Although Lassen illustrates his methods with the production of vitamins B_2 and B_1, which he specifically evaluated, he notes that his procedures apply equally to the recovery of the entire water soluble vitamin content of fish press-water.

Comparison Between Vitamin B$_2$ Content in Press-Water and Milk Whey.—The growth-promoting vitamin B$_2$ has been produced exclusively from milk whey, which contains from 30 to 40 Bourquin-Sherman units per 100 gm. of product. Fish press-water, such as sardine press-water, obtained during fish-meal production, contains more than double the amount of vitamin B$_2$ that is found in milk whey, i.e., it contains 60 to 125 Bourquin-Sherman units per 100 gm. of material.

Procedure for Concentrating B Complex Vitamins in Fish Press-Liquor.—In producing a water soluble vitamin concentrate, and specifically a vitamin B$_2$ or B$_1$ concentrate, it is essential, first, to remove from the press-liquor all insoluble substances such as proteins, protein derivatives, and oils, by any of the well known methods such as centrifuging or gravitational treatment. After removal of the insoluble material, the partially clarified liquid is run off into another container and is treated with powdered alum, which is added within the preferable range of from 0.25 to 0.50% of the weight of the liquid, precipitating, thereby, the coagulable proteins and enzymes.

The precipitated substances are then removed, leaving a very clear liquid or serum, which now has a 10 to 30 times increase in rate of filtration. The clear liquor retains practically all of the vitamin content of the original press-liquor, especially vitamin B$_2$ which was specifically evaluated. The removal of the protein solids and enzymes from the liquid also enhances its keeping quality.

The clear liquor, in an acidic state, is evaporated under vacuum, resulting in a concentrate high in the entire water-soluble vitamin content of fish press-water and particularly in vitamins B$_2$ and B$_1$. The vacuum concentration process further reduces the already mild fish odor of the clear liquor, and imparts to it a meaty aroma.

The clear liquor could be evaporated to from 10 to 30 times its original concentration of vitamin B$_2$, resulting in a concentration of from 600 to 3,-000 Bourquin-Sherman units per 100 gm. The fish press-water also contains 50 to 80 Chase-Sherman units of vitamin B$_1$ per 100 gm., which could be concentrated to from 10 to 30 times this potency.

In addition to the vitamins, the concentrate contains minerals and from 20 to 40% of easily assimilable protein hydrolyzates consisting of peptones, polypeptides, and amino acids. The concentrate could therefore be used as a food or a feed supplement.

Procedure for the Manufacture of Pure Crystalline B Complex Vitamins from Fish Press-Liquor.—Lassen (1940) describes specifically a process for the manufacture of crystalline vitamins B$_2$ and B$_1$ from fish press-liquor. He further states that the process applies equally well to the production, in crystalline form, of water soluble vitamins in fish press-liquor.

Principle of the Process.—Certain highly adsorbent inorganic compounds such as fuller's earth, bentonite, and also bleaching chars such as Darco have a particularly high adsorptive power for vitamins in the presence of an acid. Consequently, after the press-liquor has been clarified with alum, it is acidified and treated with a solid adsorbent which adsorbs the vitamins. Subsequently, the vitamins are extracted from the adsorbent with the aid of a suitable solvent. Most of the solvent is evaporated and pure vitamin B_2 crystallizes out.

Procedure.—The process described by Lassen is essentially as follows:

After the press-liquor has been clarified with alum, the clear solution is treated with one per cent of absorbent, i.e., 10 gm. per liter of solution. Hydrochloric or acetic acid is added to facilitate the adsorption. The entire contents are agitated for one hour or more. The solid adsorbent, with the vitamin content adsorbed to it, is then allowed to settle and the supernatant liquid is siphoned off.

Subsequently, the solid absorbent is agitated with a mixture consisting of one part alcohol, one part of a pyridine base, and four parts of water, to release the adsorbed vitamins from the adsorbent. After the vitamins have been released, the solid vitamin-free adsorbent is allowed to settle. The supernatant liquid which contains practically all of the vitamins is siphoned off and is concentrated under vacuum to a very small volume, which contains the vitamin B_2 concentrate.

The vitamin B_2 is then crystallized from the concentrated solution. If necessary, the vitamin B_2 crystals can be further purified. In a similar manner, all other vitamins present in press-liquor can be obtained from it without affecting their original nutritive potency.

Production of B Complex Vitamin Concentrates in Proteinaceous Residue of Fish Liver

Value of Cod Liver Residue After Oil Extraction.—The proteinaceous residue of fish livers contains an appreciable amount of B complex vitamins. Guttman (1950) summarized the results of many analyses made on meals prepared from the proteinaceous residue of cod livers, after most of the oils was removed. Results of analysis of an average meal prepared from liver residue according to Guttman are as follows: moisture, 5.1%; total nitrogen, 10.7% (moisture and oil free basis); free amino acids, 4% (expressed in nitrogen); ash, 7.6%; copper, 0.00033%; iron, 0.02%; vitamin B_1, 2.7 mg. per lb.; vitamin B_2 (riboflavin), 18 mg. per lb.; niacin, 50 mg. per lb.; pantothenic acid, 18 mg. per lb.; and total animal protein factor (APF) activity, 1.4 mg. per lb.

At the 1950 price of 20¢ a milligram of APF, Guttman estimates that a ton of this meal is worth $560, based only on its APF content.

Furthermore, processing 1,000 gal. of livers, which contain 35% oil, would yield one ton of liver meal. At the 1950 price for cod liver oil (Guttman 1950), it appears that the return from cod liver meal would be higher than that of the oil. This is apparently true today when the thiamin, riboflavin, niacin, and pantothenic acid in fish liver meal are included, in evaluating the liver meal against liver oil per ton of livers.

Recovery of Practically Undenatured Fish Liver Protein.—In order to derive the maximum nutritive value from the liver proteins, it is essential to recover the oil from the livers in a way that would leave the protein carrier in its undenatured form; accordingly, its water-soluble B complex vitamins would not be deleteriously affected. A process that fulfills these requirements is described by Vandenheuvel (1952). Essentially this process is carried out in the following four steps: (1) comminuting of livers, (2) raising temperature of comminuted livers to between 112° and 158°F., (3) adjusting pH of comminuted livers to between 7.5 and 8.5 and (4) cooling the comminuted livers to rupture the protein-water film surrounding the oil globules, thereby releasing the oil.

Both oil and protein recovered are of excellent food quality. The entire process is also continuous.

In order to understand this process better and avoid possible pitfalls in its execution, the entire procedure is discussed here, with explanations given for the various steps taken.

Vandenheuvel's Procedure.—Comminuted fish livers are heated to between 112° and 158°F., and are adjusted to pH between 7.5 and 8.5. At that alkalinity and temperature, the protein film surrounding the oil globules absorbs a maximum amount of water, resulting in the rupture of the protein-water phase on cooling, with a release of the oil. A temperature above 158°F., in the presence of high alkalinity, will cause the protein tissues to completely dissolve and while freeing the oil, will also denature the protein. The greater the oil content the lower the temperature of rupture. A pH of 8.0 is preferred. A pH above 8.5, in addition to denaturing the protein, forms emulsions.

Another procedure describes a method wherein the pH of the comminuted livers is adjusted before heating, but then the oil separation is not as efficient as in the first procedure, i.e., when pH is adjusted after heating, because the alkali does not react as readily at lower temperatures as it does at higher temperatures.

A 25 to 27% caustic soda solution is suitable to use in adjusting pH. Either caustic potash or caustic soda is preferred. However, chemically equivalent amounts of calcium hydroxide, sodium carbonate, or bi- and tri-sodium phosphate, or mixtures of alkali and alkali bases or salts can also be used. The amount of alkali to add ranges between 1 and 1.5%, depending upon the weight of livers. It should be sufficient to cause a maximum swelling of the protein surrounding the oil globules, followed by release of the oil.

TABLE 4

ORGANIC CONSTITUENTS OF LIVER EXTRACTS AND ENZYMATIC HYDROLYZATES CALCULATED ON A WATER-FREE BASIS. (GUTMAN 1955)

No.	Raw Material	Total Nitrogen, %	NH₂ Nitrogen, %	Choline base, %	Thiamin, μg./Gm.	Ribo-flavin, μg./Gm.	Folic acid, μg./Gm.	Niacin, μg./Gm.	Panto-thenic acid, μg./Gm.	Vitamin B₁₂, μg./Gm.
	Extracts									
1.	Cod liver residue	7.40	2.50	2.54	2.44	40.4	11.8	425	136	4.70
2.	Same	9.60	4.00	3.34	2.12	65.8	15.3	573	212	1.90
3.	Salmon liver frozen	11.60	5.56	0.96	7.02	55.0	7.02	581	184	2.20
4.	Pork liver, dried, defatted	9.50	4.78	5.94	9.86	433.0	19.00	1664	606	3.42
5.	Same	9.28	4.87	4.87	10.90	419.0	...	1856	614	2.78
6.	Beef liver, dried, defatted	7.67	3.12	3.32	8.06	313.0	14.50	2062	530	12.90
7.	Same	8.14	4.99	2.78	8.50	323.0	22.12	2619	698	4.50
	Enzymatic hydrolyzates									
8.	Cod liver residue, dried and defatted	7.98	3.54	1.10	7.40	35.0	9.80	247	86	0.48
9.	Same	12.87	5.27	1.26	2.95	101.0	10.50	369	89	3.80
10.	Cod liver whole	12.04	5.30	1.26	1.50	71.0	9.00	366	91	2.51
11.	Haddock liver residue, dried and defatted	11.05	5.02	2.24	1.61	73.0	15.80	321	57	0.86
12.	Salmon liver, dried and defatted	12.60	5.57	1.31	8.90	61.0	7.50	262	79	4.80
13.	Whale liver, dried and defatted	10.96	5.31	1.06	9.64	91.0	3.40	433	148	2.15
14.	Seal liver, frozen	14.6	7.22	0.24	5.30	106.0	8.20	493	342	1.27
15.	Pork liver, dried, defatted	12.30	6.23	1.86	4.48	131.0	6.48	616	231	1.35
16.	Beef liver, dried, defatted	11.1	5.72	1.75	3.92	138.0	6.54	888	261	4.79

Table Reprinted by permission of J. Fisheries Res. Board Can., Dr. J. O. Stevenson, Editor.

The water added with the alkali preferably should be below three percent of the weight of the livers and should never exceed 7 or 8%.

The objection to the use of ammonium hydroxide is twofold: first, it increased the moisture content while adjusting the pH above the point that could be absorbed by the protein, and second, the ammonium salts formed interfere with the edibility of oil and protein.

The aqueous protein suspension is neutralized with acetic, phosphoric, or hydrochloric acid. The dried and pulverized proteinaceous liver tissue is a clear yellow powder, with a pleasant aroma and is high in thiamin, riboflavin, and vitamin B anti-anemia factors as well as assimilable proteins and minerals.

A good portion of the subject discussed in this chapter is of global rather than of domestic interest, designed primarily to help developing countries that lack the technical know-how in addition to the resources, necessary to enable them to produce synthetic vitamins A and B complex. The older methods, using fishery by-products as the raw material, would be more useful to them than the most recent, complex and costly, developments prevalent in technologically advanced countries. For example, the Vandenheuval process could be useful to developing countries, but it is not an economically feasible procedure for technologically advanced countries.

Evaluations of the Nutritional Values of Concentrated and Dried Extracts and Enzymatic Hydrolyzates from Fish Liver and Mammalian Liver.—Guttman (1955) compared the nutritive values of aqueous extracts and enzymatic hydrolyzates prepared from fresh livers of salmon, cod, and haddock with corresponding products from mammalian livers. Extracts and hydrolyzates were concentrated to a syrupy consistency by vacuum distillation and then dried at a reduced temperature under vacuum. The results are summarized in Table 4.

It is evident from this table that fish liver extracts and hydrolyzates prepared from salmon, cod, or haddock compare favorably with corresponding products from mammalian livers and can, therefore, be used as additives in foods and in medicinal preparations to increase their nutritional values.

According to Tanikawa (1965), in Japan large quantities of fish and fish liver oils are subjected to molecular distillation in order to produce oils very rich in vitamin A and D. Much of this vitamin oil is exported to the United States and Europe; that which is used locally is largely used in medicine and for the enrichment of food. From an ester of vitamin A, pure crystalline vitamin A has been produced. In Japan, the concentrated vitamin oil containing vitamins A and D is less expensive than synthetic vitamin A.

BIBLIOGRAPHY

ANON 1943. Tubes, capsules and enclosures. Can. Chem. and Process. Ind. 27, 5, 248–249.

ASSOCIATION OF VITAMIN CHEMISTS. 1951. Methods of Vitamin Assay. 2nd Edition. Interscience, New York.

BAILEY, B. E. 1941. Preparation of vitamin A oils from dogfish livers. Fisheries Res. Board Can., Progr. Rept. Pacific Coast Sta. 50, 10–12.

BAILEY, B. E. 1943. Stability during household storage of vitamin A. Fisheries Res. Board Can., Progr. Rept. Pacific Coast Sta. 54, 15–17.

BAILEY, B. E. Editor. 1952. Marine Oils, with Particular Reference to Those of Canada. Bull. 89. Fisheries Res. Board Can., Ottawa.

BAIRD, F. D., RINGROSE, A. T., and MACMILLAN, M. J. 1939. Stability of vitamin A in mixed feeds. Poultry Sci. 18, 441–448.

BAXTER, J. G., and ROBESON, C. D. 1940. Crystalline vitamin A palmitate and vitamin A alcohol. Science 92, 202.

BROCKLESBY, H. N., and KUCHEL, C. C. 1938. Adsorption of vitamin A from oils by soaps formed in situ. J. Fisheries Res. Board Can. 4, 174–183.

BROCKLESBY, H. N. Editor. 1941. The chemistry and technology of marine animal oils with particular reference to those of Canada. Fisheries Res. Board Can. Bull. 59. Ottawa.

BUTLER, C. 1948. The fish-liver oil industry. U. S. Fish and Wildlife Service, Fishery Leaflet 233.

BUXTON, L. O. 1946. Concentration of fat-soluble vitamins. U. S. Pat 2,412,-561. Dec. 17.

BUXTON, L. O. 1946. Producing vitamin concentrates. U. S. Pat. 2,412,766. Dec. 17.

DRYDEN, C. E., and BUXTON, L. O. 1946. Production of fat-soluble vitamin ester concentrates. U. S. Pat. 2,404,365. July 23.

EWE, G. E. 1934. Stability of cod-liver oil under commercial distribution conditions. J. Am. Pharm. Assoc. 22, 1085–1086.

GAJJAR, I. M., and SREENIVASAYA, M. 1945. Chromatographic adsorption of shark-liver oil on activated fuller's earth. J. Sci. Ind. Res. 3, 301–302.

GUTTMAN, A. 1950. The value of cod liver residue. Fisheries Res. Board Can., Progr. Rept. Atlantic Coast Sta. No. 49, Note No. 115.

GUTTMAN, A. 1955. Extracts and enzymatic hydrolysates from fish liver and mammalian liver. J. Fisheries Res. Board Can. 12, 637–645.

GYORGY, P. 1951. Vitamin Methods. Two volumes. Academic Press, New York.

HASHIMOTO, YOSHIRO, YAMADA, SHIGEHIDI, and MORI, TAKAJIRO.. 1953. Animal protein factor and vitamin B12 in marine products. I. Aquatic animals. Bull. Japan. Soc. Sci. Fisheries. 19, No. 3, 135–140.

HICKMAN, K. C. D. 1944. Adventures in vacuum chemistry. Am. Scientist 33, 205–231.

HICKMAN, K. C. D., KALEY, M. R. W., and HARRIS, P. L. 1944. Sparing action of natural tocopherol concentrates of vitamin A. J. Biol. Chem. 152, 303–311.

HIGASHI, H., YAMAKAWA, T., KANEKO, T., and SUGH, K. 1959A. Studies on the economical manufacture of vitamin A concentrate from fish liver oil-IX. Purification of vitamin A concentrate with methanol. Bull. Japan. Soc. Sci. Fisheries. 25, No. 1, 59–66.

HIGASHI, H., *et al.* 1959B. Studies on the economical manufacture of vitamin A concentrate from fish liver oil-X. Adsorption by weakened acid clay. Bull. Japan. Soc. Sci. Fisheries. 25, No. 3, 196–203.

HOFFMAN-LAROCHE & CO. 1933. Process for the purification of vitamin A preparations. Brit. Pat. 393,883. June 15.

HOLDER, R. C., and FORD, S. K. 1939. Stability of vitamin A in mixed feeds. Poultry Sci. 18, 345–349.

HOWAT, D. D. 1942. Applications of molecular distillation. I. Commercial production of vitamin A. II. Vitamins D and E. Chem. Age 46, 41–43.

KARABINOS, J. V., ECKHARDT, E. R., and PATTERSON, W. I. 1945. Process of extracting biotin. U. S. Pat. 2,374,212. Apr. 24.

KARNOVSKY, M. L., RAPSON, W. S., and VAN RENSBURG, N. J. 1948. The transesterification and chromatographic treatment of fish-liver oils as a means of concentrating vitamin A. J. Am. Oil Chem. Soc. 25, 36–38.

KARRICK, N. L., and STANSBY, M. E. 1954. Vitamin content of fishery by-products. Part 1. Effect of processing methods on riboflavin, nicotinic acid and vitamin B_{12}. U. S. Fish and Wildlife Service Sep. No. 366.

KARRICK, N. L. 1955. Vitamin content of fishery by-products. Part 2. U. S. Fish and Wildlife Service Sep. No. 393.

KARRICK, N. L., CLEGG, W., and STANSBY, M. E. 1957. Vitamin content of fishery by-products. Part 3. Com. Fisheries Rev. 19, No. 5a (supplement), 14–23.

KUHN, R., and MORRIS, C. J. O. R. 1941. Synthesis of vitamin A. U. S. Pat. 2,-233,375. Feb. 25.

LASSEN, S. H. 1940. Process of concentrating vitamins from fish press water. U. S. Pat. 2,188,008. Jan. 23.

LASSEN, S. H. 1945. Process for treating fish press liquor. U. S. Pat. 2,372,-677. Apr. 3.

LEWIS, U. J., REGISTER, U. D., THOMPSON, H. T., and ELVEHJEM, C. A. 1949. Distribution of vitamin B12 in natural materials. Proc. Soc. Exptl. Biol. and Med. 72, 2, 479–482.

MILAS, N. A. 1945. Synthesis of Vitamin A. U. S. Pat. 2,382,085. Aug. 14.

MITCHELL, J. E. 1943. Extraction of organic materials. U. S. Pat. 2,324,012. July 13.

NATIONAL RESEARCH COUNCIL PUBL. 302, revised, 1953. Recommended Dietary Allowances. Washington, D. C.

OLIVER, T. R. 1944. Molecular distillation, a new path to separation of chemicals. Chem. Met. Eng. 51, 100–104.

PARFENTJEV, I. A. 1946. Salvage from fish viscera. U. S. Pat. 2,406,249. Aug. 20.

PARFENTJEV, I. A. 1950. Fish protein and mineral product. U. S. Pat. 2,512,-375. June 20.

PASSINO, H. J. 1949. The Solexol process. Ind. Eng. Chem. 41, 280–287.

PROCTOR, B. E., HARRIS, R. S., GOLDBLITH, S. A., and BRODY, J. 1940. Effect of processing on the vitamin B_1 content of foods. Proceedings of the First Food Conference of the Institute of Food Technologists. 109–121, Chicago.

ROBINSON, F. A. 1938. Stability of vitamin A and D to oxidation. Biochem. J. 32, 807–814.

ROSENBERG, H. R. 1942. Chemistry and Physiology of the Vitamins. Inter-science Publishers, Inc., New York.

SANFORD, F. B., and LEE, C. F. 1960. U. S. fish-reduction industry. U. S. Fish and Wildlife Service. Com. Fisheries TL14.

SEBRELL, W. H., JR., and HARRIS, R. S. 1954. The Vitamins, Chemistry, Physiology, Pathology. Three volumes. Academic Press, New York.

SHANTZ, E. M. 1946. Concentration of fat-soluble vitamins. U. S. Pat. 2,410,-590. Nov. 5.

SHIMMA, Y., and TANAKA, M. 1959. Studies on the economical manufacture of vitamin A concentrate from fish liver oil-VIII. Chromatographical separation of vitamin concentrates. Bull. Japan. Soc. Sci. Fisheries. 1959. 25, No. 1, 52–58.

STANSBY, M. E. 1953. Composition of fish. U. S. Fish and Wildlife Service. Fishery Leaflet 116.

SWAIN, L. A. 1942. Adsorption of vitamin A from treated dogfish-liver oil. J. Fisheries Res. Board Can., Progr. Rept. Pacific Coast Sta. 53, 7–9.

SWAIN, L. A. 1948. Concentrating vitamin A. J. Fisheries Res. Board Can. 7, 389–402.

TANIKAWA, E. 1965. Marine Products in Japan. Published by the author who is Professor of Marine Food Technology, Faculty of Fisheries, Hokkaido University. Hakodate, Hokkaido, Japan.

TRESSLER, D. K., and LEMON, J. M. 1951. Marine Products of Commerce. 2nd Edition. Reinhold Publishing Corp., New York, N. Y.

TRUSCOTT, B., GAGE, D. G., and HOOGLAND, P. L. 1954. Preparation of cod liver residues and vitamin B12 concentrates. J. Fisheries Res. Board Can. 11, 355–361.

VANDENHEUVEL, F. A. 1952. Treatment of fish livers. U. S. Pat. 2,588,338. March 11.

VAN ORDEN, L. J. 1946. Vitamin concentration. U. S. Pat. 2,394,968. Feb. 12.

CHAPTER 8

Salmon Egg By-Products and Other Salmon Cannery Waste

INTRODUCTION

Salmon cannery waste constitutes one third of the raw material of the plant. If this material is not properly utilized, its disposal constitutes a serious health hazard, in addition to its being an economic waste. The amount of this material available on the western coast of the United States is of tremendous proportions. For many years, from 100,000,000 to 125-000,000 lb. of salmon waste have been discarded annually in Alaska (Wigutoff 1952). The visceral portion of the salmon waste particularly the eggs, is an excellent source of proteins and vitamins (Landgraf *et al.* 1951).

In 1950, about 9,000,000 lb. of salmon eggs were discarded in Alaska (Jones, *et al.* 1950). Salmon eggs comprise about nine per cent of the entire salmon cannery waste. Large quantities of salmon eggs are discarded annually on the western coast of continental United States. This valuable raw material could be used for producing cholesterol, lipids, and proteins. Salmon eggs can be used as bait by sport fishing enthusiasts. The smaller eggs are used for caviar. Carlson (1955) described the preparation of a smoked caviar spread.

PER CENT COMPOSITION OF SALMON CANNERY WASTE

Table 5 shows the average percentage composition of the organs present in salmon cannery waste for five species of salmon. It is obvious from the data presented for a portion of the season that the head and collar comprise more than a half of the entire salmon cannery offal. The digestive tract, liver, and heart constitute much smaller portions. There are, however, seasonal variations in these figures due to the marked increase in the percentage of roe and milt during the spawning season.

USES OF SALMON CANNERY WASTE

Leekley *et al.* (1952) and Sanford (1957) have shown that salmon cannery waste and other fish waste can be utilized for mink feed.

Salmon head oil is sometimes added to canned salmon, where the oil content is low. Salmon oil is produced mostly from salmon offal. Salmon heads are used as halibut bait.

COLLECTING AND STORING RAW SALMON EGGS

The gathering of salmon eggs is relatively easy. The salmon is first passed through a machine called the "Iron Chink," which removes the

TABLE 5

PER CENT COMPOSITION OF SALMON CANNERY WASTE (STANSBY AND ASSOCIATES 1953)

Portion of fish	Per Cent of Total Salmon Cannery Waste				
	Pink	Red	Chum	King	Coho
Head and Collar	57	61	54	50	60
Tail and Fins	16	14	11	11	11
Liver	5	5	5	3	4
Roe	8	9	16	15	8
Milt	5	5	6	4	6
Digestive Tract	9	6	8	18	11
Heart	0.8	0.8	0.7	0.7	0.7

Table Courtesy of U. S. Fish and Wildlife Service.

head, tail, fins, and viscera. The salmon eggs are removed from the body cavity simultaneously with the viscera. Finally the large skeins of salmon eggs are separated by hand from the viscera, as they move along an endless conveyor (Jones *et al.* 1950).

Salmon eggs are comparatively easy to handle because each egg is encased in a tough membrane, and the entire mass is further re-enforced in a skein structure. If it is necessary to store the eggs for an extended period of time, they can be frozen, salted, or chemically preserved.

Processing of Salmon Eggs and Milts

Salmon eggs were processed at several Alaska canneries, in 1964, as red caviar for export to Japan (Anon. 1964). The procedure is as follows:

Eggs are removed after the fish are headed, then transported in open mesh baskets to the packing plant where they are salt-cured. The eggs are first washed in salt water to remove most blood and slime. They are then placed in a saturated brine solution (containing mild-cure salt plus certain color additives) and agitated mechanically for 20 min. Egg skeins are then sorted, trimmed, and graded for packing. A solid pack is made by layering individual skeins of eggs in polyethylene-lined wooden boxes with a modest sprinkling of salt between layers. Each box holds 10 kilos (22 lb.).

After packing, the boxes are cured at room temperature for about one week, again inspected, and then placed in storage at 40°F. for shipment to Japan.

Milts are frequently separated from salmon simultaneously with eggs. They are placed in 55-gal. drums and treated with seven gallons of caustic soda solution (five pounds per gallon). The caustic solution serves a double purpose: first, as a preservative, second as a reagent used in the first step of processing.

Salmon eggs and salmon milt are used in the production of certain pharmaceutical products (see Chapter 10).

It is estimated that during 1964, from $1/4$ to $1/3$ of the salmon waste in Alaska will be processed and sold.

POTENTIAL USE OF SALMON EGGS AS A SOURCE
OF OIL, PROTEIN AND CHOLESTEROL

Salmon eggs may be utilized as a source of supply for the manufacture of oil, cholesterol, or protein. These by-products will be discussed separately:

Oil from Salmon Eggs

The oil content of salmon eggs averages about 12.5% on the basis of total weight. Halpern (1945) found that the roe from sockeye salmon yielded 12.5% oil and 6.2% phospholipide. The average fat and cholesterol content of salmon eggs in six species of salmon is given in Table 6.

TABLE 6

AVERAGE CHOLESTEROL AND FAT CONTENT OF SALMON EGGS (JONES ET AL. 1950)

Species of Salmon	Cholesterol, %		Fat, %[1]
	In Raw Eggs	In Fat	
Pink	0.29	2.61	11.1
Red	0.39	2.82	13.9
Chum	0.38	3.15	11.9
Chum, dehydrated	0.86	3.06	28.0
King	0.34	2.64	12.8
Coho	0.40	3.53	11.4

Table Courtesy of U. S. Fish and Wildlife Service.
[1] Total ether extract after acid hydrolysis of sample.

Salmon eggs yield a light-colored oil. The oil contains about 45% of highly unsaturated fatty acids with molecules having 20 to 22 carbon atoms (Kyte 1958).

The iodine number of salmon egg oil is about 200. This oil could be used as a component of quick drying paints and varnishes. About one-third of the total fat is a phospholipide, probably lecithin (Stansby et al. 1953).

TABLE 7

CHOLESTEROL CONTENT OF UNSAPONIFIABLE MATTER OF FAT IN SALMON EGGS (JONES ET AL., 1950)

Species of Salmon	Unsaponifiable Residue in Fat, %[1]	Cholesterol in Fat, %	Cholesterol in the Unsaponifiable Residue, % of Total
Pink	5.44	2.16	48
Red	4.44	2.82	64
Chum	6.45	3.15	49
King	5.16	2.69	52
Coho	7.10	3.53	50

Table Courtesy of U. S. Fish and Wildlife Service.
[1] Unsaponifiable residue determined by A.O.A.C. 6th Edition, Methods of Analysis.

TABLE 8

AMINO ACID CONTENT OF SALMON EGG PROTEIN FROM PINK SALMON OF SIMILAR MATURITY (SEAGRAN 1953)

Sample	Skein Number	Amino-Acid Content (in gm. per 100 gm. of protein)[2]									
		Arginine	Histidine	Isoleucine	Leucine	Lysine	Methionine	Phenylalanine	Threonine	Tryptophan	Valine
Pink Salmon Roe	1	7.5	2.8	7.1	9.0	8.9	2.7	4.8	5.4	1.1	7.5
	2	6.8	2.8	7.0	9.0	8.8	2.7	4.7	5.2	1.0	7.9
	3	7.1	2.9	6.8	9.6	9.0	2.9	4.7	5.1	1.2	8.7
	4	7.2	2.8	6.8	9.3	8.8	3.0	4.7	5.1	1.1	8.8
	5	7.3	2.9	6.9	9.6	8.8	3.2	5.1	5.1	1.1	8.0
	6	6.9	2.8	7.1	9.5	9.1	3.3	5.2	5.0	1.1	8.4
	7	7.5	2.9	7.0	9.7	8.8	3.2	4.9	5.1	1.1	7.7
	8	7.6	2.8	6.9	9.7	8.9	3.3	5.0	5.2	1.1	7.9
Avg.[3]		7.2 ± 0.3	2.8 ± 0.1	7.0 ± 0.2	9.4 ± 0.3	8.9 ± 0.1	3.0 ± 0.3	4.9 ± 0.2	5.2 ± 0.1	1.1 ± 0.1	8.1 ± 0.5

Table Courtesy of U. S. Fish and Wildlife Service.
[1] All eggs were moderately mature and of classification 3 (egg diameter, 6.0 ± 0.5 mm.).
[2] Protein equals nitrogen times 6.25.
[3] Average values are given as the mean plus or minus the standard deviation.

Cholesterol in Salmon Eggs

Koenig and Grossfeld (1913) found that fish roe fat contains 4 to 14% cholesterol. In cholesterol content, the fat in coho salmon eggs has 3.53% and that in hens' eggs, 4.24%. The cholesterol content of the unsaponifiable fraction of salmon eggs in five species of salmon is given in Table 7 (Jones *et al.* 1950). Approximately 50% of the unsaponifiable portion of salmon egg oil is cholesterol.

Protein in Salmon Eggs

The protein of salmon eggs is of high quality. It contains all of the ten essential amino acids in substantial amounts, and is relatively high in lysine, methionine, and isoleucine as compared with soybean meal and cottonseed meal. It could, therefore, be used to supplement vegetable protein concentrates which are critically low in these amino acids (Seagran, Morey, and Dassow 1954; Kyte 1958).

It is evident that salmon egg protein is relatively high in lysine, methionine, and isoleucine. It could, therefore, be used to supplement vegetable protein concentrates which are critically low in these amino acids.

A comparison of the amino acid content of eight egg samples taken from salmon of similar maturity indicates a very close similarity. See Table 8.

Salmon egg protein might also be used whenever special physical or chemical properties are required in industrial use, such as in plastic manufacture.

CONCLUDING REMARKS

It is not feasible economically to recover only one component of salmon eggs. It is, however, thought, to be worthwhile to investigate further the gathering of salmon eggs and the recovery of fat and protein from these eggs. Furthermore, it is feasible either to isolate cholesterol and lecithin from the fats, or to use the highly unsaturated fats, wherever such fats are required.

BIBLIOGRAPHY

ANON. 1964. Salmon waste utilization. Com. Fisheries Rev. 26, No. 10, 13.

ANDERSON, L. 1945. A preliminary report on alkali process for the manufacture of commercial oil from salmon cannery trimmings. Fishery Market News 7, No. 4, 4–7 (Sep. No. 99).

BAILEY, B. E. Editor. 1952. Marine oils with particular reference to those of Canada. Bull. 89. Fisheries Research Board Can., Ottawa.

BURROWS, R. E., ROBINSON, L. A., and PALMER, D. D. 1951. Tests of hatchery foods for blueback salmon 1944–48. U. S. Fish and Wildlife Service, Special Scientific Rept: Fisheries No. 59.

CARLSON, C. J.   1955.   Preparation of a smoked salmon caviar spread.   Com. Fisheries Rev. *17*, No. 1, 13. (Sep. No. 391).
COBB, J. N.   1931.   Pacific salmon fisheries.   U. S. Bur. Fisheries Doc. 1092, 543.
CRAVEN, H. J.,   1953.   Alaska salmon potential.   National Fisheries Yearbook, 107–108, 113.
FIEDLER, R. H., and SAMSON, V. J.   1935.   Survey of fish hatchery foods and feeding practices.   Trans. Am. Fisheries Soc. *65*, 376–400.
HALPERN, G. R.   1945.   Extraction of phospholipides in salmon roe.   Nature *155*, 110.
JONES, G. I., and CARRIGAN, E. J. 1947 and 1948.   Utilization of salmon cannery waste.   Parts I and II.   OTS Reports, Cac 47-17, U. S. Dept. of Commerce, Washington, D. C.
JONES, G. I., CARRIGAN, J. E., and DASSOW, J. A.   1950.   Utilization of salmon eggs for production of cholesterol, lipide, and protein.   Com. Fisheries Rev. *12*, No. 11a, 8-14.
KOENIG, J., and GROSSFELD, J.   1913.   Fish roe as food for man.   Biochem Z. *54*, 351.
KYTE, R. M.   1957.   Enzymes as an aid in separating oil from protein in salmon eggs.   Com. Fisheries Rev. *19*, No. 4A (April-supplement), 30–34.
KYTE, R. M.   1958.   Potential by-products from Alaskan fisheries: utilization of salmon eggs and salmon waste.   Com. Fisheries Rev. *20*, No. 3, 1–5. (Sep. No. 504).
LANDGRAF, R. G. Jr., MIYAUCHI, D. T., and STANSBY, M. E.   1951.   Utilization of Alaska salmon cannery waste as a source of feed for hatchery fish.   Com. Fisheries Rev. *13*, No. 11A (November-supplement), 26–33.
LEEKLEY, J. R., LANDGRAF, R. G., BJORKE, J. E., and HAGEVIG, W. A.   1952. Salmon cannery waste for mink feed.   U. S. Fish and Wildlife Service, Fishery Leaflet 405.
MAGNUSSON, H. W., and HAGEVIG, W. H.   1950.   Salmon cannery trimmings. com. Fisheries Rev. *12*, No. 9, 11. (Sep. No. 258).
POTTINGER, S. R., and BALDWIN, W. H.   1946.   The content of certain amino acids in seafoods.   Com. Fisheries Rev. *8*, No. 8, 5–9.   (Sep. No. 145).
ROBINSON, L. A., PALMER, D. D., and BURROWS, R. E.   1951.   Tests of hatchery foods for blueback salmon, 1949.   U. S. Fish and Wildlife Service, Special Scientific Report: Fisheries No. 60.
ROBINSON, L. A., PAYNE, M. H., PALMER, D. D., and BURROWS, R. E.   1951. Test of hatchery foods for blueback salmon,   1950.   U. S. Fish and Wildlife Service, Special Scientific Report: Fisheries No. 63.
SANFORD, F. B.   1950.   Utilization of fishery by-products in Washington and Oregon.   U. S. Fish and Wildlife Service, Fishery Leaflet 370.
SANFORD, F. B.   1957.   Utilization of fish waste in northern Oregon for mink feed.   Com. Fisheries Rev. *19*, 12, 40–47. (Sep. No. 496).
SEAGRAN, H. L.   1953.   Technical Note No. 25-Amino acid content of salmon roe.   Com. Fisheries Rev. *15*, No. 3, 31–34. (Sep. No. 346).
SEAGRAN, H. L., MOREY, D., and DASSOW, J. A.   1954.   Amino acid content of roe at different stages of maturity from the five species of Pacific salmon. J. Nutr. *53*, 139–150.
SINNHUBER, R. O.   1943.   Production of salmon egg oil.   Circular 302.   Oreg. Agr. Expt. Sta., Oregon State College, Corvallis, Ore.

STANSBY, M. E.   1953.   Composition of fish.   U. S. Fish and Wildlife Service, Fishery Leaflet 116.

STANSBY, M. E., *et al.*   1953.   Utilization of Alaskan salmon cannery waste. U. S. Fish and Wildlife Service, Special Scientific Report: Fisheries No. 109.

TUNISON, V. A.   1951.   Comparison of fish food costs in federal hatcheries in 1945 and 1949.   Progressive Fish Culturist *13*, No. 3, 121–128.

WIGUTOFF, N. B.   1952.   Potential markets for Alaska salmon cannery waste. Com. Fisheries Rev. *14*, No. 8, 5–12. (Sep. No. 320).

CHAPTER 9

Insulin

INSULIN

Insulin is a hormone which maintains the blood-sugar level of man relatively constant under normal metabolic conditions. It is produced by pancreatic islets located in the epithelial tissue of the pancreas and is secreted internally by these islets and passed into the general circulation to help store and oxidize glucose and convert it into energy for the use of the various cells and tissues. These islets have been named the "islets of Langerhans" in honor of the man who first described them in 1869. Their exact function, however, was not known until 1922 (Macleod 1922).

RELATION OF INSULIN TO DIABETES

When the islets of Langerhans do not produce enough insulin, or do not render available a sufficient supply of insulin to maintain the blood-sugar level within normal range, the condition of diabetes mellitus sets in. While this disease when unchecked represents primarily a malfunction of the carbohydrate metabolism, it also affects the proper metabolism of proteins and fats.

The adage of nutrition chemistry that "fats burn in the flame of carbohydrates" indicates the interlocking mechanism of these two diet essentials from which the body derives energy. Similarly, protein metabolism and formation becomes defective. Unchecked diabetes, i.e., allowing excessive amounts of unused sugar in the blood stream and urine may lead to a number of metabolic complications which, if medically neglected, become irreversible, causing permanent damage to the body such as by atherosclerosis, arteriosclerosis, or vascular disorders.

Some of the manifestations of this insidious disease are excessive thirst and urination, rapid loss in weight as a result of the increased catabolism of proteins and fats, loss of sugar in urine, excessive hunger, fatigue, drowsiness, visual disturbances, skin infections, and the formation of an increased amount of ketonic substances such as acetone, acetoacetic acid, and β-hydroxybutyric acid as a result of an increased rate of fat catabolism. In fact, the physiological processes of every cell of the body are affected by diabetes.

Daily subcutaneous insulin injections correct the abnormal metabolic condition by lowering the increased blood and urinary sugar levels, at any early stage of the disease. The administration of insulin under proper medical supervision may, therefore, be vital to life and health (Beaser 1964).

HISTORY OF INSULIN DISCOVERY

The final discovery of the immediate source of insulin, its purification and administration to humans is directly related to research on fish carried out in the Physiology Department of the University of Toronto, Canada. As early as 1889, J. von Mehring and O. Minkowsky showed that dogs develop symptoms of diabetes mellitus after removal of their pancreas. This work indicated that the pancreas has the additional function of controlling carbohydrate metabolism besides producing digestive enzymes.

McComick (1924A) gave an account of the epoch making discovery of insulin in his bulletin: "Insulin from Fish." According to McCormick, Dr. Frederick G. Banting and Charles H. Best obtained a potent extract from a mammalian pancreas which, when injected subcutaneously in a diabetic animal or man, completely corrected and controlled their deranged carbohydrate metabolism.

This life-giving extract was named "insulin." They did not, however, pinpoint the exact focus in the pancreas from which insulin is extracted. The "missing link" for establishing the exact source of insulin was supplied by subsequent research on fish. It was finally traced down (McCormick 1924B) as follows:

The pancreas of the cartilaginous fishes, known as Elasmobranchii, such as the skate, shark, and dogfish has a regular structure with the typical islets of Langerhans embedded in its epithelial tissue and is very similar in this respect to mammalian islets. In the bony fishes, known as Teleosti, such as cod, haddock, halibut, and pollack there are no sharply defined islets.

Diamere, in 1896, observed that, in the latter species the islet tissue was shifted in its location from the pancreas and appeared as a single agglomeration readily visible to the naked eye. For example, in the cod, the insulin containing tissue appears as a "cap" at the tip of the gall-bladder. In the pollack, the "cap" of insulin containing tissue is often found at the side of the gall-bladder. These "caps" of insulin containing tissue which are discernible to the naked eye can be readily clipped off from the gall-bladder.

Rennie, in 1901, described the large islets or "principal islets" of insulin in several dozen species of fishes. Frequently, some smaller islets, or secondary islets also occurred.

Injecting a diabetic patient with an extract prepared from the large island of a monkfish, reduced his excessive blood sugar to the normal range.

Professor J. J. R. Macleod (1922), in whose laboratory insulin was discovered, further investigated his findings with the object of proving conclusively the immediate source of insulin. He continued this phase of his work in the summer of 1922, at the Atlantic Biological Station, St. Andrews, N. B., extracting large quantities of insulin from the principal and secondary islets of monkfish, sculpin, and flounder, along with a number of other fishes which were all described by Rennie, as having principal and some secondary islets filled with insulin.

As a result of this work, Macleod (1922) demonstrated the following two facts: first, the amount of insulin extracted from the principal and secondary islets, excluding the pancreas, per pound of fish is directly proportional to the amount obtained from a mammalian pancreas per pound of body weight. Second, the remainder of the pancreas of these fishes contains only traces of insulin, since their pancreas has only a few scattered microscopic islets, which resemble those found in the mammalian pancreas, known as the islets of Langerhans.

"The exception proved the rule." Consequently, Professor Macleod's experiments proved conclusively that in the mammalian pancreas, insulin is produced by the islets of Langerhans.

CHEMISTRY OF INSULIN

Insulin is a protein. Sanger (1949) and associates have shown that the insulin molecule consists of two polypeptide chains, one of 21 amino acids and the other of 30 amino acids joined by disulfide(—S—S—)linkages between their cysteine components. This structure accounts for the high sulfur content of the insulin molecule which is 3.3%. For structural formula of insulin molecule see Fig. 17.

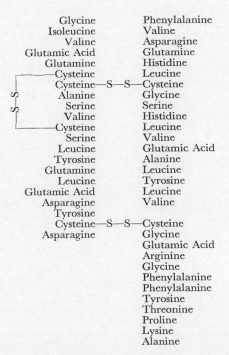

FIG. 17.   STRUCTURAL FORMULA OF INSULIN MOLECULE

Insulin contains all the commonly occurring amino acids except methionine, tryptophan, and hydroxyproline. Because of its polypeptide content, insulin cannot be taken by mouth since the strongly proteolytic enzymes of the stomach would readily hydrolyze it, splitting its peptide linkages and irreversibly inactivating the insulin.

The insulin molecule has no metal ions but it readily combines with zinc, facilitating crystallization of insulin. Crystalline insulin can be obtained by precipitating it with a weak base from a strongly buffered acetic acid solution at the isoelectric point of the insulin, when it is least soluble or more insoluble (Jensen 1938).

The speed of absorption of crystalline insulin from the tissues is relatively fast, necessitating several daily injections for the average diabetic. The annoyance of insulin therapy has been overcome by the development of several long acting and intermediate types of insulin, protamine insulin (Hagedorn *et al.* 1936), protamine zinc insulin, globin insulin, NPH insulin, and the Lente series of insulin. The rate of absorption of these is slower and one injection is generally sufficient for a 24-hr. period (Beaser 1964).

PREPARATION OF INSULIN FROM FISH

In the early stages of insulin manufacture, around 1924, it seemed, at first, less expensive to produce insulin from fish than from mammalian sources such as beef or pig pancreas. This economy of insulin production from fish appeared particularly true when the gall-bladders of cod, halibut, and pollack were used as the raw material (McCormick 1924A).

These fishes are caught in large numbers and are gutted shortly thereafter. Their large islets or "caps," which are located on the gall-bladder and contain insulin tissue, are readily noticeable (Fig. 18). The caps are very easily snipped off with scissors. This operation is very simple. One per-

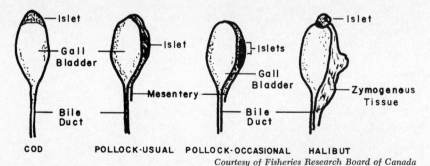

Courtesy of Fisheries Research Board of Canada

Fig. 18. Insulin "Caps" on Cod, Pollack and Halibut Gall-bladders

son can clip off 150 to 200 caps per hour from gall-bladders of fresh entrails.

A twelve year old boy, after a few minutes instruction, was able to remove the islets from codfish gall-bladders, keeping up with a team of three fish dressers who deposited the entrails in the boy's tub. This procedure applies to the open boat shore fisheries which is a seasonal operation. During the winter months shore fisheries operations cease and fishing is continued with steam trawlers.

In the United States, with a highly developed livestock industry, i.e., cattle, sheep, and pigs, insulin has been and still is being produced as a by-product of the meat packing industry. However, in sea coast countries where livestock is scarce, the production of insulin from the various types of the larger species of fishes available to them would seem to be desirable.

Directions for Collecting Insulin Material

Directions for collecting insulin material and preparing the insulin extract as given by McCormick (1924a) are essentially as follows:

Deposit entrails of fresh fish in a receptacle. Immediately thereafter, clip off with a pair of scissors the "caps" or islands which are located on the gall-bladder and which are loaded with insulin, especially the islands of cod, haddock, and halibut, and preserve the insulin containing tissue in 95% alcohol, acidified with 0.3% of mineral acid, preferably hydrochloric acid. Do not include any bile, gall-bladder, or pancreatic tissue with the insulin.

Collect the tissue in a 4-oz. wide-mouth bottle, half filled with the preserving fluid, and forward it daily to the central collecting station. Do not expose it to direct sunlight. This size container will hold insulin islets from approximately 4000 lb. of fish.

The alcohol concentration should not exceed approximately 75%. Should delays in shipment arise, then store bottles in cracked ice during transit for not more than 18 to 24 hr. The islets of cod, pollack, halibut, etc., may all be collected in the same container.

It should be noted that preserving the insulin tissue in an acidified alcoholic solution was the method used during the early days of insulin production. A more desirable alternative procedure is to freeze the tissue with solid carbon dioxide and to ship it in frozen form (Fisher 1964).

Preparation of the Insulin Extracts

The alcohol is filtered through muslin and the tissue is squeezed to dryness, weighed, and ground thoroughly in a mortar and re-extracted in supernatant alcohol which has been adjusted to a 75% alcohol concentration in the mixture of tissue and fluid. After the tissue is completely macerated, the mixture is allowed to remain at room temperature for about $1^1/_2$ hr. and the alcohol is again drained off through the muslin.

In this fashion the residue is extracted three times. The composite of the three alcoholic extracts is filtered through thin paper into porcelain trays and the alcohol is evaporated by vacuum distillation. The residual oil found in the aqueous insulin solution is extracted several times with ether, in a separatory funnel.

This insulin preparation has proved highly potent, but in a few instances it showed undesirable local irritations. To prevent this untoward effect, the alcoholic extract is further purified by conversion into insulin hydrochloride by Dudley's process. Subsequently, the extract is concentrated and adjusted to a suitable potency, which is determined by the standard procedure using rabbits or mice (Hill and Howitt 1936).

Extensive chemical and physiological tests carried out on cod insulin proved it to be similar to insulin extracted from beef or pork. Furthermore, clinical tests carried out by Dr. W. R. Campbell on diabetic patients in the Toronto General Hospital proved very successful (McCormick 1924a).

With the advent of oral antidiabetic agents such as the sulfonylurea and biguanide drugs, the demand for insulin might appear to be considerably reduced. This might be particularly true in view of the fact that diabetes primarily affects the middle aged and the older population. About 75% of diabetics are between the ages of 40 and 70, and it is to this group that the oral therapy is largely applied with great success. Actually there has been a shortage of sources of commercial insulin and the oral agents have only temporarily helped balance supply and demand. Eventually new sources of insulin will be welcome due to the relatively fixed sources of supply as compared with an expanding population (Beaser 1964).

Cost of Insulin

Another consideration that might well justify the extraction of insulin from fishes is its cost as compared with the cost of the oral agents or of insulin obtained from animal sources, particularly as it applies to patients of technologically under-developed countries. For example, the June, 1963 cost of Orinase was $6.00 for 50 tablets, one-half gram each, or 12¢ per tablet. The average adult diabetic usually takes two to four tablets a day at a cost of 24 to 48¢ per day for Orinase. This cost amounts to $1.68 or $3.36 a week, or $87.36 or $174.72 a year.

To a diabetic patient in the technologically developing countries, whose total annual income is only several hundred dollars, the cost of this life-saving drug would be almost prohibitive. However, developing seacoast countries could supply their diabetic patients with insulin from fish obtainable "around the corner," i.e., from locally caught fish at relatively reduced cost.

According to Tanikawa (1965), two factories manufacture insulin from fish and whales in Japan. The principal raw materials of marine origin used in making insulin in Japan are derived from bonito (*Katsuonus vagans*) and whales. Some raw material is obtained from albacore and yellow fin tuna. The percentage yield of insulin from the whale pancreas is less than that from beef pancreas but the whale's pancreas is much greater in size; this makes its manufacture commercially practical.

BIBLIOGRAPHY

BEASER, S. B. 1964. Personal communication. Boston, Mass.

FISHER, A. M. 1964. Personal communication. Toronto, Canada.

HAGEDORN, H. C., JENSEN, B. N., KRARUP, N. B., and WODSTRUP, I. 1936. Protamine insulinate. J. Am. Med. Assoc. *106*, 177–180.

HILL, D. W., and HOWITT, F. O. 1936. Insulin: Its Production, Purification and Physiological Action. Hutchinson, London.

JENSEN, H. F. 1938. Insulin: Its Chemistry and Physiology. Commonwealth Fund, New York.

MACLEOD, J. J. R. 1922. The source of insulin. J. Metabolic Res. *2*, No. 2, 149–172.

McCORMICK, N. A. 1924A. Insulin from fish. Bull. Biol. Board Can.

McCORMICK, N. A. 1924B. The distribution and structure of the islands of Langerhans in certain fresh-water and marine fishes. Trans. of the Roy. Can. Inst.

McCORMICK, N. A., and NOBLE, E. C. 1924. Insulin from fish. J. Biol. Chem. *59*, Proc. Soc. Biol. Chem., p. 29.

McCORMICK, N. A., and NOBLE, E. C. 1924. Further sources of insulin. Contrib. to Can. Biol., New Series, *2*.

SANGER, F. 1949. Terminal peptides of insulin. Biochem. J. *45*, 563–574.

TANIKAWA, E. 1965. Marine Products in Japan. Published by the author who is Professor of Marine Food Technology, Faculty of Fisheries, Hokkaido University, Hakodate, Japan.

CHAPTER 10

Biochemical and Pharmaceutical Products of Special Interest

POTENTIAL SOURCES OF BIOCHEMICAL PRODUCTS

Introduction

A substantial number of biochemical products may be derived from various organs and tissues of fish. Stansby *et al.* (1953) stated that salmon cannery wastes could serve as a potential source for the production of a number of useful biochemical products. They also indicated that "full and efficient utilization of salmon wastes rest upon the instigation of a comprehensive and long term research program in order to fully ascertain the possibilities of the lesser known constituents."

Although Stansby *et al.* (1953) limited their survey principally to salmon cannery waste, it is, nevertheless, logical to assume, with some reservations, that these biochemical substances could be derived from other fish, such as cod. In fact, Dugal and Lafromboise (1955) have done considerable research on bile derived from cod gall-bladder.

Some of these biochemical products, namely, nucleic acids and nucleosides, protamines, strepogenin, glutathione, cortisone, bile salts, and proteolytic enzymes will be discussed briefly.

Nucleic Acids and Nucleosides

Nucleic acids are essential components of cell nuclei. The nucleic acid molecule consists of purine and pyrimidine bases, carbohydrate, and phosphoric acid. Nucleic acids combine with proteins to form nucleoproteins, and are produced by a mild hydrolysis of nucleoproteins. Nucleosides are formed by heating nucleic acid at 356°F. with dilute ammonia for $3^1/_2$ hr., during which reaction phosphoric acid is split off. Glandular organs and sperm cells are good sources of nucleic acids.

The milt of salmon is very high in a readily available supply of nucleic acids and nucleosides (Stansby *et al.* 1953). Fish spermatozoa contain over 70% nucleic acids, on a dry basis. During the spawning season, the enlarged salmon testes contain from 5 to 10% sperm. These enlarged mature testes could be mechanically removed from salmon and the sperm could serve as an excellent natural source of nucleosides and nucleic acids.

Protamines

Protamines are simple proteins, consisting of a polypeptide structure. On hydrolysis, they yield principally diamino acids which render the protein hydrolyzate basic in reaction. Protamines have been found in various fish sperm combined with nucleic acids. For example, the following basic proteins have been isolated from fish sperm: "salmin" from salmon sperm; "clupein" from herring sperm; "sturin" from sturgeon sperm, and "cyprinin" from carp sperm. "Salmin" contains 88% of arginine. Salmon milt which contains the salmon sperm, can be readily separated from salmon cannery waste in the same way that salmon eggs are separated.

Protamines are soluble in water and precipitate other proteins from an aqueous solution. Compounds of insulin and protamines have been prepared for improving the treatment of diabetics.

Hagedorn *et al.* (1936) combined protamine and insulin and formed a suitable compound for the treatment of diabetes. This compound slows down the action of the injected insulin, by decreasing the rate of absorption of the insulin from the tissues of the diabetic, and therefore, markedly prolonging the effectiveness of the insulin.

Strepogenin

Certain proteins, such as purified casein, appear to have a growth promoting factor which is an aid to a more efficient protein metabolism. This substance is called strepogenin (Gortner and Gortner 1950). It is also referred to as the "protein utilization factor."

Strepogenin appears to be a growth-promoting factor for certain microorganisms such as some of the better known lactobacilli, e.g., *Lactobacillus bulgaricus* (Woolley 1941). Fish flesh seems to be an excellent source of this substance.

Glutathione

Glutathione, in either the reduced or oxidized form, is present in all body tissues. In the reduced form glutathione is a tripeptide consisting of the three amino acids glycine, cysteine, and glutamic acid. It seems to act as a coenzyme in carbohydrate metabolism and it probably plays an important part in intracellular oxidation-reduction processes. It is also likely that glutathione may play an important role of detoxification in man (Gortner and Gortner 1950, p. 499).

It has been shown that the glutathione content is high in the kidney, spleen, heart, and liver of salmon. Fish waste, in general, is a plentiful and inexpensive source of glutathione (Stansby *et al.* 1953).

Cortisone

Cortisone, a steroid compound, is used to alleviate the pain caused by certain collagenous diseases, such as rheumatoid arthritis. It has an anti-inflammatory action.

Idler *et al.* (1958) reported the isolation of cortisol(I) and cortisone(II) from blood samples obtained from Fraser River sockeye salmon just before spawning. Steroids were obtained from plasma by extraction with ethyl acetate. By the use of paper chromatography, they ascertained the presence of $17\mu g$ of cortisol(I) and $37\mu g$ cortisone(II) per 100 ml. of plasma, constituting about 60 to 70% yield.

Consequently, cortisone, which has many diversified therapeutic uses, can be derived from fish plasma.

Bile Salts

Bile is produced in the liver. It is concentrated and stored in the gall-bladder, which releases the bile on contraction and squeezing and secretes it into the intestine through the bile duct. The bile salts emulsify fats, thus aiding the digestion and absorption of fats from the intestines.

Bile salts have recently been utilized in medicine and in synthetic organic chemistry (Stansby *et al.* 1953). Sex hormones, for example, are synthesized from bile acids obtained from mammalian gall-bladders. This synthesis, is possible because of the structural similarity of bile acids, sex hormones, and cholesterol.

Fish bile contains cholic acid and deoxycholic acid (Dugal and Lafromboise 1956). Cholic acid is combined in the liver with taurine and sodium to produce the bile salt, sodium taurocholate.

Recovery of Salmon Gall-Bladder.—Since the salmon gall-bladder is very small, the cost of manual separation of this organ from the viscera would be prohibitive as compared with the cost of obtaining ox bile (Dugal and Lafromboise 1955). Removal of salmon gall-bladder would be justifiable only when several other organs are simultaneously separated from the viscera, or if the gall-bladder could be removed mechanically.

Recovery of Cod Gall-Bladder.—The gall-bladder of cod can be readily recognized and segregated from the viscera. It is generally a dark-greenish oval-shaped organ, about 0.5 to 0.75 in. in its longitudinal axis and about 0.25 to 0.5 in. in its shorter diameter. The cod gall-bladder yields from 3 to 6.1 gm. of bile, although some individual gall-bladders average as much as 29.7 gm. (Dugal and Lafromboise 1956). Deoxycholic acid concentration averages about 0.30% per gall-bladder while the cholic acid concentration averages about six per cent. It appears, therefore, that cod bile is a potential raw material for the preparation of pure cholic acid.

Collecting Bile from Cod Gall-Bladder.—It is a very delicate operation to collect bile by mechanical removal of the gall-bladder. Even a slight incision in the gall-bladder would result in a loss of bile. Accordingly, suction produced by an aspirator seems to be a more efficient way of recovering bile from gall bladders.

Apparatus for Collecting Cod Bile.—An apparatus for collecting bile from cod gall-bladders, as devised by Dugal and Lafromboise (1955), consists of an injection needle *C* (See Fig. 19) to connect the apparatus with the gall-bladder; a suction flask *B* to collect the bile and an aspirator *A* to produce the vacuum. Frothing in the suction flask was at first prevented by a partial break in the vacuum through an opening in the con-

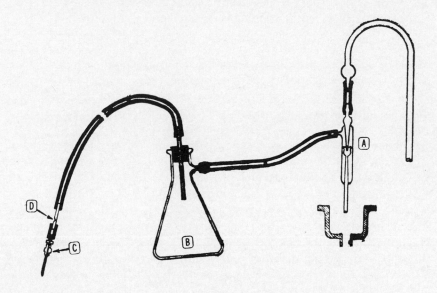

Courtesy of Fisheries Research Board of Canada

FIG. 19.   SUCTION APPARATUS FOR COLLECTING COD BILE

necting tubing at *D*, the opening and closing of which is readily controlled with one finger. Subsequently, frothing was prevented with a silicone anti-foam agent. This method of bile recovery proved to be efficient.

COST COMPARISON BETWEEN COD BILE AND OX BILE

The cost of labor is the main criterion in deciding whether to use cod or ox gall-bladders as the source for bile (Dugal and Lafromboise 1956). One or two ox gall-bladders are sufficient to produce one pound of bile, whereas 170 cod gall-bladders are required to produce the same quantity of bile. Consequently, the recovery of cod bile can be resorted to when the price of bile is high.

It would also be worthwhile to recover cod bile or bile from other species of large fishes, in sea coast countries where the cattle industry is not extensively developed because of poor grazing areas, or because of other geographic and climatic limitations. Under such conditions, bile from various species of fish similar to cod in size and in accessibility to their gall-bladders, might constitute the best source of supply.

PROTEOLYTIC ENZYMES FROM PYLORIC CAECA OF FISH

Introduction

Enzymes are organic catalysts produced by the living cells of all forms of life, i.e., animals, plants, and microorganisms. The function of enzymes is to accelerate biochemical reactions in all living cells and tissues under conditions of temperature, pH, and moisture content which are compatible with their carrier, better known as substrate.

Without enzymes, biochemical reactions would proceed at an exceedingly low rate. Like all catalysts, enzymes act only as agents without combining with the new products formed or without being used up in the process.

"A little goes a long way"—a small amount of enzyme is sufficient to hydrolyze a large amount of substrate. Enzymes are specific in their actions. Their action is analogous to a key and lock arrangement, i.e., enzymes which hydrolyze proteins do not hydrolyze fats or carbohydrates.

Enzymes are protein in nature, therefore they generally become inactivated under conditions which bring about protein denaturation. Some enzymes such as the proteinases behave like albumins. Trypsin and pepsin are simple proteins, i.e., they are composed entirely of amino acids. Others are conjugated proteins, where the enzyme is bound to a prosthetic group such as hematin, riboflavin, or phosphate. Most enzymes are either soluble or dispersible in water.

The proteolytic enzymes, with which we are principally concerned in fish, occur in the pyloric caeca. Since enzymes are proteins, they contain some free amino and carboxyl groups and therefore act as ampholytes, or amphoteric electrolytes, which ionize with changes in pH and charge the enzyme molecule. Enzymes, therefore, have an optimum activity at a certain pH value and their activity drops off on both sides. They are destroyed by strong acid or alkali. The rate of enzymatic reactions is accelerated by heat within definite limits. Generally, enzymes become inactivated when held at approximately 170°F. for from 15 to 20 min.

PYLORIC CAECA OF FISH

The pyloric caeca of fish are blind tube-like sacs attached to the stomach near the pyloric end. The structure of the pyloric caeca of each species of fish is typical for the species. In fact, this structural difference serves as a means for differentiating two species of fish that might appear similar in all other respects (Blake 1960). The pyloric caeca constitute about 1.1% of the weight of fish as landed. The function of the pyloric caeca in fish is similar to that of the mammalian pancreas, i.e., they elaborate proteolytic enzymes. The proteolytic enzyme activity of the pyloric caeca enzymes closely resembles that of trypsin, or tryptic enzymes. These enzymes, obtainable from various species of fish, can be used largely for leather bating. They can also be used for preparing protein hydrolyzates and peptones.

USE OF PROTEOLYTIC ENZYMES IN LEATHER BATING

One of the most important uses of proteolytic enzymes, especially trypsin, is in leather "bating." This essential step in the manufacture of leather is carried out as follows: First, hair and excessive flesh are removed from hides. Subsequently, the hides are bated, i.e., they are subjected to the action of proteinases, especially tryptic enzymes, which render then more plump and more porous (see Chapter 4). The increase in permeability allows better penetration of the tanning agents into the hides. It is sufficient that the enzymes used for bating should be able to hydrolyze certain hide proteins into proteoses, rather than break them down to the amino acid state. A bate should remove all the elastin fibers. The value of a bate is usually determined by its proteolytic activity on casein.

OTHER USES FOR FISH CAECAL ENZYMES

Enzymes obtained from the pyloric caeca of fish can have, in addition to their use in leather bating, applications similar to those of other proteolytic enzymes. Such uses, for example, are those of degumming silk, chillproofing beer, or tenderizing meat.

Brody (1963) described procedures for liquefying meat by the use of either proteolytic or catheptic enzymes, with the view of providing a meat product which is easily digestible and assimilable and is particularly adaptable to consumption by the ill or infirm or by infants. Such a product is also suitable to serve as emergency ration by the military or for other uses.

PROTEOLYTIC ENZYME ACTIVITY OF THE PYLORIC CAECA OF COD AND HADDOCK

Johnston (1937) found that the proteolytic activity of enzymes obtained from the pyloric caeca of cod and haddock compared very favorably with the activity obtained from hog pancreas or commercial bates. These enzymes showed their maximum proteolytic activity at approximately pH 8 and temperature 112°F., which practically coincide with optimum conditions for trypsin. He also found that the pyloric caeca showed some lipolytic, peptic, and rennet activity but no amylolytic activity. Therefore, a suitable leather bate could be prepared from cod and haddock pyloric caeca.

Preparation of a "Standard" Enzyme Extract from Pyloric Caeca of Cod and Haddock

A "standard" enzyme extract was prepared by Johnston (1937) as follows: pyloric caeca were cut from fresh fish and kept frozen overnight and were ground up while still frozen. They were then treated with a solution amounting to 150% of their weight, containing 90% acetone and 10% ether. The entire mixture was allowed to stand for about 30 min.

Subsequently, the solid portion was pressed to remove as much of the extract as possible and the residual solids were again treated in the same manner as in the first extraction. The solids remaining after the two extractions and pressings were then spread out and dried at room temperature. It would be even better to dry the remaining solids by evaporation under partial vacuum. The dried caeca were ground to a 20 mesh. The resulting yellowish powder was about 30% water soluble.

Total Proteolytic Activity of the Digestive Organs of Cod, Haddock, Hake, and Mackerel

Johnston (1941) tried to determine the total proteolytic activity of the digestive organs of cod, haddock, hake, and mackerel. He found that only the pyloric caeca and the intestinal mucosa of these fish showed sufficiently high proteolytic activity to render their industrial application feasible. Mackerel caeca showed the highest tryptic activity and yield of any organ of the four species of fish examined. Furthermore, the pyloric caeca yielded about four times as much tryptic activity as did the intestine.

The preparation of the pyloric caeca enzymes was made in the same manner as that described by Johnston in 1937, except that the ground tissue was treated with a solution, containing 90% acetone and 10% ether, in an amount equal to 350%, instead of 150%, of the weight of the tissue.

PROTEOLYTIC ENZYME ACTIVITY OF THE PYLORIC CAECA OF SALMON

Cooke and Chowdhury (1948) found that the pyloric caeca of the four species of salmon—spring, pink, sockeye, and chum—can be used as a source of tryptic enzymes. These enzymes showed their maximum activity at pH between 8.0 and 8.5 at about 105°F. These conditions are optimum for a mammalian trypsin and, therefore, the enzymes obtained from the salmon pyloric caeca can be used effectively for leather bating.

PROTEOLYTIC ENZYME ACTIVITY OF THE PYLORIC CAECA OF REDFISH

Redfish, also known as ocean perch, is involved in an important segment of the New England fishery industry and has minimized the ill effect of the critical drop in the codfish catch. Redfish is one of the few species of fish caught all year round, in very large quantities, off the New England coast.

An investigation was carried out by Stern and Lockhart (1953) on the proteolytic activity of an enzyme preparation from the pyloric caeca of redfish. They found that when using casein as a substrate, the optimum conditions for proteolytic activity were 122°F. and pH 8.75. This pH is slightly higher than the optimum pH of trypsin. The relative proteolytic activities of a number of enzyme preparations, with the activity of trypsin taken arbitrarily as 100, are as follows: pancreatin, 95; dried redfish caeca, 77; papain, 32; commercial bate, 13; and hog intestinal mucosa, 10.

These comparative figures indicate that the pyloric caeca of redfish could be used as a suitable raw material source for the preparation of leather bate.

Similarly, other species of fish caught in large quantities in various localities could, no doubt, yield important proteolytic enzymes from their pyloric caeca.

The potential use of proteolytic enzymes from pyloric caeca of fish, described here, has not, as yet, reached a commercial scale in the United States. One of the main reasons for not using pyloric caeca of fish as a source of enzymes is the unavailability of the raw material because viscera of the larger types of fish, such as cod and haddock, are thrown overboard immediately after the fish are gutted. The viscera, together with the skeletal remains of the smaller types of fish, such as redfish, are converted into fish meal and fish oil.

PRESENT STATUS OF THE BIOCHEMICAL AND PHARMACEUTICAL PRODUCTS FROM FISH

It is significant to note that, notwithstanding the potential usefulness of the biochemical and pharmaceutical products described in this chapter, which could be derived from fish, none has, as yet, been put into production except protamine. Apparently, it is not economically feasible or possible in the United States at the present time (1965), to manufacture these products from fish in competition with the highly developed animal (or meat packing) industry.

Developing sea coast countries that have a serious shortage of farm animals, could resort to the utilization of fish as the next best source of these products.

FOUR BIOCHEMICAL OR PHARMACEUTICAL PRODUCTS
CURRENTLY MANUFACTURED

Biochemical or pharmaceutical products, which are commercially derived from fish are protamine, 5-iododeoxyuridine, desitin, and cholesterol depressants (Stansby 1964).

Protamine and 5-iododeoxyuridine are derived from salmon milt. The latter is a drug which shows promise of benefit to terminal cancer patients (Anon. 1960). It is produced by an enzyme process. Over 100 lb. of salmon sperm is required to produce one ounce of 5-iododeoxyuridine.

Desitin is produced from unsaturated fish oil fatty acids and used as an ointment for skin irritations. It is manufactured by Desitin Chemical Co., Providence, R. I. Cholesterol depressants are derived from fish oil fatty acids or their esters.

BIBLIOGRAPHY

ANON. 1960. Growth recipe: be unconventional. Chem. Eng. News. 38, No. 15, 46.

BEASER, S. B. 1964. Personal communication. Boston, Mass.

BLAKE, C. 1960. Personal communication. Boston, Mass.

BODANSKY, M. 1938. Physiological Chemistry. 4th Edition. John Wiley and Sons, New York.

BRODY, J. 1963. Method of preparing a liquid meat product. U. S. Pat. 3,113,-030. Dec. 3.

COOKE, N. E. 1947. A note on the cost of salmon bile. Fisheries Res. Board Can., Progr. Rept. Pacific Coast Sta. No. 70, 18.

COOKE, N. E., and CHOWDHURY, N. K. 1948. Utilization of fish wastes. Commercial enzymes from the pyloric caeca of fish. Fisheries Res. Board Can., Progr. Rept. Pacific Coast Sta. No. 75, 51–54. Vancouver, B. C.

DIXON, M., and WEBB, E. C. 1958. Enzymes. Academic Press, New York.

DUGAL, L. C., and LAFROMBOISE, A. 1955. Recovery of cod bile. Fisheries Res. Board Can., Progr. Rept. Atlantic Coast Sta., Issue No. 62, 10–12, St. Andrews, N. B., Canada.

DUGAL, L. C., and LAFROMBOISE, A. 1956. The bile acids of cod bile. Fisheries Res. Board Can., Progr. Rept. Atlantic Coast Sta., Issue No. 65, 21–22. St. Andrews, N. B, Canada.

DUNN, C. G. 1964. Personal communication. Cambridge, Mass.

FRUTON, J. S., and SIMMONDS, S. 1960. General Biochemistry. 2nd Edition. John Wiley and Sons, New York.

GORTNER, R. A., JR., and GORTNER, W. A. 1950. Outlines of Biichemistry. 3rd Edition, John Wiley and Sons, New York.

HAGEDORN, H. C., JENSEN, B. N., KRARUP, N. B., and WODSTRUP, I. 1936. Protamine insulate. J. Am. Med. Assoc. 106, 177–180.

HARPER, H. A. 1959. Review of Physiol. Chem. 7th Edition. Lange Medical Publications. Los Altos, Calif.

HARRISON, R. W., ANDERSON, A. W., POTTINGER, S. R., and LEE, C. F. 1939. Pacific salmon oils. U. S. Bur. Fisheries Inves. Rept. No. 40, 1-21.

HARROW, B., and MAZUR, A. 1962. Textbook of Biochemistry. 8th Edition. Saunders. Philadelphia.

IDLER, D. R., RONALD, A. P., and SCHMIDT, P. J. 1958. Isolation of cortisone and cortisol from the plasma of Pacific salmon. Fisheries Res. Board Can., Technol. Sta., Vancouver, B. C.

JOHNSTON, W. W. 1937. Some characteristics of the enzymes of the pyloric caeca of cod and haddock. J. Biol. Board Can. 3, No. 5, 473–485.

JOHNSTON, W. W. 1941. Tryptic enzymes from certain commercial fishes. J. Fisheries Res. Board Can. 5, No. 3, 217–226.

JONES, G. I., and CARRIGAN, E. J. 1947. Possibility of development of new products from salmon cannery waste. Dep't of Commerce, Office of Technical Services Report, "Utilization of salmon cannery waste—Part I." Cac-4717.

KOENIG, J. and GROSSFELD, J. M. 1913. Fish roe as food for man. Biochem. Z. 54, 351–394.

KYTE, R. M. 1955. Study of pharmaceutical and other industrial products from salmon eggs. Com. Fisheries Rev. 17, No. 2, 14–15. (Sep. No. 394).

KYTE, R. M. 1958. Potential By-Products from Alaska Fisheries: Utilization of salmon eggs and salmon waste. Com. Fisheries Rev. 20, No. 3, 1–5 (Sep. No. 504).

MACKAY, M. E. 1929. Note on the bile in different fishes. Biol. Bull. 56, No. 1, 24–27.

MIYACHI, S. 1937. Glutathione content of salmon. Japan. J. Med. Sci., II, Biochem. 3, 267–268.

NORRIS, E. R., and Elam, D. W. 1939. Crystalline salmon pepsin. Science 90, 399.

STANSBY, M. E., et al. 1953. Utilization of Alaskan salmon cannery waste. U. S. Fish and Wildlife Service, Special Scientific Report: Fisheries No. 109.

STANSBY, M. E. 1964. Personal communication. Seattle, Wash.

STERN, J. A., and Lockhart, E. E. 1953. A study of the proteolytic enzyme activity of the pyloric caeca of redfish. Contrib. No. 148 from the Dep't of Food Technology, M.I.T., Cambridge, Mass.

SUMNER, J. B., and Somers, G. F. 1953. The Chemistry and Methods of Enzymes. 3rd Edition. Academic Press Inc., New York.

TAUBER, H. 1950. The Chemistry and Technology of Enzymes. 2nd Printing. John Wiley and Sons, New York.

WOOLLEY, D. W. 1941. The nutritive requirements of bacteria. J. Bacteriol. 42, 155–163.

CHAPTER 11

Fish Meal Production

INTRODUCTION

Fish meal is a highly concentrated, nutritious feed supplement consisting principally of high-quality proteins, minerals, and B complex vitamins. It also contains other ingredients which contribute to animal growth and which are usually referred to as "unknown growth factors" (Stansby and Dassow 1963).

Fish meal has won wide acceptance in the feed trade because of its proved nutritional value. It is obtained through the "fish reduction process," which consists essentially of grinding, cooking, pressing, and drying of fish scrap obtained from filleting or canning operations, or by processing whole fish such as herring, menhaden, pilchards (California sardine), or trash-fish (Fig. 20).

Fish scrap consists of the skeletal remains of fish which have been gutted and filleted and it includes the head, the entire fish skeleton, and its adhering proteinaceous tissues. When the raw stock consists of small fish, grinding may not be necessary.

The production of fish meal and the production of fish oils are usually started simultaneously, particularly when fatty fish such as herring, menhaden, pilchard, or salmon cannery waste is used. For the sake of clarity, however, it seems best to describe these two important fishery by-products and their overlapping processes in two separate chapters, devoting this chapter to fish meal. Fish-body oil production is the subject of Chapter 13.

Importance of Fish Meal Production

In the United States, fish meal is manufactured in larger quantity than any other fishery by-product. Comparing the total U. S. production figures of fish meal with those of fish oils, in terms of short tons, for the period 1953 through 1959, we find that the amount of fish meal produced was about three times that of fish oils (Table 9).

Comparing production of fish meal by the major producing countries during 1948, 1953, 1958, and 1959 (Table 10), we find that the United States produced more fish meal than any other country up to 1959 when Peru exceeded U. S. production by approximately 20%.

The imports of fish meal to the United States by country of origin during 1953–1959 is shown in Table 11.

TABLE 9

U. S.: PRODUCTION OF FISH MEAL AND FISH OIL BY TYPE OF PRODUCT (IN SHORT TONS) 1953–1959 (J. A. SMYTH 1961)

Product	1953	1954	1955	1956	1957	1958	1959
Fish meal							
Menhaden scrap and meal	174,752	183,091	190,628	210,582	172,388	158,074	223,893
Herring meal	206	6,973	7,671	11,298	13,891	10,277	11,963
Pacific sardine meal	144	6,513	6,966	2,809	1,474	10,756	2,927
Tuna and mackerel meal	20,029	21,576	23,396	26,266	25,716	25,311	25,380
Other meal[1]	38,720	38,814	35,841	44,838	50,616	43,722	42,388
Total	238,851	256,967	264,502	295,793	264,085	248,140	306,551
Fish oil							
Menhaden oil	66,844	69,904	79,620	84,105	59,243	63,994	77,355
Herring oil	2,696	2,854	4,091	6,840	7,054	6,600	7,504
Pacific sardine oil	48	2,835	3,367	1,264	330	2,779	705
Tuna and mackerel oil	2,471	2,194	2,044	2,644	2,768	2,351	2,254
Other marine oil[2]	3,278	3,318	3,424	3,776	4,706	5,092	3,772
Total	75,337	81,105	92,546	98,629	74,101	80,816	91,590

Table courtesy of U. S. Fish and Wildlife Service.
Source: Bureau of Commercial Fisheries, Canned Fish and Byproducts, 1959.
[1] Chiefly offal, waste, and scrap fish from the groundfish industry; includes also crab meal (9,206 tons in 1959), seal meal (330 tons in 1959), shrimp meal (627 tons in 1959), and whale meal (1,881 tons in 1959).
[2] Chiefly groundfish, ocean perch, and anchovy oils; also includes alewife, seal, salmon, and whale oils. Source: Bureau of Commercial Fisheries.

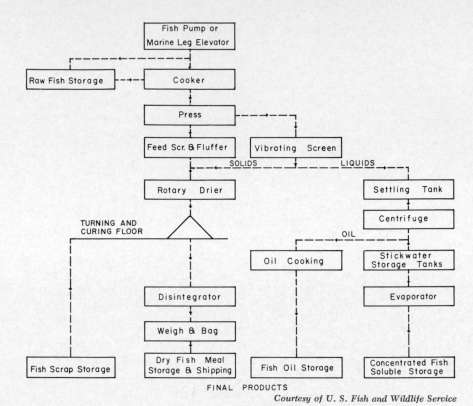

FINAL PRODUCTS

Courtesy of U. S. Fish and Wildlife Service

FIG. 20. FLOW SHEET FOR FISH REDUCTION PLANT

TABLE 10

PRODUCTION OF FISH MEAL (IN SHORT TONS) BY MAJOR PRODUCING COUNTRIES 1948, 1953, 1958, 1959 (J. A. SMYTH, 1961)

Country	1948	1953	1958	1959
Angola	15,653	46,631	52,679	61,916
Morocco	[1]	18,073	22,811	19,526
South Africa	11,795	96,170	109,258	143,722
Canada	45,856	51,856	72,393	77,177
United States	215,500	238,851	248,140	306,551
Chile	882	8,218	20,725	33,811
Peru	...	13,330	139,854	366,351
Japan	37,809	105,374	231,530	258,468
Denmark	11,904	30,986	72,319	78,242
Federal Republic of Germany	18,298	77,205	83,335	98,078
Iceland	45,415	28,660	48,170	71,640
Norway	177,801	176,755	131,035	141,060
United Kingdom	66,248	92,314	87,743	87,696
U.S.S.R.	12,015	26,896	[1]	[1]
Total[2]	659,176	1,011,319	1,319,992	1,744,238

Table courtesy of U. S. Fish and Wildlife Service, Washington 25, D. C.
Note: For some countries data may include wet or dry solubles.
Source: Food and agriculture organization, Yearbook of Fishery Statistics.
[1] Not available.
[2] Totals do not include smaller quantities produced in many other countries. The amount of fishmeal produced in 1959 in countries not listed above is estimated at about 250,000 short tons.

TABLE 11

UNITED STATES: IMPORTS OF FISH MEAL (IN SHORT TONS) BY COUNTRY OF ORIGIN, 1953–1959

Country	1953	1954	1955	1956	1957	1958	1959
Angola	33,589	30,130	12,138	5,063	9,708	18,062	20,738
Canada	28,733	39,740	41,661	57,127	42,823	27,777	39,033
Chile	2,019	823	5,282	1,366	1,108	8,160	5,104
Denmark	6,586	9,103	3,119	...	...	1,092	2,266
Morocco	6,229	4,404	2,815	1,157	...	...	...
Norway	21,748	34,154	14,568	10,965	2,930	1,184	141
Peru	10,685	17,596	8,734	7,766	16,817	33,371	49,923
Union of South Africa	14,072	4,794	3,545	3,470	4,015	7,345	9,727
Other	7,812	5,033	6,141	3,507	3,795	3,361	5,993
Total	131,473	145,777	98,003	90,421	81,196	100,352	132,925

Table courtesy of U. S. Fish and Wildlife Service.
Source: Bureau of Commercial Fisheries; compiled from Bureau of the Census Data.

Effect of Imports upon the United States Fish Meal Industry

By mid-1959, U. S. fish meal manufacturers began to feel the pinch of serious foreign competition in the industry, particularly because of the steadily increasing importation of fish meal from Peru and Chile. Early in 1960 foreign competition forced a reduction in the price of fish meal to $70 per ton, while U.S. manufacturers had to sell for at least $110 to $120 per ton to realize a fair return. In most instances, the imported fish meal was inferior in quality to the American product; still the price differential was great enough to induce feed manufacturers to buy imported rather than domestic fish meal.

By the middle of 1960, almost all fish-meal producers in the United States were either forced out of business or had to curtail their operations very drastically. The steady increase in imports of foreign fish meal and of fish solubles is very graphically shown in Figure 21 taken from C.F.S. No. 3454 for the period 1953-1963.

As a result of this upheaval, hardly any technological advances have been made in this field since 1959.

Twelve Reasons for Fish Meal Popularity

1. Fish meal possesses exceptionally good nutritional values. It furnishes, in concentrated form, high-quality proteins which contain all of the essential amino acids and it is particularly high in lysine. Since this essential amino acid is low in the cereal grains, which constitute the major components in poultry and swine rations, the addition of at least three per cent fish meal to such feed blends balances their protein value.

2. It furnishes some of the B complex vitamins, namely, riboflavin, niacin, pantothenic acid, choline, and B_{12}.

3. Fish meal is high in mineral content ranging from about 12% for a high protein meal to about 33% for a low protein meal. It is particularly high in the

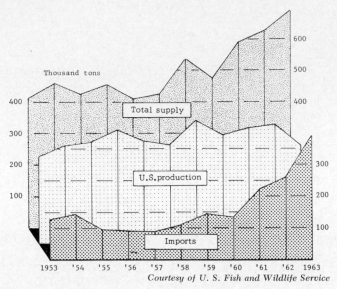

Courtesy of U. S. Fish and Wildlife Service

FIG. 21.   UNITED STATES SUPPLY OF FISH MEAL AND SOLUBLES,
1953–1963

bone and tooth building minerals, i.e., calcium and phosphorus.   It also contains
most of the minerals that are necessary for building up and maintaining the animal body, namely, iron, copper, and some trace elements.

4. Fish-body oil, another very useful by-product, is simultaneously obtained
during fish-meal production, whenever fatty fish such as menhaden, pilchard, or
herring is processed.

5. The production of fish meal furnishes another very nutritious by-product,
namely "fish solubles," when the wet-reduction method is used.

6. Fish meal is low in fiber content, which is a desirable property.

7. The biological value of fish-meal protein is very high, rendering its use in
feeds efficient.

8. From a technological standpoint fish meal is relatively easy to produce.
The basic principles of the procedures for production are well-known, and the
details of the process customarily used are widely disseminated in the trade
literature.   Several basic problems involved in the procedures, however, still
plague the industry.

9. Large quantities of fish meal and its accompanying products, namely, fish
oils and fish solubles, can be produced with a small staff at a relatively low cost,
particularly when the continuous wet-reduction process is used.

10. In general, fish meal has a ready and well-established market as a supplement to poultry, swine, and other animal feeds, and in particular to enrich the
nutritional value of "broiler," "starting," and "breeder" mashes, helping to promote rapid growth.   Fed to poultry, it improves productivity and hatchability
of eggs.

11. Fish meal is a low-cost feed supplement and is generally regarded as a
"good buy" for its intrinsic nutritive value.

12. Fish meal has unknown growth factors (see p. 120) which amplify its value in feed rations.

It is estimated (Borgstrom and Heighway 1961) that about ten per cent of poultry protein is derived from menhaden protein conversion.

A schematic drawing of production equipment for fish meal, fish scrap, and press liquor by the wet-reduction process is shown in Fig. 22.

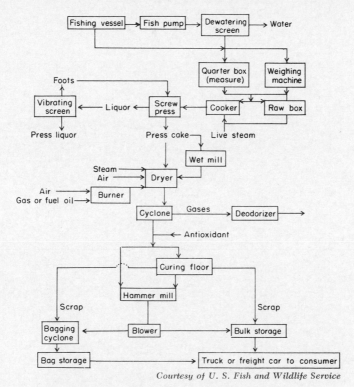

Courtesy of U. S. Fish and Wildlife Service

FIG. 22.   SCHEMATIC DRAWING FOR PRODUCTION OF FISH MEAL, FISH SCRAP, AND PRESS LIQUOR BY WET REDUCTION

Sources of Raw Material for Fish Meal Production

Fish meal can be prepared from fish offal such as the skeletal remains of filleted fish, also known as "gurry," and fish cannery waste. It can also be prepared from whole fish which are generally regarded as inedible, such as trash fish or industrial food fish, menhaden, certain varieties of herring, pilchards (California sardine), and carcasses of sharks and grayfish.

The statistics for the production of fish meal in the United States from menhaden, herring, sardine, tuna, mackerel, etc., during the period, 1941 to 1963 are shown in Table 12.

TABLE 12

PRODUCTION OF FISH MEAL 1941–1963. c.f.s. no. 3454

Year	Menhaden Dried Scrap and Meal		Herring Meal		Sardine (Pacific) Meal	
	Tons	Value	Tons	Value	Tons	Value
1941	75,316	$4,008,355	12,520	$847,116	97,979	$5,942,272
1942	50,504	3,362,279	5,591	386,059	71,828	5,310,037
1943	66,357	4,766,672	9,170	690,280	75,611	5,775,932
1944	69,170	4,913,224	14,212	1,044,861	86,196	6,582,600
1945	77,451	5,483,377	14,344	1,120,042	60,860	4,643,694
1946	94,622	8,605,118	19,505	2,248,942	36,899	5,233,075
1947	98,602	10,883,852	18,453	2,649,474	16,715	2,556,038
1948	103,819	11,548,038	17,686	2,065,042	19,076	2,614,616
1949	112,641	17,773,491	5,298	973,445	39,278	6,219,717
1950	103,260	12,855,651	17,797	2,138,776	43,009	5,269,696
1951	115,426	13,877,636	9,631	1,370,083	17,225	2,266,968
1952	143,968	17,844,511	9,864	1,314,361	390	51,741
1953	174,752	21,767,205	5,206	717,472	144	18,966
1954	183,091	23,783,364	6,973	928,862	6,513	842,649
1955	190,628	25,457,512	7,671	1,163,464	6,966	968,908
1956	210,582	27,439,634	11,298	1,562,622	2,809	369,867
1957	172,388	21,725,888	13,891	1,861,961	1,474	183,330
1958	158,074	20,698,929	10,277	1,457,982	10,756	1,390,200
1959	223,893	26,391,987	11,963	1,589,237	2,927	323,999
1960	218,423	19,201,716	9,151	834,426	3,508	316,463
1961	247,551	25,852,498	5,268	619,934	2,518	257,171
1962	239,707	28,249,566	5,095	688,984	702	73,260
1963	181,750	21,961,625	7,537	856,432	...	...

	Tuna and Mackerel Meal		Other Meal, Acidulated, Dried and Green Scrap		Total, Scrap and Meal	
	Tons	Value	Tons	Value	Tons	Value
1941	8,693	$484,886	42,336	$1,812,944	236,844	$13,095,573
1942	7,144	465,481	36,013	2,101,903	171,080	11,625,759
1943	7,766	505,199	31,499	1,891,069	190,403	13,629,152
1944	9,648	644,458	33,921	2,057,879	213,147	15,243,022
1945	10,273	705,976	37,747	2,452,249	200,675	14,405,338
1946	13,584	1,743,189	35,011	2,609,099	199,621	20,439,423
1947	19,761	2,998,321	32,908	3,292,666	186,439	22,380,351
1948	21,305	2,757,778	37,658	4,103,260	199,544	23,088,734
1949	19,139	3,073,742	60,824	7,611,747	237,180	35,652,142
1950	25,377	3,268,594	50,511	5,721,018	239,954	29,253,735
1951	23,147	3,021,720	44,327	4,837,490	209,756	25,373,897
1952	21,951	2,892,874	45,230	5,058,167	221,403	27,161,654
1953	20,029	2,622,631	38,720	4,433,379	238,851	29,559,653
1954	21,576	2,850,605	38,814	4,348,517	256,967	32,753,997
1955	23,396	3,120,302	35,841	4,039,282	264,502	34,749,468
1956	26,266	3,355,069	44,838	5,159,699	295,793	37,886,891
1957	25,716	3,037,436	50,616	5,783,140	264,085	32,591,755
1958	25,311	3,185,772	43,722	5,025,696	248,140	31,758,579
1959	25,380	2,847,204	42,388	4,773,438	306,551	35,925,865
1960	26,499	2,318,877	32,556	2,610,106	290,137	25,281,588
1961	21,243	2,056,426	34,685	3,153,807	311,265	31,939,836
1962	26,559	2,578,761	40,196	3,982,259	312,259	35,572,830
1963	26,957	2,943,109	37,208	4,177,588	253,452	29,938,754

Table courtesy of U. S. Fish and Wildlife Service.

Effect of Raw Material Quality on Fish Meal

It would seem on first thought that the better the condition of the raw fish stock the higher the quality of the manufactured fish meal. Yet a great deal of evidence exists that the condition of the fish is not the determining factor in nutritive value of the meal, although the condition of the fish affects the yield. If use of decomposed fish affects nutritive value at all, it is minor compared to effects that occur during processing (Karrick 1964).

FISH-MEAL MANUFACTURING PROCEDURES

Butler (1956) describes two general types of processes for fish-meal production: (a) wet-reduction and (b) dry-rendering.

A description of these two processes follows.

Outline of Procedure for the Wet-Reduction Method or the "Continuous Process"

The wet-reduction method for the manufacture of fish meal applies primarily to the processing of fatty fish such as menhaden, redfish, sea-herring, pilchard (California sardine), and salmon cannery offal, whereby fish meal and fish-body oil are simultaneously produced. Since it is a continuous process, it is particularly adaptable to the reduction of large quantities of fish.

Essentially, the wet-reduction process consists of the following operations: (1) grinding or "hogging" of fish offal or of whole fish of the larger variety, which step may be omitted when processing small fish (Fig. 23), (2) heating or cooking the ground or hogged fish, or small whole fish, with live steam under pressure to soften the flesh and bones and to release the oil, Fig. 24), (3) pressing the cooked fish to expel the liquid portion, known as press liquor, and retaining, in the filter-press, the semi-dry portion known as press cake (Fig. 25), (4) screening out the suspended fish solids from the press liquor by passing it over a shaker-screen or a vibratory screen, or using other devices for separating suspended solid particles from the fluid carrier, and returning the wet solids to the press cake, (5) fluffing up the press cake to facilitate its drying, (6) drying the press cake, (7) grinding and sacking the dried meal, (8) heating and centrifuging the screened liquor, from which the suspended solid particles have been removed, to separate the oil from it,[1] (9) further purifying the

---

[1] The practically oil-free, screened or clarified liquor or "stickwater," consists of about 95% water and approximately 5% solids. The solids portion consists of dissolved, dispersed, and finely suspended fish proteins, minerals, B complex vitamins, and unknown growth factors. Some of the proteins are present in the various forms of protein degradation products, namely proteoses, peptones, polypeptides, and amino acids.

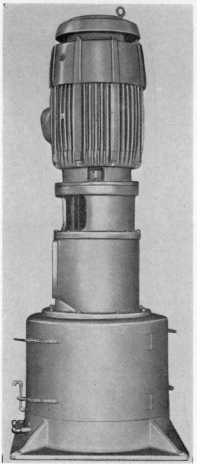

Courtesy of Enterprise Engine and Machinery
Co., a subsidiary of General Metals Corp.,
Oakland, Calif.

FIG. 23.   VERTICAL MILL (EVM-18)

oil by passing it through an oil polishing centrifuge, and (10) discarding
the stickwater or better still concentrating this nutritionally valuable fluid
portion from approximately 5% solids to a syrupy consistency containing
approximately 50% solids.[2]

A flow sheet for a typical fish reduction plant is shown in Fig. 26.

---

[2] Stickwater, which is press-liquor freed from most of its residual oil and suspended
solid particles, is referred to as "fish solubles" when concentrated to approximately
50% solids.   Some manufacturers restore the solubles to the meal and thus produce
"whole" meal.

Courtesy of Edw. Renneburg and Sons, Co., Baltimore, Md.

FIG. 24. CONTINUOUS COOKER

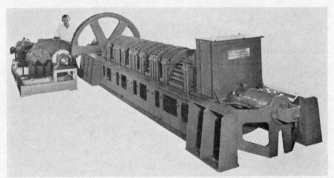

Courtesy of Edw. Renneburg and Sons, Co., Baltimore, Md.

FIG. 25. SCREW PRESS

The equipment to carry out the above enumerated processes consists essentially of a "hogger" or grinder when processing large material, conveyors, cooker, press, fluffer, meal drier, centrifuge or settling tanks, vacuum evaporator, dry meal disintegrator, and a grinding and sacking device.

Description in Detail of a Wet-Reduction or Continuous Process

Butler (1956) described the processing of ten tons of raw stock per hour, essentially as follows:

The **Continuous Cooker** portion of the unit consists of a stationary horizontal steel cylinder 24 in. in diameter and about 30 ft. long. Fresh raw fish or fish

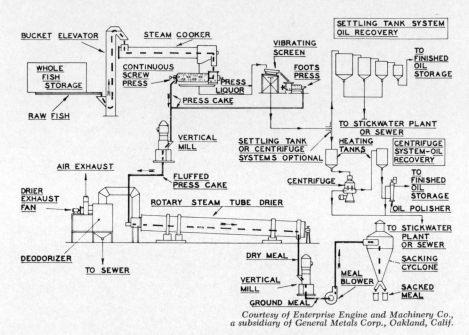

*Courtesy of Enterprise Engine and Machinery Co.,
a subsidiary of General Metals Corp., Oakland, Calif.*

FIG. 26.   FLOW SHEET FOR TYPICAL FISH REDUCTION PLANT

offal are transported continuously from a holding bin, through a hopper, at one end, to a cooker by means of a bucket elevator or an augur-type conveyor, at a predetermined rate. If the material consists of large pieces it is coarsely ground before being admitted to the cooker. The fish is moved at the pre-determined rate through the cooker by a revolving screw conveyor which is fixed to the central shaft. Steam used for cooking is admitted into the cooker from a manifold that runs parallel to the cooker, through a series of jets that serve as perpendicular steam conduits connecting the manifold with the cooker. Suitable arrangements at the feed and discharge ports of the cooker, known as steam chokes, prevent the escape of steam from the cooker. As the cooked mass is being pushed forward by the revolving augur toward the outlet of the cooker, the expressed fluid portion is allowed to escape through a screen on the bottom half of the steel cylinder.

The cooked fish drop at the discharge end through a hopper to the continuous screw press positioned directly below.

Bailey (1952), points out that the cooking process should be carried out correctly, since the pressing properties of the cooked material depend on this. Proper cooking releases oil and coagulates the protein. Overcooking yields a soft mass which will not develop a "head" in the press, inhibiting thereby adequate pressing. Undercooking tends to retain the fluids in the proteinaceous portion, interfering thereby with the proper expression of oil and water from the cells.

Cooking conditions may be controlled by varying the steam pressure usually between 5 and 10 p.s.i., depending on the type of raw material used, and by changing the speed of the augur-type conveyor. For whole herring or pilchard, the pressure is about 10 p.s.i. on the feed end and about 5 p.s.i. on the discharge end of the cooker. Sometimes lower pressures are used.

Salmon cannery offal needs considerably more cooking. In fact, frequently the cooking time is almost doubled. Hogging or grinding helps processing of such offal because it breaks up its solid bony structure, facilitating its subsequent cooking. Dogfish carcasses and skates require a very short cooking period, otherwise they soften up to such an extent that pressing becomes impossible.

Whole herring, pilchard (California sardine), or similar fish, or their cannery waste, do not require any preliminary grinding. In general, when cooking is adequate, the fish flesh should come off the larger bones easily on shaking. There is usually a 10 to 15% increase in weight of the cooked fish due to the condensed steam during cooking.

The Continuous Press.—The cooked fish passes into a continuous press. One type of press consists of a cast-steel screw tightly encased in a cylindrical screen. The pitch of the flights progressively decreases so that the pressure exerted becomes greater as the water and oil content of the press cake becomes less. At the discharge end, the pressure developed may be regulated to produce the desired characteristics in the press cake.

The cylinder screen may have perforations of approximately $3/64$ in. diameter at the inlet end section and of approximately $1/32$ in. diameter at the discharge end section. The press-liquor is dropped into a receptacle and pumped over a rapidly vibrating fine screen for the removal of small fish particles which are returned to the screw press and combined with the press-cake. The stickwater is raised to approximately 195°F., then centrifuged to separate most of the oil from it. The rest of the stickwater, after the oil removal, is either discarded or concentrated under vacuum to fish solubles.

The press-cake, which contains ordinarily from 40 to 60% water, is fluffed and transported to a fish-meal drier where the moisture content is further reduced to about eight per cent.

Continuous Centrifugal Filtration.—The separation of fish meal from press-liquor may be accomplished by centrifugal sedimentation, using the Continuous Solid Bowl Centrifuge (Fig. 27). This machine will separate solids that have the following two characteristics: (a) specific gravity greater than the liquid in which they are suspended, and (b) sufficient mass to respond to centrifugal separating forces up to 1700 times gravity.

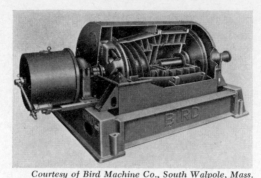

Courtesy of Bird Machine Co., South Walpole, Mass.

FIG. 27.   CONTINUOUS SOLID BOWL
CENTRIFUGE

Operation of the Continuous Solid Bowl Centrifuge.—Press-liquor enters the machine through a stationary feed pipe shown on the right-hand side of the picture.   There are two working elements in this machine; one is a rotating bowl which acts as a settling vessel and the other is a conveyor which discharges the solids as soon as they have settled out in the bowl.   The screw conveyor rotates inside the bowl, in the same direction as the bowl, but at a somewhat reduced speed thus effecting the discharge.   The solids are steadily moved along by the conveyor as fast as deposited by centrifugal force and are retained for a short interval before leaving the bowl, to allow maximum drainage.   Discharge of both solids and filtrate is continuous.

After the solids are removed from the press-liquor, the fish oil is next removed from the liquor by the conventional procedures already described in this chapter.

There are several advantages in using this type of separator: (a) separation of solids from liquids is quick and continuous, (b) operation is completely under cover, (c) machine has a wide range of capacity, (d) minimum floor space is required, and (e) none of the auxiliary parts that go with conventional filters, i.e., filter pads or filter aids, is required.

Dry-Rendering or Dry-Reduction of Fish Meal

The dry-rendering or dry-reduction method of fish meal production is principally applied to the conversion of fish or fish offal of a nonoily type, such as cod or haddock filleting waste, or carcasses of shark or grayfish. It is a batch process and is easier to manipulate than the continuous or wet-reduction process.

The first two steps involved in carrying out dry-rendering, are (1) coarse grinding of the fish scrap and (2) treating the ground material in a steam-jacketed cooker-drier which is equipped inside with a power-driven stirring device. Sometimes a press is used to extract residual oil; settling tanks for the oil, hydraulic presses, driers, and press-cake disintegrators are used sometimes also.

The cooker-drier may be operated at atmospheric pressure or under a partial vacuum to facilitate the drying. The cookers and presses handle one charge at a time.

Since this process has a limited capacity and is used only for producing small batches, labor costs in this process are higher than in the continuous process. Also the dry-reduction process yields a comparatively dark oil which is of inferior quality.

However, this process has several advantages over the wet-reduction method. First, the water-soluble materials are retained in the meal, thereby increasing the meal yield per ton of raw material. Furthermore, the batch process is not as rigid an operation as the continuous process. It allows for changes in operating conditions such as different cooking times and temperatures when a variety of raw material is processed, permitting each batch to be processed under its optimum conditions.

Batch cookers are constructed in different forms. Some cookers use live steam with optimum pressures of from 10 to 20 p.s.i. Higher temperatures tend to darken the product. Other cookers are jacketed and can operate under either pressure or vacuum.

Pressure cooking under steam pressure varying from 40 to 80 p.s.i. in the jacket, depending on the type of raw material used, is a relatively rapid operation and it tends to break down the "gel" and the adhesiveness of the cooked fish, but the dry rendered oil is very dark.

Vacuum cooking may require 6 to 7 hours for drying the meal, after which the oil is pressed out of the dried material. The oil usually contains some finely divided proteinaceous particles and some water. These impurities settle out from the impure oil when it is stored in a tank heated with closed steam coils.

Fish meal should be cooled as soon as it leaves the drier. Cooling can be carried out readily by putting the meal into small piles and turning them over until their excess heat has dissipated. This precaution should particularly be adhered to in order to prevent spontaneous combustion, when fish meal is produced in large quantities.

DehydrO-Mat Drier.—A relatively recent development in fish-meal production is Renneburg's DehydrO-Mat Drier (Fig. 28). According to Renneburg, it is designed principally to minimize the damaging effect of high temperatures on heat-sensitive material such as fish meal.

Principle of the DehydrO-Mat Drier.—Moisture from the surface of heat sensitive material can be removed rapidly by applying a high temperature

Courtesy of Edw. Renneburg and Sons, Co., Baltimore, Md.

FIG. 28.   DEHYDRO-MAT DRIER

for a short period of time, without any damaging effect to the product. But the removal of internal moisture as drying progresses is much more difficult because case hardening or surface drying reduces the rate of evaporation, which in turn, requires a reduction of the temperature of drying to avoid scorching.

Reduction in temperature of drying requires an increase in time of drying to allow the internal moisture to diffuse slowly through the surface of the fish-meal particles and vaporize. DehydrO-Mat attains this end by using a multi-diameter cross-section drier, where a one-pass shell changes the velocity of air and solids as they travel through it. Thus, both product retention time is automatically controlled and temperature is regulated in each section to produce optimum drying conditions. This design prevents overheating the product during any stage of its drying cycle.

Drying Cycles of the DehydrO-Mat.—Drying a heat-sensitive product in a DehydrO-Mat involves subjecting it to three stages.

First, the material is introduced into the drier through a narrow-diameter throat, at the feed end and it is rapidly conveyed by the surrounding hot air through the first compartment.

In this hot zone, the initial drying is rapid, resulting in minimum damage to the surface of the heat-sensitive product because of the protective action or cooling effect that the large amount of moisture exerts during evaporation.

Second, the material is passed through a larger diameter section of the drier, resulting in expansion of the hot air which, in turn, reduces the velocity and temperature of the material but prolongs the time required for the meal particles to pass through this section of the drier.

Finally, the partially dried meal moves into the largest diameter section where it is held for a longer period of time, and at reduced temperature, than in either of the other two compartments, allowing a slow moisture removal at a minimum damage to the product. After the fish meal is sufficiently dried, it is automatically discharged.

A schematic drawing of DehydrO-Mat (varying diameter drier) is shown below:

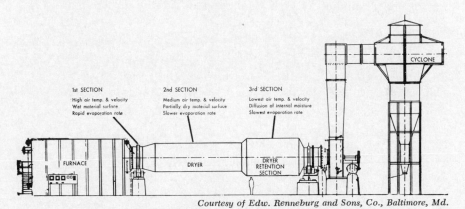

Courtesy of Edw. Renneburg and Sons, Co., Baltimore, Md.

FIG. 28. DEHYDRO-MAT

VARYING DIAMETER DRIER

Advantages and Disadvantages of Dry-Rendering and Wet-Reduction Methods

Method of Production	Advantages	Disadvantages
Dry-rendering	1. Yield of oil in meal is somewhat larger even with low-oil fish which is the only type of fish to which this process is applicable (Karrick 1964). 2. Suitable for small batch operations. 3. Easier to manipulate. 4. Permits greater flexibility in operating conditions and is therefore more suitable for handling a large variety of raw material.	1. Oil is darker and of inferior quality because of its additional heat exposure. 2. Installing and operating cost for the same capacity are generally higher. 3. Batch reduction method tends to slow up production. 4. More expensive to operate.

Method of Production	Advantages	Disadvantages
Wet-reduction	1. Quality of oil is better. 2. A continuous process is usually faster. 3. Installing and operating costs for the same capacity are generally lower. 4. More suitable for processing large quantities of raw material. 5. Yields a valuable by-product: "fish solubles." 6. Less expensive to operate.	1. Meal is low in water-soluble material, unless the solubles are added back. 2. Yield is lower. 3. Operating conditions are more rigid.

Approximate Amounts of Fish Meal Supplementation in Poultry and Animal Rations

Fish meal should be used as a stock feed supplement at relatively low levels so that no objectionable "fishy" odors and flavors are imparted to the animal tissues and carried over to their end products such as eggs, milk, or meat. Fish meal can be used as a feed supplement (Anon. 1945) in the following amounts:

Poultry: Not more than 10% of total ration for hens and not more than 5% of total for chicks.
Cattle: 2 lb. per day for every 1,000 lb. live weight.
Pigs: $1/4$ to $1/2$ lb. per day according to weight.
Sheep: $1/10$ to $1/5$ lb. per day for every 100 lb. live weight.

Proximate Chemical Composition of Fish Meal

Fish meals differ considerably in composition because they can be processed in several different ways utilizing a variety of raw material (Sanford and Lee 1960). Accordingly, wide ranges exist in results of fish-meal analyses as may be seen from the following proximate content of protein, fat, ash, and moisture of fish meals derived from different types of raw stock processed by different methods.

Proteins: The protein content varies from 55 to 70% by weight. Herring meals have the highest protein values. Fish scrap meals have the lowest values (Nilson 1950). Most meals contain between 60 and 65% protein.
Fat: The fat content may vary from 5 to 10 per cent, but is preferably not more than eight per cent. When the fat content is low, the meal is dusty. When the fat content is high there is danger of oxidation (Nilson 1950).
Ash: The mineral content of fish meals varies from about 12% for high-protein meal to about 33% for low-protein meal or meal made from fillet waste containing a high proportion of bones. About 18% ash is satisfactory.
Moisture: An average of eight per cent moisture is preferred with an allowable range of from 6 to 10 per cent. Fish meal containing 12% moisture is sub-

ject to mold growth. Heating will occur when the moisture content is less than six per cent.

Crude Fiber: The crude fiber content is less than one per cent. Fish meal is therefore regarded as a low-fiber feed.

The range of composition in proximate analyses of 200 fish meal samples is shown in Table 13.

TABLE 13

PER CENT RANGE OF COMPOSITION IN PROXIMATE ANALYSES OF 200 FISH MEALS
(SANFORD AND LEE 1960)

Meal	Portion of fish used	Protein	Oil	Ash	Moisture
Herring	Whole fish and scrap	60–77	8–12	8–11	6–10
Menhaden	Whole fish	50–65	5–15	16–25	5–12
Ocean perch	Fillet scrap	50–60	8–12	20–24	5–10
Salmon	Cannery scrap	55–65	10–14	12–30	6–10
Tuna	Cannery scrap	60–65	5–10	20–23	7–10

Table Courtesy of U. S. Fish and Wildlife Service.

Fish Meal Proteins.—Fish meal proteins contain all of the ten essential amino acids as well as the eleven dispensable amino acids in sufficient amounts which in conjunction with the other necessary nutrients, produce a balanced diet. The essential amino acids content of cod, flounder, haddock, Atlantic, and Pacific herring, and Pacific salmon (chinook) are given in Table 14.

TABLE 14

ESSENTIAL AMINO ACIDS CONTENT (IN GM.) OF VARIOUS FISH PER 100 GM. OF EDIBLE PORTION
(ORR AND WATT 1957)

Item →	Cod	Flounder	Haddock	Herring (Atlantic)	Herring (Pacific)	Salmon (Chinook) (Pacific)
% Protein → Amino Acids	16.5	14.9	18.2	18.3	16.6	17.4
Tryptophan	0.164	0.148	0.181	0.182	0.165	0.173
Threonine	0.715	0.646	0.789	0.793	0.720	0.754
Isoleucine	0.837	0.756	0.923	0.928	0.842	0.883
Leucine	1.246	1.125	1.374	1.382	1.254	1.314
Lysine	1.447	1.306	1.596	1.605	1.455	1.526
Methionine	0.480	0.434	0.530	0.533	0.483	0.507
Phenylalanine	0.612	0.553	0.676	0.679	0.616	0.646
Valine	0.879	0.794	0.970	0.975	0.884	0.927
Arginine	0.929	0.839	1.025	1.031	0.935	0.980
Histidine	. . .	. . .	. . .	. . .	. . .	. . .

Table courtesy U. S. Dept. of Agriculture.

The dispensable amino acids present in fish meal are glycine, alanine, cystine, serine, tyrosine, norleucine, aspartic acid, glutamic acid, hydroxyglutamic acid, proline, and hydroxyproline.

Fish-meal protein is particularly valuable nutritionally because of its relatively high content of lysine. The cereal grains which are used in feed rations are deficient in this essential amino acid. Supplementing these rations with a minimum of three per cent of fish meal balances off the cereal grains deficiency.

Vitamin Content of Fish Meal.—Fish meal (Nilson 1950) contains approximately the following vitamins in milligrams per pound:

Name of Vitamin	Milligrams per pound
Riboflavin	3
Niacin	30
Pantothenic acid	3
Choline	1,500
B_{12}	0.1–0.33

Because of the nutritionally valuable composition of fish meal, it serves as a very important supplement in all types of feed rations, in general, and in poultry and swine feeds in particular.

AN INEXPENSIVE METHOD FOR THE PRODUCTION OF FISH MEAL

Introduction

Sea coast countries that are not as technologically advanced as the United States or the other great powers and cannot afford to buy the latest fish reduction machinery that embody efficiency and mass production ca-

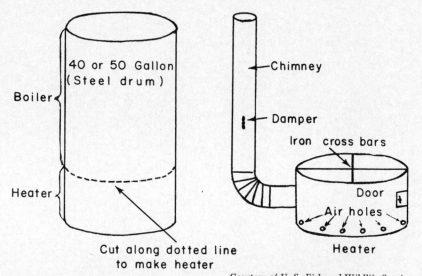

Courtesy of U. S. Fish and Wildlife Service

Fig. 30.   Heater and Boiler

pacities can, nevertheless, produce fish meal for local consumption using very simple home-made equipment. Such simple equipment is described in Fishery Leaflet 135 (Anon. 1945). Simple as this equipment and procedure appear to be, they are, nevertheless, very ingenious and could serve a very useful purpose when used under limited conditions such as exist in technologically under-developed countries. A description is, therefore, reproduced here, by courtesy of U. S. Fish and Wildlife Service:

Sharks as a Source of Fish Meal for Poultry and Stock

Fish meal is now in very great demand. It is an extremely valuable source of protein for feeding stock. At one time people were afraid to use it because they were afraid that it would give a "fishy" flavor to the meat, milk, and eggs. We now know that this is not true. Of course, if you feed enormous quantities of

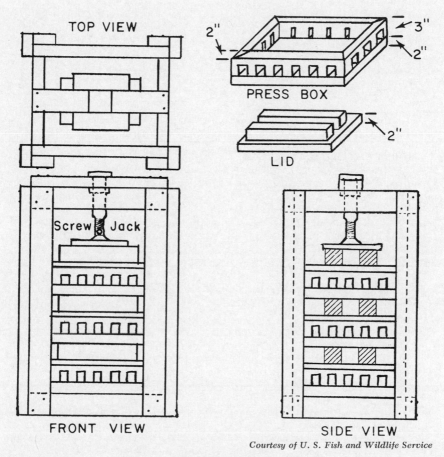

Courtesy of U. S. Fish and Wildlife Service

FIG. 31. PRESS

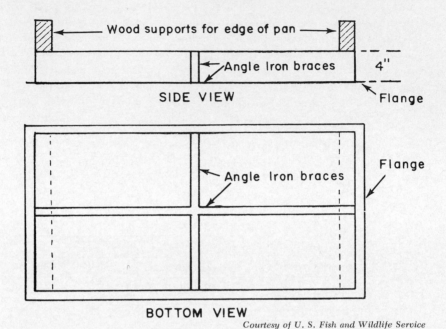

SIDE VIEW

BOTTOM VIEW

Courtesy of U. S. Fish and Wildlife Service

FIG. 32.   DRIER

the material to animals, this "fishy" flavor may appear, but since fish meal is such a concentrated source of protein, it should be used sparingly anyway.

Fish meal can be made from the parts of the shark (and other fish) which are unsuitable for other purposes, and the general scheme for preparing it is very simple. Absolutely fresh scrap meal, offal, and bones of the shark are boiled in water to cook the flesh and get rid of the oil. The cooked scrap is then pressed to remove the rest of the water and oil. Next it is dried over a fire, taking care to avoid scorching, and lastly, the dried material is ground up to a coarse powder. To carry this process out, a few pieces of simple equipment are necessary. It will now be explained how you can make these pieces of equipment simply and cheaply with materials at present available to you. These pieces of equipment are (a) a heater, (b) a boiler, (c) a press, (d) a drier, and (e) a grinder.

(a) **Heater and (b) Boiler.**—[Fig. 30]—You can make the heater and boiler very easily out of a 40- to 50-gal. steel drum. To make the heater cut off the bottom third of the drum, add a chimney to it, cut a door for adding fuel and punch air holes around the bottom. On the top, to support the boiler, either place a piece of black iron sheet or two pieces of stout iron bar crossed. This heater will work well with wood or charcoal.

The other two thirds of the drum, turned upside down, will do for the boiler and will hold about 25 to 30 gal.

(c) **Press.**—[Fig. 31]—The press consists of a set of boxes in which the material to be pressed is placed and a frame in which these boxes are pressed.

Make five or six boxes (Fig. 31) using $1^1/_2$ in. or 2 in. thick wood. The boxes should be 3 ft. × 2 ft. × 3 in. inside measurement. The lid should be reinforced and just fit smoothly inside the box. On the lid attach two pieces of 3- × 3-in. wood just a little shorter than the length of the lid—about 2 ft × 10 in.

Through the sides and ends of the boxes, make a number of holes through which the liquid can escape as it is squeezed out. These holes should start from the bottom of the box and be 2 in. high. As the sides are 3 in. high, this will leave 1-in. solid wood above. These holes are made wider outside than inside so that they will not get stopped up. On the inside the holes should be $1/4$ in. wide and on the outside $3/4$ in. wide.

A good sturdy frame of 2- × 4-in. lumber is made of such a size that the boxes just fit snugly inside. Near the bottom of the frame are stops which prevent the bottom box from going through. At the top of the frame is either an ordinary large screw-jack or a stout, long-handled lever, to give the pressure for squeezing the meal in the boxes. At the bottom of the jack is attached a 3-in. board 2 × 2 ft. which pushes down squarely on the 3- × 3-in. bars on the lid of the top box.

(d) **Drier.**—[Fig. 32]—The drier consists of two large trays but quite shallow. When in use, the bottom tray rests on the heaters and the top tray rests on the bottom one. Each tray can be made of sheet iron, black iron, or galvanized "corrugated" iron rolled out flat. A good-sized tray is made by riveting two 6 × $2^1/_2$-ft. sheets together, giving one sheet about 6 × 4 ft.

For the lower tray, turn up the edge 4 in. with a 1-in. flange for the upper tray to rest on. The tray can be stiffened with angle iron or iron bar riveted in place. If stiff iron bars are continued as a cross over the top of this tray, this will better support the upper tray.

The upper tray is made in the same way as the bottom one except that the turn-up need be only 3 in. with no flange, and it can be stiffened by nailing 3- × 2-in. wood round it (on the inside). If the lower pan has been fitted with iron bars crossed over the top, there is no need to stiffen the bottom of the upper tray.

When in use, the top pan is placed on the bottom pan, and this is supported on two of the heaters described in (a) above. For better and more even heat, a piece of sheet iron should be placed between the heater and the bottom of the lower pan. If it is to be used as a water heater it must be made water tight and should be made of galvanized material. It should also be fitted with two steam escape pipes 2 in. in diameter by 1 ft. long to take the excess steam away from the drying meal. When used as a water heater, the bottom bath should not be filled more than half full, and care should be taken to see that it does not boil dry.

If the lower pan is to be used as an air heater, it is best to make it of black iron. In this case, care must be taken to avoid overheating the drying meal.

In any case, galvanized iron is the best material for the upper pan, although this is not essential.

(e) **Grinder.**—[Fig. 33]—A good grinder can be made from a stout barrel with both ends intact. Take a piece of sound, square lumber, about 3 × 3 in., and around the center of each end of the barrel cut a hole to fit this bar tightly. Pass the bar of 3 × 3 in. through both holes so that it sticks out about 15 in. at each end. A couple of stout nails driven into the bar of wood will hold the barrel in this position.

About 6 in. clear of the barrel at each end, round the 3- × 3-in. bar for a distance of about 3 in.

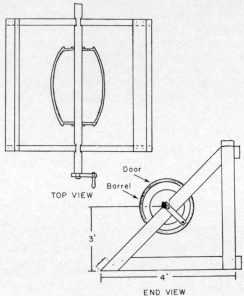

FIG. 33.   GRINDER

Next cut a hole about 6 × 6 in. in the middle of the side of the barrel.   This is for putting things into and taking them out of the barrel.   It must be fitted with a snug cover that will not fall off or out.

Take reasonably heavy pieces of lumber and make a frame similar to the one shown in Fig. 33.   Let the rounded part of the bar through the barrel turn in a notch cut in the lumber as shown in the figure.   Nail a strip of leather, metal or lumber over the top of the notch to prevent the bar from slipping out.   A suggested bearing to place in this notch can be made from a piece of tin or by nailing in a piece of bacon rind.

On one end of the bar through the barrel, now the axle, fit a simple handle for turning the barrel.

For grinders inside the barrel put several good, heavy solid stones.   These should be as nearly round as possible.   The best type of stone to use is heavy volcanic stone or granite.   In some places where such stones do not occur naturally they can be found where ships dumped ballast.   Ordinary coral rock is useless, but hard limestone will do for want of something better.   In some places round suitable pieces of scrap metal are available.

If the ends of the barrel are not completely firm, they should be strengthened with wood around the hole through which the axle passes.

Of course these instructions need not be followed strictly.   Where one thing is not available there is always something else that will do.   With a little thought and imagination, this equipment can be built anywhere at little cost.

The method described above is very simple.   There are many elaborate machines for making fish meal.   At the present time this machinery would be difficult if not impossible to get. Besides, even the smallest set of equipment would cost thousands of dollars, and to make it pay you would have to handle between 3,000 and 6,000 tons of scrap a year. If you ever reach this stage, it will be worth your while to make inquiries. The simple equipment described above requires a good deal more labor than the modern machines but it produces just as good fish meal.

Making Fish Meal—Boiling and Cooking—Put about 12 gal. of water into the boiler and bring it to a boil. Add about 150 lb. of chopped meat and refuse and broken up bones. Cook for 20 to 25 min. with occasional stirring. Allow to cool for 10 min. without stirring. Draw off the surface water.

At one time it was thought that oil in fish meal was harmful to stock; it is now known that with the possible exception of growing chicks, this is untrue and that the oil is an advantage in feed. As this fact has been known for only the last ten years, you will still find people who will not buy meal with a high oil content. For this reason and for the reason that low-oil meal is more easily prepared and stored, keep your oil content down—if necessary by prolonging the boiling of the scrap.

Take out the cooked material (a wire basket of about $1/8$-in. wire mesh is often useful here). Pick the flesh off the bones and pack the flesh and the bones into separate boxes for the press.

Pressing—Press the material to get out as much of the liquid as possible. A slow pressure is best and when the final pressure is reached, allow it to remain there for 10 min. to drain.

Drying—Spread the pressed material on the upper part of the drier. While it is drying rake it about and make sure that it does not scorch. The flesh will dry out faster than the bones so it should be removed first by shaking through a $1/2$-in. sieve. Leave the bones on the drier till they are crisp and brittle. Total drying should take from 4 to 5 hr.

Grinding—Transfer the material to the grinding barrel. A good sized barrel will hold from 15 to 20 lb. of dried material, and it should not be filled too full. The grinding takes about 10 to 15 min. but bones may take longer.

The yield is about $1/6$ to $1/8$ the weight of the original scrap.

If the process is done thoroughly, the protein content should be between 50 and 60%, and the water content should be not more than eight per cent. The resulting meal is of good quality and equal in value to most of the meal which is on the market.

To Make Good Fish Meal Remember:—(1) Use only fresh material. Do not waste time with decaying stuff. (2) Keep everything clean and sanitary. Wash out the boiler and the drying tray at least once a day. (3) Get all the oil and water out that you can before drying. Although the oil is really useful stock food, some people do not know this yet and will not buy meal with a high oil content. (4) Dry thoroughly. You will not get paid for water you leave in, and it will tend to make the meal become mouldy and spoil. At the same time, do not let the meal scorch and become too dark. (5) Store in a dry place and do not expose to air any more than you have to.

CONCLUDING REMARKS

Notwithstanding the extensive advancement made in the technology of fish meal production, the ideal procedure, i.e., that of economically manufacturing fish meal on a large scale without the use of heat and with retention of most of the nutritive value of the raw stock, has not been developed.

BIBLIOGRAPHY

ANDERSON, A. W., HARRISON, R. W., and POTTINGER, S. R. 1935. Studies on drying cod and haddock waste. U. S. Fish and Wildlife Service, Investigational Rept. 32.

ANON. 1941. Utilization of fish cannery wastes. Food Manuf. *16*, 49.

ANON. 1945. Guide to commercial shark fishing in the Caribbean area. U. S. Fish and Wildlife Service, Fishery Leaflet 135.

ANON. 1949. Fish meal and oil. Fishing Gazette *66*, No. 6, 64–66.

BAILEY, B. E. Editor. 1952. Marine Oils, with Particular Reference to Those of Canada. Bull. *89*. Fisheries Res. Board Can., Ottawa.

BIRD, H. R., and KARRICK, N. L. 1957. Determination of unknown growth factors in fish meals by chick-growth tests. Com. Fisheries Rev. 19, 5a (supplement), 1–3.

BISSETT, H. M., and TARR, H. L. A. 1954. The nutritive value of herring meals II. The effect of heat on availability of essential amino acids. Poultry Sci. *33*, 250–254.

BORGSTROM, G., and HEIGHWAY, A. J. Editors. 1961. Atlantic Ocean Fisheries. Fishing News (books) Ltd., London.

BORGSTROM, G. Editor. 1962. Fish as Food. Volumes I and II. Academic Press, New York.

BUREAU of COMMERCIAL FISHERIES. 1951. Suggested code for fish meal. U. S. Fish and Wildlife Service. Technical Note No. 12. Sep. No. 299.

BUTLER, C. 1956. Fish reduction processes. U. S. Fish and Wildlife Service. Fishery Leaflet No. 126.

CAMP, A. A., CARTRITE, H. T. QUISENBERRY, J. H., and COUCH, J. R. 1955. Further information concerning unidentified chick growth factors. Poultry Sci. *34*, No. 3, 559–566.

CARVER, J. H. 1954. A comparative study of fish meals made from haddock offal. U. S. Fish and Wildlife Service. Sep. No. 388.

DANIEL, E. P., and McCOLLUM, E. V. 1931. Studies of the nutritive value of fish meals. Investigational Rept. 2. U. S. Fish and Wildlife Service.

EVAN, R. E. 1959. The minimum amount of whitefish meal required to supplement the proteins in some vegetable-protein concentrates. J. Agr. Sci. *53*, No. 2, 230–246.

FIEDLER, R. H. 1939. The factory ship. Proc. of Sixth Pac. Sci. Cong. *3*, 273. University of Calif. Press, Berkeley.

GRAU, C. R., and WILLIAMS, M. A. 1955. Fish meals as amino acid sources in chick rations. Poultry Sci. *34*, No. 4, 810–817.

GRAU, C. R., KARRICK, N. L., LUNDHOLM, B. D., and BARNES, R. N. 1959. Nutritional values of fish-meal proteins and their relation to processing variables. U. S. Fish and Wildlife Service. Sep. No. 557.

GRAU, C. R., OUSTERHOUT, L. E., LUNDHOLM, B. C., and KARRICK, N. L. 1959. Progress on investigations of nutritional value of fish-meal protein. Com. Fisheries Rev. *21*, 2a (supplement).

HARRISON, R. W. 1939. Some aspects of fish meal manufacture and distribution. Proc. of Sixth Pac. Sci. Cong. 3, 309, Univ. of Calif. Press, Berkeley.

KARRICK, N. L. 1955. Literature review of factors that may affect processed feeds quality. U. S. Fish and Wildlife Service. Sep. No. 404.

KARRICK, N. L. 1963. Fish meal quality. In Industrial Fishery Technology, M. E. STANSBY with editorial assistance of JOHN A. DASSOW. Reinhold Publishing Corp., New York.

KARRICK, N. L. 1964. Personal communication. Seattle, Wash.

LANHAM, W. B. JR., and NILSON, H. W. 1947. Some studies on the feeding value of fish meals. U. S. Fish and Wildlife Service. Com. Fisheries Rev. 9, 8.

LEA, C. H., PARR, L. J. and CARPENTER, K. J. 1958. Chemical and nutritional changes in stored herring meal. Brit, J. Nutr. 12, No. 3, 297–312.

LOVERN, J. A. 1948. The fishing industry of North America. Part IV—Fish Meal and Oil. Food Manuf. 23, 323–327.

MARCH, B. E., STUPIEH, D., and BIELY, J. 1949. The evaluation of the nutritional value of fish meals and meat meals. Poultry Sci. 28, No. 5, 718–724.

McFEE, E. P. 1954. Stabilization of fish press liquor. U. S. Pat. 2,667,416.

NILSON, H. W. 1946. Feeding fish meal to ducklings. U. S. Fish and Wildlife Service. Sep. No. 142.

NILSON, H. W. 1950. Feeding value of fish meals. U. S. Fish and Wildlife Service. Sep. No. 269.

NILSON, H. W., and SNYDER, D. G. 1957. Feeding studies with menhaden press cake. Com. Fisheries Rev. 19, No. 4, 11–12.

ORR, M. L., and WATT, B. K. 1957. Amino acid content of foods. Home Economics Research Report No. 4. U.S. Dept. Agr., Washington, D. C.

OUSTERHOUT, L. E., GRAU, C. R., and LUNDHOLM, B. 1959. Biological availability of amino acids in fish meals and other protein sources. J. Nutr. 69, No. 1, 65–73.

OUSTERHOUT, L. E., and SNYDER, D. G. 1961. Effect of processing on the nutritive value of fish products in animal nutrition. FAO International Conference on Fish in Nutrition.

POTTINGER, S. R., and BALDWIN, W. H. 1939. The content of certain amino acids in seafood, Proc. of the Sixth Pac. Sci. Cong. 3, 353. Univ. of Calif. Press, Berkeley.

POWER, E. A. 1963. Advance report on the fisheries of the U. S., 1962. U. S. Fish and Wildlife Service. C. F. S. No. 3150.

RAND, N. T., COLLINS, V. K., VARNER, D. S., and MOSSER, J. B. 1960. Biological evaluation of the factors affecting the protein quality of fish meals. Poultry Sci. 39, No. 1, 45–53.

RUNNELS, T. D. 1959. Supplementary effect of fish meal and fish solubles in chick diets. Summary Report, Symposium for Nutritionists. Technological Leaflet No. 20.

RUNNELS, T. D., SNYDER, D. G., and NEALIS, S. W. 1959. The optimum level of menhaden fish meal and solubles as sources of growth factors in broiler diets. Summary Report, Symposium for Nutritionists. Technological Leaflet No. 20, 3–11.

SANFORD, F. B. 1950. Utilization of fishery by-products in Washington and Oregon. U. S. Fish and Wildlife Service. Fishery Leaflet No. 370.

SANFORD, F. B., and LEE, C. F.   1960.   U. S. Fish reduction industry.   U. S. Fish and Wildlife Service, Technical Leaflet No. 14.

SMYTH, J. A.   1961.   World production and trade in fish meal and oil.   U. S. Fish and Wildlife Service.   Fishery Leaflet 507.

STANSBY, M. E., and CLEGG, W.   1955.   Determination of oil in fish meal.   U. S. Fish and Wildlife Service.   Sep. 401.

STANSBY, M. E., with editorial assistance of J. A. Dassow.   1963.   Industrial Fishery Technology.   Reinhold Publishing Corp., New York, N. Y.

SUMERWELL, W. N.   1955.   Unidentified growth factors in fish by-products.   U. S. Fish and Wildlife Service.   Sep. No. 411.

TARR, H. L. A., BIELY, J., and MARCH, B. E.   1954.   The nutritive value of herring meals.   I.   The effect of heat.   Poultry Sci. 33, 242.

TRESSLER, D. K.   1923.   Marine Products of Commerce.   1st Edition.   Reinhold Publishing Corp., New York, N. Y.

TRESSLER, D. K., and LEMON, J. M.   1951.   Marine Products of Commerce.   2nd Edition.   Reinhold Publishing Corp., New York, N. Y.

U. S. FISH and WILDLIFE SERVICE.   Bureau of Commercial Fisheries.   1962.   Industrial fishery products—1961, Annual Summary.   C. F. S. No. 2863.

CHAPTER 12

General Considerations of Fish Oils

OCCURRENCE AND DISTRIBUTION OF FISH OILS

Fish oils may be obtained commercially from the following two classes of fish: first, the teleostomi, or the teleost fishes which constitute the common food fishes, such as cod, haddock, halibut, herring, pilchards, and salmon; second, the selachii, e.g., sharks, rays, and skates. Anatomically, these two classes differ in that the former have a calcified internal skeleton, and the latter have a cartilaginous internal skeleton.

Some of the teleost fishes, e.g., cod, haddock, and hake, have practically all of their oil localized in their fairly large livers, and relatively little in their muscle tissue; while other members of the teleost class, such as salmon, herring, and pilchard, have most of their fat distributed in their muscle tissue, but very little in their relatively small livers. Aside from these generalizations, the fat content in fish fluctuates with feeding habits, season, species, spawning cycle, and water temperature (Bailey 1952).

In addition to the fat depots described in the preceding paragraph, in some fish, fats are deposited in other locations. For example, lingcod, red cod, black cod, salmon, some soles, and flounders store a substantial amount of their fat in the tissues of the intestine and mesentery. Depending upon the status of the fish in regard to spawning, the eggs of most species of salmon have a high percentage of oil. This oil has different characteristics from the oil found in muscle, intestine, or mesentery.

Sharks, rays, and skates, in general, have large oily livers that may comprise 10 to 15% of their body weights. Unlike the teleost fishes, the shark may have a considerable amount of oil in its muscle tissue, in addition to at least 50% of oil in its large liver.

GENERAL COMPOSITION OF FISH OILS

Fish oils are principally esters of fatty acids and glycerol. They are noted for possessing the following general composition: (a) the oils contain about 25% of saturated fatty acids, and about 75% highly unsaturated fatty acids, (b) the various unsaturated fatty acids of fish oils vary substantially in chain length and most of the unsaturated fatty acids are C_{16}, C_{18}, C_{20}, and C_{22} acids, (c) fish oils vary considerably in the composition of their unsaponifiables, (d) fish liver oils contain a relatively high amount of cholesterol, while fish body oils have a low cholesterol content, (e) in general, the glyceride structure of fish oils is far more complex than that of land animal fats and vegetable fats because fish oils consist of long chains of highly unsaturated fatty acids (Bailey 1952).

GENERAL COMPOSITION AND PROPERTIES OF FATTY ACIDS IN FISH OILS

Most fatty acids in fish oils are normal straight-chain compounds with an even number of carbon atoms. Isovaleric acid is an exception to this rule. It is a fish oil fatty acid with an odd number of carbon atoms and is also a branched-chain acid.

The highly unsaturated structure of some fatty acids renders them unstable and therefore difficult to isolate and purify.

Brief Summary of Saturated Fatty Acids in Fish Oils

Among the better known saturated fatty acids found in fish oils, palmitic acid, $C_{16}H_{32}O_2$, stearic acid, $C_{18}H_{36}O_2$, and myristic acid, $C_{14}H_{28}O_2$ occur widely in fish oils. Lignoceric acid, $C_{24}H_{48}O_2$, occurs only in traces in some sardine and herring oils.

A description of fatty acids found in teleost fish oils is given in Tables 15, 16 and 17.

TABLE 15

SATURATED FATTY ACIDS FOUND IN MARINE OILS (BAILEY, 1952)

Common Name	Formula	Molecular Weight	Melting Point (°C.)	Boiling Point (°C. at 760 mm.)	Solubilities (Gm./100 Gm. Solvent at 10 °C.)		
					Water	Ethanol (95%)	Acetone
Iso-valeric	$C_5H_{10}O_2$	102.1	−37.6(−51)	176.7	...	∞	∞
Caprylic	$C_8H_{16}O_2$	144.2	16.3	239.7	0.056	1035	975
Capric	$C_{10}H_{20}O_2$	172.3	31.3	270.0	0.012	93.5	112
Lauric	$C_{12}H_{24}O_2$	200.3	44.2	298.9	0.0046	34.0	21.9
Myristic	$C_{14}H_{28}O_2$	228.4	52.3	326.2	0.0017	7.64	6.50
Palmitic	$C_{16}H_{32}O_2$	256.4	63.1	351.5	0.0059	2.10	1.94
Stearic	$C_{18}H_{36}O_2$	284.5	69.6	376.1	0.0023	0.65	0.80
Arachidic	$C_{20}H_{40}O_2$	312.5	75.4	...	...	...	...
Behenic	$C_{22}H_{44}O_2$	340.6	80.0	...	...	...	...
Lignoceric	$C_{24}H_{48}O_2$	368.6	84.2	...	...	...	...

Table reprinted by permission of Fisheries Research Board of Canada. Dr. J. C. Stevenson, Editor.

Brief Summary of Unsaturated Fatty Acids in Fish Oils

Among the better known unsaturated fatty acids found in all fish oils, oleic acid, $C_{18}H_{34}O_2$, occurs as the major constituent. It has one double bond. Clupanodonic acid, which has five double bonds, also occurs in practically all fish as an important component. It is generally believed that the characteristic odor of fish oils is partly due to the presence of the

TABLE 16

UNSATURATED FATTY ACIDS FOUND IN MARINE OILS (BAILEY, 1952)

Acid Common Name	Formula	No. of Double Bonds	Position of Double Bonds	Iodine Value	Molecular Weight	Boiling Point (°C.)
Caproleic	$C_{10}H_{18}O_2$	1	9	149.1	170.1	142/15 mm.
Lauroleic	$C_{12}H_{22}O_{11}$	1	9	128.0	198.2	...
Myristoleic	$C_{14}H_{26}O_2$	1	9	112.2	226.2	...
	$C_{14}H_{26}O_2$	1	5	112.2	226.2	...
Palmitoleic	$C_{16}H_{30}O_2$	1	9	99.8	254.2	...
Hiragonic	$C_{16}H_{26}O_2$	3	6, 10, 14	304.2	250.2	180–190/15 mm.
Oleic	$C_{18}H_{34}O_2$	1	9	89.9	282.2	286/100 mm. 153/0.1 mm.
Vaccenic	$C_{18}H_{34}O_2$	1	11	89.9	282.2	...
	$C_{18}H_{32}O_2$	2	...	181.1	280.2	...
	$C_{18}H_{30}O_2$	3	...	273.7	278.2	...
Moroctic	$C_{18}H_{28}O_2$	4	4, 8, 12, 15	367.5	276.2	...
Gadoleic	$C_{20}H_{38}O_2$	1	9	81.7	310.3	220/6 mm.
Gondoic	$C_{20}H_{38}O_2$	1	11	81.7	310.3	...
	$C_{20}H_{36}O_2$	2	11, 14	164.6	308.3	...
	$C_{20}H_{34}O_2$	3	8, 11, 14	248.6	306.3	...
	$C_{20}H_{32}O_2$	4	4, 8, 12, 16	333.7	304.2	...
	$C_{20}H_{32}O_2$	4	6, 10, 14, 18	333.7	304.2	...
	$C_{20}H_{30}O_2$	5	4, 8, 12, 15, 18	419.9	302.2	...
Cetoleic	$C_{22}H_{42}O_2$	1	11	75.0	338.3	...
	$C_{22}H_{40}O_2$	2	11, 14	150.7	336.3	...
	$C_{22}H_{38}O_2$	3	8, 11, 14	227.8	334.3	...
Clupanodonic	$C_{22}H_{34}O_2$	5	4, 8, 12, 15, 19	384.2	330.3	236/5 mm.
	$C_{22}H_{32}O_2$	6	..	463.8	328.3	...
Selacholeic	$C_{24}H_{46}O_2$	1	15	69.2	366.4	...
Scoliodonic	$C_{24}H_{38}O_2$	5	...	354.2	358.3	...
Nisinic	$C_{24}H_{36}O_2$	6	4, 8, 12, 15, 18, 21	427.5	356.3	...
Bonitonic	$C_{24}H_{34}O_2$	7	...	501.4	354.3	...
Shibic	$C_{26}H_{42}O_2$	5	...	328.5	386.3	...
Thynnic	$C_{26}H_{40}O_2$	6	...	396.3	384.3	...

Table reprinted by permission of Fisheries Research Board of Canada. Dr. J. C. Stevenson, Editor.

highly unsaturated fatty acids. In fact, when fish oils are hydrogenated, they lose their characteristic odor.

Examples of weight percentage distribution of fatty acids in fish liver oils are given in Table 18.

FACTORS AFFECTING COMPOSITION AND QUANTITY OF OILS IN FISH

Introduction: General Considerations

Fat is utilized by the animal body for energy requirements. When the fat intake by an animal is higher than what is needed by the body for energy conversion, the excess is generally stored as a reserve food in the adipose tissues for future use. The characteristics of the deposited fat depend to a large extent on the characteristics of the ingested fat. Since any fish species lives on a more or less specific diet, the characteristics of its in-

Table 17

WEIGHT PERCENTAGE DISTRIBUTION OF CONSTITUENT FATTY ACIDS IN FISH OILS (BAILEY 1952)

	Unsap. matter %	Saturated			Unsaturated[1]					
		C14	C16	C18	C14	C16	C18	C20	C22	C24
Pisces (Teleostomi)										
Family Clupeidae										
Pilchard, *Sardinops caerulea* (British Columbia), body oil	1.0	5.1	14.4	3.2	0.1(2.0)	11.7(2.0)	17.7(3.3)	17.9(4.1)	13.8(8.5)	15.2(10.9)
Herring, *Clupea harengus* (Iceland), body oil	1.3	7.0	11.7	0.8	1.2(2.0)	11.8(2.4)	19.6(3.5)	25.9(5.2)	21.6(4.3)	0.1(3.8)
(Irish sea), visceral oil	0.75	5.8	15.7	2.0	1.4(2.0)	10.5(2.5)	31.8(2.6)	22.4(7.1)	9.3(10.5)	...
Menhaden, *Brevoortia tyrannus* (North Atlantic), body oil	0.6–1.0	6.0	16.0	1.5	...	15.5(2)	30.0(4)	19.0(10)	12.0(10)	...
Family Salmonidae										
Salmon, *Salmo salar* (Scotland)										
Flesh	0.9	5.0	11.3	1.1	0.5	9.1(2.0)	25.7(2.7)	26.5(4.7)	20.8(6.4)	...
Mesentery	...	3.6	14.4	2.3	0.1	7.1(2.4)	25.3(2.9)	28.4(4.6)	18.8(6.1)	...
Liver	...	2.7	10.9	1.6	0.7	12.3(2.0)	32.8(2.9)	25.8(5.7)	13.2(7.8)	...
Immature ova	8.8	3.1	16.0	0.5	0.1	12.6(2.0)	23.7(4.0)	27.2(8.0)	16.8(10.4)	...
Ripe eggs	7.2	2.3	12.9	2.2	...	9.6(2.0)	34.8(2.7)	23.2(7.6)	15.0(11.2)	...
Family Pleuronectidae										
Halibut, *Hippoglossus hippoglossus* (North Sea), flesh	1.3	4.0	14.8	0.7	trace	6.5(2.6)	23.8(3.0)	26.9(5.2)	23.3(6.5)	...
Turbot, *Rhombus maximus* (North Sea), flesh	2.1	3.4	15.1	2.1	0.3	8.9(2.6)	21.7(3.4)	26.6(6.0)	21.9(7.7)	...
Family Scombridae										
Bluefin tuna, (tunny), *Thynnus thynnus* (North Sea)										
Flesh	0.7	4.2	18.6	3.5	...	6.2(2.7)	26.0(3.2)	23.5(5.5)	18.0(6.8)	...
Liver	...	0	17.9	8.9	...	3.4(2.5)	23.5(2.8)	28.2(5.5)	18.1(7.4)	...
Pyloric caeca	...	3.4	18.4	2.7	...	6.3(2.7)	21.9(3.7)	25.5(5.5)	21.8(6.2)	...
Spleen	...	0	21.0	7.0	...	7.0(>2.0)	27.0(3.1)	22.0(5.4)	16.0(?)	...
Heart	...	0	25.0	3.0	...	4.0(>2.0)	26.0(3.4)	25.0(5.4)	17.0(7.5)	...
Family Acipenseridae										
Sturgeon, *Acipenser sturio* (Atlantic)										
Peritoneum	...	7.1	14.0	0.8	0.6	23.8(2.0)	35.8(2.9)	12.1(7.4)	5.8(8.6)	...
Liver	...	3.0	19.2	0	0	19.5(2.0)	39.6(2.7)	11.8(7.1)	6.9(10.0)	...

Table reprinted by permission of Fisheries Research Board of Canada. Dr. J. C. Stevenson, Editor.
[1] Numbers in brackets are the unsaturations in terms of —H.

gested fat are specific within these limits, and the stored fat is similar to the ingested fat.

When an animal ingests small amounts of foreign fats which are different in character than that already stored, the animal body will try to modify the foreign fat, and render it similar to the stored fat. When an animal is fed large quantities of foreign fats, then only a portion of it is modified to resemble its characteristic type of fat and the balance is deposited in the adipose tissues in its unchanged form.

In addition to these general considerations which affect the character and quantity of oils in fish, the following four influencing factors are important: (a) species, (b) food, (c) spawning cycle and feeding habits, and (d) temperature of the sea water (Bailey 1952).

Salinity of the sea water might also affect fish fats, although the changes which fish undergo during their spawning migration from salt to fresh water or vice versa is most likely a matter of sexual maturity. A brief summary of these four influencing factors as outlined in Bulletin 89 follows:

Species

The species of fish from which oil is prepared is, undoubtedly, one of the most important factors that control the nature of fish oils. While feeding habits play an important role, what is more important is the ability of the fish to modify ingested fats to the extent and form most suited to its own needs. In some fish, the main fat storage depot is the liver, while in others the oil is deposited in the fish body. In commercial fish oil production, the fat depot of the species should be taken into consideration in setting up an oil extraction method.

There is, in general, a linear relationship between the iodine value and the refractive index in fish oils. The higher the refractive index the greater the degree of unsaturation of the oil. Oils which have different iodine values or different refractive indices also differ in their composition. The converse, however, is not true, i.e., when two oils have the same iodine value or the same refractive index, they do not necessarily have the same composition.

Oils that are derived from like organs in the same species of fish and that have similar iodine values and refractive indices will be alike in properties and composition. Other analytical constants, such as the content of unsaponifiable matter of fish oils, exist to the same extent in samples taken from the same species of fish.

The fact that the same species of fish produces depot fats with the same characteristics, implies either that the fish can modify their ingested fats or that they select their diets.

TABLE 18

WEIGHT PERCENTAGE DISTRIBUTION OF CONSTITUENT FATTY ACIDS IN FISH LIVER OILS (BAILEY 1952)

	Unsap. matter, %	Saturated			Unsaturated[1]					
		C_{14}	C_{16}	C_{18}	C_{14}	C_{16}	C_{18}	C_{20}	C_{22}	C_{24}
Pisces (Teleostomi)										
Family Gadidae										
Cod, *Gadus morrhua*										
(Newfoundland)	0.8–1	6.0	8.5	0.5	0.1	20.0 (2.3)	20.0 (2.8)	26.0 (6.0)	10.0 (6.9)	...
(North Sea)	0.8–1	3.5	10.0	...	0.5	15.5 (2.0)	25.0 (2.9)	31.5 (6.1)	14.0 (4.4)	...
(Norway)	0.8–1	5.0	6.5	0.2	0.5	16.0 (2.0)	31.0 (2.8)	3.5 (5.1)	10.5 (?)	...
Haddock, *Gadus aeglifinus*										
(North Sea)	0.7	4.3	14.1	0.3	0.5	12.4 (2.0)	30.5 (2.6)	29.3 (5.9)	8.6 (7.3)	...
Pollack *Gadus pollachius*										
(North Sea)	...	2.1	13.0	1.4	...	10.9 (2.0)	34.2 (2.7)	25.4 (5.4)	13.0 (6.5)	...
Family Merluccidae										
Hake, *Merluccius merluccius*										
(North Sea)	1.3	4.5	12.0	0.5	...	12.0 (2.0)	27.0 (3.0)	30.0 (4.1)	14.0 (5.4)	...
Family Pleuronectidae										
Halibut, *Hippoglossus hippo-glossus*										
(North Sea)	6.6	3.9	15.1	0.5	...	18.7 (2.0)	34.4 (2.0)	13.8 (5.5)	13.6 (7.6)	...
Turbot, *Rhombus maximus*										
(North Sea)	8.0	7.6	14.9	0.8	1.5 (2.0)	21.4 (2.1)	27.1 (2.5)	14.0 (6.1)	12.7 (6.7)	...
Family Scombridae										
Bluefin tuna (tunny)										
Thynnus thynnus	...	...	17.9	8.9	...	3.4 (2.5)	23.5 (2.8)	28.2 (5.5)	18.1 (7.4)	...

Selachii (Elasmobranchii)

Species										
Family Lamnidae										
Basking shark, *Cetorhinus maximus* (Atlantic)	32-48	2.1	13.6	3.2**	0.5(2.0)	11.9(2.0)	12.8(2.3)	23.2(4.0)	20.0 (3.6)	5.6(5.9)
Family Squalidae										
Dogfish, *Squalus acanthias* (Atlantic)	10.0	6.0	10.5	3.0	...	9 (2.0)	24.5(2.3)	29.0(3.3)	12.0 (4.0)	6.0(2.0)
Shark, *Centrophorus* (Atlantic)	50-80	1.0	13.0	2.5	trace	3.5(2.0)	35.5(2.1)	16.4(2.2)	15.8 (2.3)	12.0(3.0)
Family Scymnorhinidae										
Shark, *Scymnorhinus lichia* (Europe)	70-80	1.2	14.6	3.6	0.5	3.7(2.0)	29.1(2.0)	10.6(2.0)	25.9 (2.1)	10.0(2.0)
Family Scylliidae										
Small spotted dogfish, *Scyllium canicula*	2.0	1.7	15.7	3.3	...	4.0(2.2)	25.3(3.0)	24.4(6.4)	24.8 (9.2)	trace
Large spotted dogfish, *Squalus catulus* (g) (South Africa)	...	3.2	15.7	2.0	1.7(2.0)	12.6(2.0)	40.3(2.8)	10.7(6.0)	13.8(10.4)	...
Family Alopiidae										
Thresher shark, *Alopecia vulpes*	1.8	7.4	11.0	0.5	1.5	12.0(2.0)	19.0(3.4)	31.0(6.6)	17.3(10.5)	...
Family Squatinidae										
Monk-fish, *Squatina angelus*	1.5	1.4	17.0	2.0	...	6.5(2.0)	20.7(3.0)	21.9(6.0)	30.5(10.2)	...
Family Rajidae										
Skate, *Raja maculata*	0.3	4.0	14.0	...	Trace	10.5(2.0)	20.5(3.3)	32.5(7.3)	18.5 (9.5)	...
Family Chimeridae										
Ratfish, *Chimaera monstrosa*	37.0	...	8.4	7.2†	...	2.5(2.0)	50.6(2.2)	19.6(2.9)	7.9 (3.5)	2.1(?)

Table reprinted by permission of Fisheries Research Board of Canada. Dr. J. C. Stevenson, Editor.
[1] Numbers in brackets are the unsaturations in terms of —H. ** Plus 3.6, C_{20}; 3.2, C_{22}; 0.4, C_{24}. † Plus 1.3% C_{20} and 0.4% C_{22}.

Food

In general the more fish eat, the greater their fat content. Some exceptions to this rule apply to certain species of fish, e.g., cod and haddock. As they feed, the fish fatten up in preparation for the spawning period when their only source of energy is their reserve fat supply.

Phytoplankton, the minute floating plants, are the basis for life in the sea. These minute plants which float near the surface of the sea synthesize carbohydrates, proteins, and fats from carbon-dioxide and water with the aid of sunlight and chlorophyll.

The plankton crustaceans and other minute animal organisms in the sea feed on this plant material. These minute animal organisms are the main food supply of the smaller fish and of many of the larger ones. The larger carnivorous fishes live on the smaller ones. The fat formation in marine organisms has been traced through this feeding cycle, indicating the effect of diet on the type of fat in fishes.

Spawning Cycle and Feeding Habits

The spawning cycle of fish has a very great influence on their feeding habits. Usually fish stop feeding before spawning and there is a very great drain on the reserve food supply—the stored fat, for two reasons: first, because they stop feeding, and second, because of their rapidly maturing sex organs.

This depletion of reserve food supply, which is largely the stored fat, applies both to fish that store their fat in muscle tissue, such as salmon, herring, and pilchard, and to those fish that store their oil in the liver, such as cod. The dogfish is an exception to this general rule.

The spawning season varies with the type of fish. The British Columbia herring for example, spawns between February and April, while the pink salmon spawns during July and August.

Temperature

Fish caught in the northerly regions exhibit a higher degree of unsaturation in their oil than fish of the same species caught in warmer latitudes.

SPOILAGE OF FISH OILS AND PREVENTATIVE MEASURES

Introduction

Fish oils may deteriorate before processing, during processing, or during storage after processing. The undesirable changes may be brought about by either chemical, enzymatic, or microbial activity. Spoilage manifests itself by formation of free-fatty acids through oxidative rancidity, which is largely responsible for loss of vitamin A potency, or by flavor reversion, i.e., a tendency of some oils to develop off-flavors after deodorization.

The general concensus is that harmful effects may result when an animal ingests deteriorated fish oils. It is, therefore, essential to understand the various causative agents that deteriorate fish oils, as well as to point out preventive measures. These subjects will be treated in two sections under the headings: (1) various types of oil deterioration, and (2) methods for controlling deterioration of oils.

Various Types of Oil Deterioration

The various types of deterioration (Bailey 1952) that oils may be subject to are as follows: (1) development of free-fatty acids by lipases, (2) development of oxidative rancidity, and (3) flavor reversion. A discussion of each of these factors follows.

Development of Free-Fatty Acids by Lipases.—Lipases, or fat-splitting enzymes, are ever present in fish tissue, particularly in fish entrails, including the livers. They become especially active after the death of the fish. Lipases are elaborated by microorganisms, that might contaminate the oil.

Jensen and Grettie (1937) have shown that, while moisture-free oil would not support microbial activity, yet, as little as 0.3% moisture in oil would enable microbes to grow. Oils prepared from decomposed material are, therefore, high in free fatty acids.

Drummond and Hilditch (1930) have shown that the storage duration of cod livers at 41°F. has a marked effect on the quality of oils produced from them, i.e., the longer the storage period the higher the free-fatty acid and color content and the lower the quality of the oil. This is due largely to the presence of enzymes in the livers. The storage time of the livers has hardly any effect on the vitamin A content of the oil.

Oil in muscle tissue of fish is also subject to relatively rapid enzymatic hydrolysis. Brocklesby (1933) found that storage of coho salmon, both in the minced condition and "in the round," at temperatures respectively of 55° and 52°F., resulted in increase of free-fatty acid content. Fish stored "in the round" increased in its free-fatty acid content tenfold, i.e., from 0.2 to 2.0 per cent, in approximately 50 hr., while it took only 30 hr. to carry out a similar change when the fish was in minced condition. It required more time for the fish "in the round" to undergo the same change because it was less contaminated and it was stored at a somewhat lower temperature.

Similar results were obtained in the Pacific Fisheries Experiment Station, Vancouver, B. C., during their investigation on the effect of time and temperature of storage of whole herring on the oil produced from them. They showed that the free fatty acid content of fresh herring stored at 35.6°F. for 3 and 7 days increased respectively from an initial value of 0.2 to 0.4 and 2.0.

Ono (1935) investigated the enzymatic hydrolysis of mackerel and sardine oil stored at 8.6°F. He found that the iodine value does not change during cold storage, but the free-fatty acid content increases rapidly. Furthermore, the hydrolysis of a neutral fat is caused by the tissue lipases but not by microorganisms.

Sizer and Josephson (1942) have demonstrated that at —94°F. lipolytic activity is practically at a standstill, but at 86°F., the enzymes resume their normal rate of lipolysis.

Development of Oxidative Rancidity.—Oxidative rancidity, or simply "rancidity" refers to oxidation of the fatty acid molecule. It is a much more serious problem when rancidity is caused by atmospheric oxidation than when it is brought about by the action of lipoxidases. Rancidity is largely responsible for loss of vitamin A potency in fish oils. Rancidity can be brought about by two types of oxidations: (a) atmospheric oxidation, and (b) enzymatic oxidation by lipoxidases. A further explanation follows.

Atmospheric Oxidation.—Atmospheric oxidation under ordinary conditions of temperature and pressure affects unsaturated oils readily and, to a lesser extent, saturated fatty acids. The latter react with oxygen most effectively at elevated temperatures and in the presence of a suitable catalyst. Most of the rancid flavor and odor develops soon after an initial slow change. The rate of atmospheric oxidation increases considerably in the presence of various metals (Ziels 1945), and organic substances such as fatty peroxides.

Enzymatic Oxidation by Lipoxidases.—Lipoxidases are naturally-occurring enzymes in fish tissues. They produce oxidation products, while lipases produce only free-fatty acids (Banks 1937). Lipoxidases can also be produced by bacteria, but the oil must contain at least 0.3% moisture to enable bacterial growth and multiplication (Jensen and Grettie 1937).

Oxidation products formed by lipoxidases are much more difficult to eliminate than the formation of free-fatty acids which are the end products of the lipases. The latter can be easily removed by alkali refining, but oxidation products are difficult to remove. Lipoxidases also reduce the vitamin A potency in the oil.

Both types of enzymes, namely, the lipases and the lipoxidases, are inherently present in fish oils produced without heating, such as by application of the cold process for the oil extraction. These enzymes are, however, readily inactivated by heating their carrier to 176°–212°F., for about 15 or 20 min. Hence lipolytic hydrolysis offers no problem to oils extracted by heat. However, oils produced by the cold process should be subjected to sufficient heat to inactivate the enzymes.

Flavor Reversion.—Deodorized fish oils tend to redevelop a fishy odor and flavor which may or may not be similar to the original off-flavor. This phenomenon is primarily due to a slight oxidation occurring after deodorization. Davies and Gill (1936) attributed fishiness in oils to a possible chemical combination of the nitrogenous compound with the highly unsaturated triglycerides, in the presence of peroxides. Flavor reversion takes place even after prolonged vacuum-steam deodorization designed primarily to remove the nitrogenous compounds.

Methods for Controlling Deterioration of Oils

There are three approaches for controlling deterioration of oils, in addition to the use of heat for the inactivation of enzymes. One process obtains stabilization of edible oils and fats by means of a very slight halogenation. It is described by Renner (1944). The second method is by the use of antioxidants. Although these are primarily used to prevent oxidation of vitamin A in oils, they are also applied for the prevention of oxidative deterioration of oils. The third method involves the use of inert atmospheres, such as nitrogen gas, often used in packaging labile products.

Antioxidants.—There are two forms of antioxidants (Bailey 1952). They are (1) synthetic and (2) naturally occurring antioxidants in animal and vegetable tissues. Synthetic antioxidants for fatty oils are hydroquinone, pyrogallol, catechol, alpha-naphthol, para-aminobenzoic acid, butylated hydroxyanisole, and others. The naturally occurring group includes tocopherols, phosphatides, some seed flours and extracts, nordihydroguaiaretic acid (N.D.G.A.), gallic acid, gallates, gum guaiac, ascorbic acid and its esters, and others.

Synergism plays an important role among antioxidants. This phenomenon represents a beneficial effect on one antioxidant by another. When two antioxidants are added simultaneously, the beneficial effect is far greater than the sum of the two when they are added individually at the same concentration. When certain substances, which by themselves have little or no antioxidant properties, are added to oils along with an antioxidant, they exert a markedly synergistic effect on the antioxidant. For example, ascorbic acid exerts a synergistic effect with a number of antioxidants; also, hydroquinone acts synergistically with lecithin when both are added jointly in a 0.1% concentration.

Naturally Occurring Antioxidants.—The following is a brief description of some naturally occurring antioxidants which are more fully described by Bailey (1952).

Tocopherols are fairly widely distributed in the oily portion of plant seeds, particularly in wheat germ. They are also found in fish oils. All of the four isomeric forms of tocopherol exert antioxidant effects on fatty acids in varying degrees. The phenol oxygen and pyran oxygen of a fused phenolpyran nucleus of tocopherols constitute the chemically active parts of tocopherols. Phosphoric acid, and also phosphatides and ascorbic acid, either directly or in their ester forms, have been used as synergists to tocopherol.

Phosphatides.—Cephalin is one form of phosphatide which is used as an antioxidant and is particularly effective as a synergist when used in conjunction with tocopherols. It constitutes about 40% of the soybean phosphatide. The naturally occurring phosphatides with lecithin similarly act as synergists for tocopherols.

Musher (1940) described a method for stabilizing fatty oils including cod liver oil, halibut liver oil, mackerel oil, herring oil, etc., against rancidity by adding to the oils antioxidant mixtures consisting of various amounts of sugar or molasses and a phosphatide and then heating the entire mixture. The following are examples of such antioxidant mixtures containing phosphatides: (a) equal parts of lecithin and sucrose, (b) 30% lecithin and 70% crude cane sugar, (c) 5% lecithin and 95% black-strap molasses. These antioxidant mixtures may be added to oils in from 0.05 to 5.0% concentrations with or without heat, although maximum effectiveness is obtained when the mixtures are heated at temperatures within the wide range of 180°–400°F.

Nordihydroguaiaretic acid (*N.D.G.A.*), in 0.1% concentration, exerts antioxidant effect on salmon oils. The addition of either 0.005% citric acid or 0.01% phosphoric acid acts as a synergist to N.D.G.A., and increases markedly its antioxidant activity for oils of low concentration.

Gallic acid and gallates are powerful antioxidants by themselves and can also act as synergists with other antioxidants (Golumbic and Mattill 1941). Sabalitschka and Bohm (1941) describe the use of methyl, ethyl, propyl, and butyl gallates as antioxidants for fats and oils. Gallic acid and propyl gallate are most effective at 0.02% concentrations, without any synergist. Adding 0.2% isoascorbyl palmitate, as a synergist, to fats containing 0.02% of gallic acid and several gallates increased the effectiveness about 50%. Under the same conditions, it doubled the effectiveness of N.D.G.A. as an antioxidant.

Ascorbic Acid and Its Esters.—Ascorbic acid serves a double function with respect to its protective action on oils. First, it possesses antioxidant properties; second, it acts synergistically with some antioxidants, notwithstanding the fact that it is only very slightly oil-soluble. Mattill and Golumbic (1943) stated that not more than 0.1% of ascorbic acid plus a similar amount of tocopherol-like substances such as hydrocoumarans, hydrox-ychromans, tocopherols, etc., can be used as an antioxidant.

In order to overcome the relative insolubility of ascorbic acid in oils, which tends to reduce its antioxidant effectiveness, Wells and Riemen-schneider (1945) developed fat-soluble fatty acid esters of ascorbic acid for use as antioxidants in fats and oils.

Riemenschneider and Turer (1945A) describe the use of from 0.01 to 0.20% of alpha-tocopherol as an antioxidant together with from 0.05 to 0.12% ascorbyl monoester of a fatty acid as the synergist. The same inventors (1945B) describe a procedure for combining three antioxidants to produce a synergistic effect. The following ternary synergistic antioxidant combination, i.e., three antioxidants acting together, in the following amounts, was found particularly effective: d-isoascorbyl stearate, 0.12%; alpha-tocopherol, 0.001%; soybean phospholipids (commercial lecithin) 0.03%.

Three patents were granted to Norris (1945A, B, C) for stabilizing fatty products by the use of multiple synergistic combinations of various synergists with ascorbic acid or other compounds containing an ene-diol group. Thus, U. S. Patent 2,377,029 involves the use of 0.1% of para-aminobenzoic acid, 0.02% of tocopherol, and 0.1% of a compound with an ene-diol grouping, such as l-ascorbic acid. U. S. Patent 2,377,030 covers the stabilization of fats with 0.1% of mono-, di-, or tri-ethanolamine by itself or in synergistic combination with 0.1% of l-ascorbic acid or other ene-diol grouping compounds. U. S. Patent 2,377,031 describes the stabilization of edible fats and oils by combining para-aminobenzoic acid, with an ene-diol group compound and one of several heterocyclic oxygen compounds. The antioxidants used do not exceed 0.1% in concentration.

Gum Guaiac.—The use of gum guaiac as an antioxidant for animal fats and oils, and probably for fish oils, is described by Newton and Grettie (1933). It is very effective in stabilizing animal fats and oils and probably fish oils as well. Gum guaiac is not effective with vegetable oils. It can be applied advantageously only to hot oils, since it is practically insoluble in cold oils.

Brown (1945) covers the use of gum guaiac as an antioxidant after it is dissolved in higher fatty acid esters containing at least one hydroxyl group.

Miscellaneous Naturally Occurring Antioxidants.—Other naturally occurring substances that have shown stabilizing activities on fats and oils are the following: citric and tartaric acids, orthophosphoric and pyrophosphoric acids, the aliphatic amino acids glycine, asparagine, aspartic and glutamic acids, all at 0.01 to 0.10% concentration (Lea 1936), also tannic acid, (Musher 1942A) and phosphoric acid (Richardson et al. 1935).

Musher (1942B) stated that the addition of 0.05% tyrosine or its esters to gurry of fat fish, such as mackerel heads and tails, retards oxidative deterioration.

Synthetic Antioxidants.—Synthetic antioxidants are limited in their application. Hydroquinone at a 0.1% concentration by itself or as a synergist with lecithin, also at 0.1% concentration, was used earlier as an antioxidant for fish oils. Other synthetic antioxidants are pyrogallol and catechol. Alpha-naphthol at 0.1% concentration is effective. Butylated hydroxyanisole (BHA) may be used up to 0.02% concentration.

BIBLIOGRAPHY

AENLLE, E. O.   1944.   Distribution of fatty acids on the oils of the ruffe (*Perca cernua*) and of the liver of the spotted dogfish at the coast of Africa. Ion *4*, No. 32, 161–169.

ARMSTRONG, E. F., and ALLEN, J.   1924.   Neglected chapter in chemistry: the fats. J. Soc. Chem. Ind. *43*, 207–218.

ARMSTRONG, J. G., and MCFARLANE, W. D.   1944.   Flavor reversion in linseed shortening. Oil and Soap *21*, 322–327.

BAILEY, A. E.   1951.   Industrial Oil and Fat Products. 2nd Edition.   Interscience Publishers Inc., New York.

BAILEY, A. E.   1946.   Flavor reversion in edible fats. Oil and Soap *23*, 55–58.

BAILEY, A. E.   1950.   Melting and Solidification of Fats. Interscience Publishers Inc., New York.

BAILEY, B. E.   1934.   Seasonal variation in the vitamin D potency of pilchard oil. Pacific Biol. Sta. B. C. Progr. Rept. No. 19, 5–6.

BAILEY, B. E.   1935.   Vitamin A potency of liver oils from some miscellaneous Pacific Coast fishes. Biol. Board Can., Pacific Progr. Rept. *26*, 17–18.

BAILEY, B. E. Editor.   1952.   Marine Oils with Particular Reference to Those of Canada. Fisheries Res. Board Can., Bull No. *89*, Ottawa.

BANKS, A.   1937.   Changes in fat of cold-stored herring. Dept. Sci. Ind. Res., Rept. Food Invest. Board 77–79.

BAUDART, P.   1942.   III.   Separation and constitution of arachidonic acid. Bull. Soc. Chim. 9, 919–922.

BJARNASON, O. B., and MEARA, M. L.   1944.   The mixed unsaturated glycerides of liquid fats. J. Soc. Chem. Ind. *63*, 61T–63T.

BROCKLESBY, H. N., and DENSTEDT, O. F.   1933.   Industrial chemistry of fish oils with particular reference to those of British Columbia. Bull. Biol. Board Can., Bull. No. 37.

BROCKLESBY, H. N.   1933.   Hydrolysis of the body oil of the salmon. Contrib. Can. Biol. Fisheries 7, 507–519.

BROCKLESBY, H. N.   1936.   Fatty acids and their esters. Can J. Res. *14B*, 222–230.

BROCKLESBY, H. N., and HARDING, K. F.   1938.   The approximate composition of the fatty acids of the oil of pilchards. J. Fisheries Res. Board Can. *4*, 59–62.

BROCKLESBY, H. N. Editor.   1941.   The Chemistry and Technology of Marine Animal Oils with Particular Reference to Those of Canada. Fisheries Res. Board Can., Bull 59, Ottawa.

BROWN, L. C.   1945.   Stabilization of fatty material.   U. S. Pat. 2,377,610. June 5.

BUCHER, D. L.   1945.   Antioxidants for fish oils.   Fishery Market News 7, No. 7, 17–18.   . .

CARLSON, A. J., and BREWER, N. R.   1948.   Summary of Toxicity Studies on Hydroquinone.   University of Chicago, Chicago, Ill.

COLLIN, G., DRUMMOND, J. C., HILDITCH, T. P., and GUNTER, E. R.   1934.   The fatty constituents of marine plankton.   II.   General character of the plankton oils.   J. Expt. Biol. 11, 198–202.

DAVIDSON, F. A., and SHOSTROM, O. E.   1936.   Physical and chemical changes in the pink salmon during the spawning migration.   U. S. Bur. Fisheries Invest. Rept. 33, 1–37.

DAVIES, W. L., and GILL, E.   1936.   Investigations on fishy flavor.   J. Soc. Chem. Ind. 55, 141T–146T

DENSTEDT, O. F., and BROCKLESBY, H. N.   1936.   Fish oils.   VI.   Structure and properties of pilchard-oil films.   J. Biol. Board Can. 2, 1, 13–40.

DEUEL, H. J.   1951.   The Lipids, Vol. I.   Interscience Publishers, Inc., New York.

DRUMMOND, J. C., and HILDITCH, T. P.   1930.   The Relative Value of Cod Liver Oils from Various Sources.   H. M. Stationery Office, London, Gr. Brit. Empire Market Bd. Rept. 35, 1–29.

ELLIS, G. W.   1932.   Autoxidation of the fatty acids.   I.   The oxygen uptake of elaidic, oleic and stearic acids.   Biochem. J. 26, 791–800.

EVERS, N., JONES, A. G., and SMITH, W.   1936.   Characteristics of halibut-liver oils.   Analyst 61, 7–11.

FARMER, E. H., and SUTTON, D. A.   1943.   Course of auto-oxidation reactions in polyisoprenes and allied compounds.   V.   Observations on fish-oil acids.   J. Chem. Soc. 119–122.

FRITZ, J. C., et al.   1942.   Oxidative destruction of vitamin D.   Ind. Eng. Chem. 34, 979–982.

GOLUMBIC, C., and MATTILL, H. A.   1941.   Antioxidants and the autoxidation of fats.   J. Am. Chem. Soc. 63, 1279–1280.

GREEN, C. W.   1919.   Biochemical changes in the muscle tissue of king salmon during the fast of spawning migration.   J. Biol. Chem. 39, 435–456.

GRIEWAHN, J., and DAUBERT, B. F.   1948.   Alpha-Tocopherol as an antioxidant in lard.   J. Am. Oil Chem. Soc. 25, 26–27.

GUHA, K. D., HILDITCH, T. P., and LOVERN, J. A.   1930.   Composition of the mixed fatty acids present in the glycerides of cod-liver and certain other fish-liver oils.   Biochem. J. 24, 266–290.

HARRISON, R. W., ANDERSON, A. W., POTTINGER, S. R., and LEE, C. F.   1939.   Pacific salmon oils.   U. S. Bur. Fisheries Invest. Rept. 40, 1–21.

HART, J. L., TESTER, A. L., BEALL, D., and TULLY, J. P.   1938.   Chemical analyses of herring.   Fisheries Res. Board Can., Pac. Progr. Rept. 37, 19–21.

HART, J. L., TESTER, A. L., BEALL, D., and TULLY, J. P.   Proximate analysis of British Columbia herring in relation to season and condition factor.   J. Fisheries Res. Board Can. 4, 478–490.

HICKMAN, K. C. D.   1948.   Molecular distillation.   Arch. Biochem. 19, 360–363.

HILDITCH, T. P.   1944.   Fats, fatty oils and detergents.   Rept. Soc. Chem. Ind. Progr. Applied Chem. 26, 259–278.

HILDITCH, T. P. 1947A. Mechanism of oxidation and reduction of the unsaturated groups in drying oils. J. Oil and Color Chem. Assoc. *30*, 1–16.

HILDITCH, T. P. 1947B. The Chemical Constitution of the Natural Fats. 2nd Edition. Chapman and Hall Ltd., London.

HILDITCH, T. P., and HOLBROOKE, A. 1928. Composition of the fatty acids present glycerides in elasmobranch oils. Analyst *53*, 246–257.

HILDITCH, T. P., and MADDISON, L. 1942. The mixed unsaturated glycerides of liquid fats. J. Soc. Chem. Ind. *61*, 169–173.

HILDITCH, T. P., and PATHAK, S. P. 1948. Component acids of herring visceral fat. Biochem. J. *42*, 316–320.

HOLMES, A. D., and CLOUGH, W. Z. 1927. Chemical and physical characteristics of cod-liver oil. Oil Fat Ind. *4*, 403–409.

JENSEN L. B., and GRETTIE, D. P. 1937. Action of microorganisms of fats. Food Res. *2*, 97–120.

KARNOVSKY, M. L., *et al.* 1948. South African fish products XXVII. Composition of the liver oils of the basking shark and the spiny shark. J. Soc. Chem. Ind. *67*, 104–107.

KORNER, J., and LOOMIS, H. P. 1946. Stabilization of vitamin A and vitamin A containing material. U. S. Pat. 2,394,456, Feb. 5.

LEA, C. H. 1936. Antioxidants and the preservation of edible fats. Dept. Sci. Ind., Rept. Food Invest. Board. 38–43. Cambridge, England.

LEMON, H. W. 1944. Flavor reversion in hydrogenated linseed oil. The production of an isomer of linoleic acid from linolenic acid. Can. J. Res. *22F*, 191–198.

LIPS, H. J., LEMON, H. W., and GRANT, G. A. 1947. Flavor reversion in hydrogenated linseed oil. IV. Further processing studies. Can. J. Res. *25F*, 44–50.

LOVERN, J. A. 1938. Fat metabolism in fishes. XII. Seasonal changes in the composition of herring. Biochem. J. *32*, 676–680.

LOVERN, J. A. 1943. The nation's food. VI. Fish as food. 3. Vitamin and mineral content of fish. Chem. Ind. 328–330.

LOVERN, J. A. 1948. The fishing industries of North America. Part IV. Fish meal and oil. Food Manuf. *23*, 323–327.

LOVERN, J. A. 1951. The chemistry and metabolism of fats in fish. The biochemistry of fish Symposium No. 6, 49. The Biochemical Society, Cambridge, England.

LOVERN, J. A. 1958. The nutritional significance of fish lipids. Proc. Nutr. Soc. England and Scotland *17*, 161–164.

LUNDBERG, W. O. 1947. A survey of present knowledge, researches, and practices in the U. S. concerning the stabilization of fats. The Hormel Inst. of the University of Minnesota, Publication No. 20, 1–45. Austin, Minn.

MARKLEY, K. S. 1947. Fatty Acids. Interscience Publishers Inc., New York.

MATTILL, H. A., and GOLUMBIC, C. 1943. Antioxidants for fats and oils. U. S. Pat. 2,333,655. Nov. 9.

MATTILL, H. A. 1947. Antioxidants. Ann. Rev. Biochem. *16*, 177–192.

MATUDA, S., and UENO, S. 1938. Bonito oil. J. Chem. Soc. Japan. *59*, 289–294.

MILBY, T. T., and THOMPSON, R. B. 1944. The stability of D-activated animal sterol when pre-mixed with common poultry feed ingredients. Poultry Sci. *23*, 405–407.

MORRIS, S. G., KRAEKEL, L. A., HAMMER, D., MYERS, J. S., and RIEMENSCHNEI-
DER, R. W. 1947. Antioxidant properties of the fatty alcohol esters of gallic
acid. J. Am. Oil Chem. Soc. *24*, 309–311.

MUSHER, S. 1940. Inhibiting oxidative deterioration of compositions containing glyceride oils and fats. U. S. Pat. 2,176,022. Oct. 10.

MUSHER, S. 1942A. Preservation of oils. U. S. Pat. 2,282,811. May 12.

MUSHER, S. 1942B. Stabilization of foods. U. S. Pat. 2,290,064. July 14.

NEWTON, R. C., and GRETTIE, D. P. 1933. Antioxidant for fats and oils. U. S.
Pat. 1,903,126. Mar. 28.

NORRIS, F. A. 1945A. Stabilization of fat products. U. S. Pat. 2,377,029.
May 29.

NORRIS, F .A. 1945B. Stabilization of fatty products. U. S. Pat. 2,377,030.
May 29.

NORRIS, F. A. 1945C. Stabilization of fat products. U. S. Pat. 2,377,031.
May 29.

OLCOTT, H. S. 1934. Antioxidants and autoxidation of fats. II. J. Am.
Chem. Soc. *56*, 2492–2493.

OLCOTT, H. S., and MATTILL, H. A. 1941. Constituents of fats and oils affecting the development of rancidity. Chem. Rev. *29*, 257–268.

ONO, T. 1935. Enzymatic hydrolysis of mackerel and sardine oil, stored at
8.6°F. Bull. Japan. Soc. Sci. Fisheries *3*, 255.

PRIVETT, O. S., JORGENSEN, A. E., Holman, R. T., and Lundberg, W. O. 1959.
The effect of concentrates of polyunsaturated acids from tuna oil upon essential fatty acid deficiency. J. Nutr. *67*, 3, 423–432.

RENNER, H. O. 1944. Treating fatty material. U. S. Pat. 2,349,377. May 23.

RICHARDSON, A. S., VIBRANS, F. C., and ANDREWS, J. T. R. 1935. Composition
of fatty matter and stabilizing same. U. S. Pat. 1,993,181. Mar. 5.

RIEMENSCHNEIDER, R. W., and TURER, J. 1945A. Antioxidant compositions.
U.S. Pat. 2,375,250. May 8.

RIEMENSCHNEIDER, R. W., and TURER, J. 1945B. Ternary synergistic antioxidant composition. U. S. Pat. 2,383,815. Aug. 28.

RIEMENSCHNEIDER, R. W. 1947. Oxidative rancidity and the use of antioxidants. Trans. Am. Assoc. Cereal Chem. V, 50–63.

ROBESON, C. D., and BAXTER, J. G. 1943. Mimeographed copy of paper presented at 104th meeting of A. C. S., Buffalo, N. Y., 14B. J. Am. Chem. Soc.
65, 940–943.

SABALITSCHKA, T., and BÖHM, E., 1941. Stabilizing high-molecular fat acids,
animal and vegetable fats and oils, and fish oils. U. S. Pat. 2,255,191.
Sept. 9.

SIMMONS, R. O. 1958. Variation in physical and chemical characteristics of
herring, menhaden, salmon, and tuna oils. Com. Fisheries Rev. *20*, No. 11a
(supplement), 15–17.

SIZER, I. W., and JOSEPHSON, E. S. 1942. Kinetics as a function of temperature
of lipase, trypsin and invertase activity from −93 to 122°F. Food Research
7, 201–209.

SWAIN, L. A. 1947. Vitamin A loss in dogfish livers. Fisheries Res. Board
Can., Pacific Progr. Rept. *73*, 48–49.

SWERN, D., SCANLAN, J. T., and KNIGHT, H. B. 1948. Mechanism of the reactions of oxygen with fatty materials. J. Am. Oil Chem. Soc. *25*, 193–200.

SWIFT, C. E., ROSE, W. G., and JAMIESON, G. S. 1942. Factors affecting the stability of cottonseed oil. A study of the antioxygenic activity of alpha-tocopherol. Oil and Soap *19*, 176–180.

TARR, H. L. A. 1947. Control of rancidity in fish flesh. I. Chemical antioxidants. J. Fisheries Res. Board Can. 7, 137–154.

TSUJIMOTO, M. 1932. Liver oils of elasmobranch fish. J. Soc. Chem. Ind. *51*, 317–323T. Japan.

WATERMAN, H. I., and VLODROP, C. VAN. 1936. Transformations of esters of unsaturated acids with and without hydrogenation catalysts in the absence of hydrogen. J. Soc. Chem. Ind. *55*, 320–344.

WELLS, P. A., and RIEMENSCHNEIDER, R. W. 1945. Antioxidant. U. S. Pat. 2,-368,435. Jan. 30.

ZIELS, N. W. 1945. U. S. Quartermaster Corps. Manual 17-7, 104–112.

CHAPTER 13

Fish-Body Oil

INTRODUCTION

Fish-body oils are generally extracted from whole fish or fish offal by the wet-reduction method (see Chapter 11). This process is particularly suited for the extraction of oil from fatty fish such as sea herring, menhaden, pilchards, and redfish or from salmon cannery offal all of which have high oil content (Table 19). It is also used for the recovery of oil from fish

TABLE 19

OIL AND PROTEIN CONTENT OF THE EDIBLE PORTION OF FISH (STANSBY 1953)

Species	Average Oil Content %	Protein Content %
Fish		
Alewives	5	19
Cod	0.4	17
Croaker	3	18
Flounder	0.6	16
Haddock	0.3	18
Halibut	5	19
Herring, sea	11	19
Mackerel, common	13	18
Mullet	5	19
Pollock	0.8	20
Salmon, king[1]	16	18
Salmon, sockeye[1]	11	21
Salmon, coho[1]	8	21
Salmon, pink[1]	6	21
Salmon, chum[1]	5	21
Sardine (pilchard)	13	23
Squeteague (sea trout)	2	19
Tuna, skipjack[1]	4	22
Whiting	0.4	17
Shellfish		
Clams	1	9
Crab	2	17
Oysters	1	7
Shrimp	1	25

Courtesy U. S. Fish and Wildlife Service.
[1] Canned.

that are low in their oil content such as trash fish, or the skeletal remains of cod and haddock after filleting, especially when large quantities of fish are processed.

When small quantities of nonoily fish are available, dry rendering is preferred. The fish-body oil can then be recovered by the use of hydraulic presses or by solvent extraction.

The oil content of fish varies more than any other constituent of fish, while the protein content changes the least. The quantity of oils in fish is affected by the feeding habits, spawning cycle, season, and species. An increase in oil content is compensated by a corresponding decrease in moisture content. The vitamin content of fish-body oils is low as compared to the generally high vitamin potencies of fish-liver oils.

RECOVERY OF FISH-BODY OILS BY THE WET REDUCTION PROCESS

The first three steps in the wet reduction process for the extraction of fish-body oils from whole fish or fish offal, i.e., grinding, cooking with live steam, and pressing, are carried out simultaneously with fish-meal production, using the same raw material. When small fish are used, grinding may be omitted. The divergence in the procedure for fish meal and fish oil production by the wet reduction method takes place after pressing the cooked fish. The pressing operation separates the cooked fish into two distinct portions, namely, press-cake and press-liquor. The press-cake is used for fish meal production (see Chapter 11). The press-liquor is used for the manufacture of fish-body oils and fish solubles as well as for the recovery of suspended solids in the liquor.

U. S. Production of Fish Oils 1941–1963

Annual production of fish oil in the United States for the period of 1941–1963 is shown in Table 20.

Wet Reduction Process.—The method of producing fish-body oil from the press-liquor is essentially as follows:

The press-liquor is passed through a vibrating screen or is passed through any other separatory device, such as a suitable type of centrifuge, to remove the suspended solid particles from the fluid carrier. The recovered solid particles are returned to the press-cake. The liquid portion, called stickwater, is heated and then separated into fish-body oil and fish solubles.

The separation can be accomplished either by centrifuging or by using a system of settling tanks. The oil is further purified by passing it through an oil polishing centrifuge. The fish solubles are then discarded or better still, the solubles are concentrated to approximately 50% solids, or are added to the press-cake and dried to produce a whole fish meal [see Fig. 34].

DESCRIPTION OF FISH-BODY OIL PRODUCTION
BY THE WET REDUCTION PROCESS[1]

The recovery of fish-body oils from press-liquor, obtained after cooking and pressing whole fish or fish offal may be carried out by the use of three different types of centrifuges, in the following sequence:

---

[1] DeLaval Separator Co., Poughkeepsie, N. Y.

TABLE 20

u. s. production of fish oils, 1941–1963. (c. f. s. no. 3454)

Year	Menhaden Oil Thousand Pounds	Menhaden Oil Value	Herring Oil Thousand Pounds	Herring Oil Value	Sardine (Pacific) Oil Thousand Pounds	Sardine (Pacific) Oil Value
1941	45,255	$2,829,441	22,810	$1,563,545	135,939	$9,879,290
1942	38,466	3,200,129	7,390	646,565	93,817	8,067,750
1943	43,010	3,892,142	12,956	1,129,446	104,605	9,301,593
1944	45,503	3,725,498	17,920	1,603,078	135,742	11,722,950
1945	62,513	5,656,550	19,977	1,786,040	88,898	7,926,147
1946	73,190	9,033,032	26,494	4,292,776	36,499	6,843,376
1947	63,550	11,425,497	29,063	4,144,643	15,780	2,677,453
1948	65,730	10,132,179	27,327	4,004,250	17,464	2,457,858
1949	62,204	3,407,510	5,425	394,297	45,924	2,872,532
1950	76,575	5,866,554	24,821	2,366,005	46,415	4,693,550
1951	94,028	9,771,154	11,346	1,205,384	14,569	1,545,937
1952	96,665	5,785,395	8,115	517,538	157	10,815
1953	133,684	8,806,317	5,390	360,533	98	6,402
1954	139,811	9,755,320	5,707	434,347	5,669	420,531
1955	159,241	12,195,454	8,183	668,681	6,733	521,566
1956	168,211	14,092,275	13,681	1,141,911	2,530	180,544
1957	118,484	9,466,198	14,106	1,138,978	656	54,615
1958	127,986	9,434,108	13,203	882,119	5,556	426,695
1959	154,712	10,743,781	15,004	988,994	1,409	91,691
1960	183,403	11,582,027	11,499	668,295	1,201	78,066
1961	235,167	12,913,447	6,135	416,710	646	36,221
1962	232,619	10,059,839	5,086	237,897	161	10,442
1963	167,635	9,739,117	5,709	292,966	...	...

Year	Tuna and Mackerel Oil Thousand Pounds	Tuna and Mackerel Oil Value	Liver Oil Thousand Pounds	Liver Oil Value	Total Oil Thousand Pounds	Total Oil Value	Grand Total, Value
1941	1,879	$100,048	9,249	$14,871,588	219,627	$29,594,214	$56,801,074
1942	1,612	112,042	7,507	10,034,907	154,343	22,579,602	50,896,862
1943	1,643	131,906	6,389	14,841,970	173,372	29,812,854	59,136,266
1944	2,379	177,774	7,491	13,237,435	212,422	31,008,781	63,298,553
1945	2,281	173,452	6,032	11,202,207	183,764	27,235,722	58,210,606
1946	2,696	395,475	67,19	13,478,590	150,233	34,702,132	76,642,850
1947	5,610	958,998	6,244	11,643,468	125,497	31,750,662	80,592,327
1948	4,954	622,110	5,551	12,507,652	128,127	30,982,807	79,865,623
1949	4,485	265,736	6,258	9,845,455	132,719	17,364,977	78,472,495
1950	6,633	553,231	2,484	3,431,090	163,229	17,472,709	77,188,366
1951	5,345	525,552	2,247	2,579,347	136,292	16,623,643	69,313,027
1952	5,586	367,585	2,074	2,075,014	120,708	9,391,368	67,991,631
1953	4,944	314,586	1,532	1,436,627	152,206	11,480,906	74,371,996
1954	4,386	243,446	1,775	1,391,921	163,985	12,805,444	82,427,136
1955	4,087	264,225	1,642	588,739	186,734	14,868,614	83,335,402
1956	5,290	359,144	2,143	625,337	201,500	17,251,672	91,736,841
1957	5,537	397,334	1,145	542,031	152,615	12,619,229	81,380,968
1958	4,704	319,183	381	234,899	165,210	12,333,190	79,883,049
1959	4,508	190,938	247	300,503	187,334	13,091,976	82,215,526
1960	3,819	175,047	245	349,813	209,143	13,386,472	66,595,152
1961	5,719	278,160	52	54,546	258,118	14,372,886	74,568,974
1962	5,008	235,528	44	40,819	250,075	11,001,408	75,677,169
1963	5,735	267,952	193	35,019	185,827	10,745,221	68,018,482

Table courtesy of U. S. Fish and Wildlife Service.

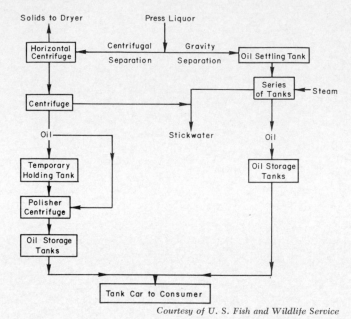

Courtesy of U. S. Fish and Wildlife Service

FIG. 34.   FLOW CHART FOR THE PRODUCTION OF FISH OILS
FROM PRESS LIQUOR

First, the press-liquor is clarified by passing it through a continuous meal recovery centrifuge for the recovery of fine high protein meal which is dried with the regular press cake.

Second, the clarified press-liquor is passed through a three-way separator which divides it into oil, water, and a fine aqueous suspension or dispersion of fish solubles. These three components are discharged through three separate outlets.

Third, the oil is passed through an oil purifier or oil polisher, thus removing residual moisture and impurities, and yielding a bright, clean oil with only traces of impurities.

The DeLaval Separator Co. has provided the flow chart for a fish oil and fish-meal recovery plant (Fig. 35). They describe the fish oil recovery process, essentially, as follows:

The press-liquor obtained after cooking and pressing whole fish or fish offal is heated by means of live steam to approximately 190°F. The liquor is then passed through a continuous meal recovery centrifuge called Desludger (Fig. 36) for recovery of fine high-protein meal from the press-liquor. The continuous meal recovery centrifuge has a horizontally revolving bowl inside of which a screw conveyor rotates at a reduced speed. As the fine high-protein meal is deposited on the wall of the bowl by centrifugal force, the conveyor moves it to the discharge ports. At this point the recovered meal is sufficiently dried to be mixed with the regular press-cake for final drying. The discharge of both meal and clarified press-liquor is continuous.

The clarified press-liquor contains fish oil, dissolved protein, protein degradation products, some finely divided fish meal, vitamins, and minerals. It is heated to approximately 200°F. by means of live steam and it is passed through a Nozzle-Matic fish oil separator. In this machine, continuous three-way separation of oil, water, and solids is made (Fig. 37).

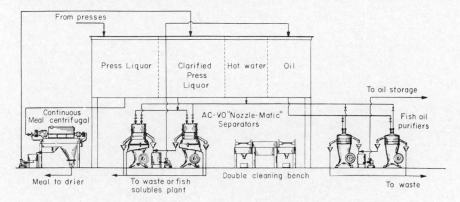

Courtesy of DeLaval Separator Co., Poughkeepsie, N. Y.

Fig. 35. Flow Chart of Fish Oil and Fish Meal Recovery Plant

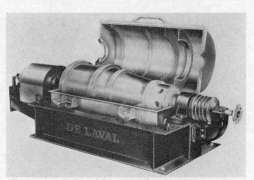

Courtesy of DeLaval Separator Co., Poughkeepsie, N. Y.

Fig. 36. Desludger. Stage I

This machine will run practically continually if it is fed clarified press-liquor at a uniform rate, but in practice the bowl is cleaned at the end of each run. Very seldom is it operated longer than 48 hr. continuously without cleaning. The stickwater normally is concentrated to a 50% syrupy consistency, referred to as fish solubles; the concentrate may be blended and dried with the fish meal to make a whole fish-meal or the unconcentrated stickwater may be discarded.

Finally, the oil obtained from the Nozzle-Matic separator is further purified, to yield a bright clean oil by heating it to approximately 200°F., and feeding it into a fish oil purifier, or oil polisher (Fig. 38) along with a stream of hot water at the same temperature. Water washing removes from the oil fine residual meal particles.

A typical analysis of a sample of sardine oil which has been water washed and polished is as follows:

Moisture and volatile matter	0.11%
Insoluble impurities	0.01%
Free-fatty acids (as oleic)	0.01%
Color	Light

Fish oil that contains such a low content of impurities is stable and should show no increase in fatty acids on storage.

Courtesy of DeLaval Separator Co.,
Poughkeepsie, N. Y.

FIG. 37. NOZZLE-MATIC FISH OIL
SEPARATOR. STAGE II

Courtesy of DeLaval Separator Co.,
Poughkeepsie, N. Y.

FIG. 38. FISH OIL POLISHER.
STAGE III

DESCRIPTION OF FISH-BODY OIL PRODUCTION BY THE WET REDUCTION PROCESS[2]

Figure 39 is a schematic flow diagram of a typical fish oil and fish-meal plant for the recovery of fish body oil from press-liquor obtained after cooking and pressing whole fish or fish offal. The Sharples description of the flow diagram is as follows:

---

[2] The Sharples Company, Philadelphia, Pa., a division of Pennsalt Chemicals Corp.

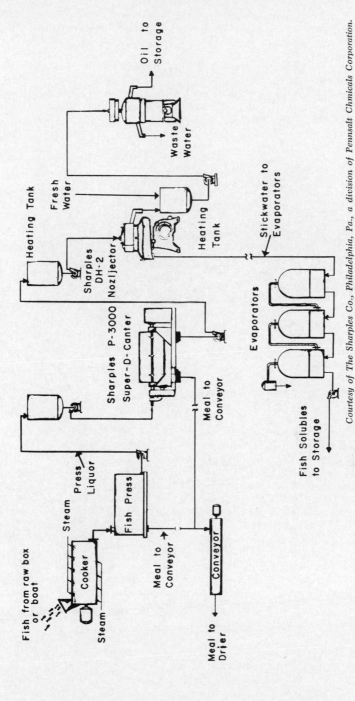

Courtesy of The Sharples Co., Philadelphia, Pa., a division of Pennsalt Chemicals Corporation.

Fig. 39. Schematic Flow Diagram of a Typical Fish Meal and Fish Oil Plant Using the "Wet Reduction" Method

After receipt in the bins the fish are carried by screw conveyors to the cooker. The fish are continuously cooked by direct or indirect steam or both. They are then fed to the press, where the first separation of liquids from solids takes place.

The solids are transported directly to the drier. Grinding follows the drier. The meal is then bagged.

The liquid phase (called press-liquor) from the press still contains insoluble solids. It is therefore fed to a horizontal type centrifuge (Super-D-Canter) where the bulk of the insoluble solids are removed (Fig. 40). These solids are then mixed with the press-cake and fed to the drier.

Courtesy of The Sharples Co., Philadelphia, Pa.,
a division of Pennsalt Chemicals Corporation.

FIG. 40.   SUPER-D-CANTER

The liquid effluent of the solids separator (clarified press-liquor) still contains a small amount of fine solids, as well as the water and oil. It is fed to a Nozljector to recover the oil. (Fig. 41).

The separator splits the feed into oil and water. By employing nozzles around the circumference of the bowl, the separator is enabled to continuously discharge solids. These solids are minute in size and less than one per cent of the feed. Nevertheless if they were not eliminated the bowl would soon have to be stopped for cleaning.

The oil is discharged in an oil-water emulsion. It is subsequently fed to a Super-Centrifuge to eliminate the water (Fig. 42).

The nonoil discharge from the oil separator (now called stickwater) is fed to an evaporator for solubles concentration. Concentrated solubles are usually fed with the press-cake to the drier for whole meal production.

THE WESTFALIA SEPARATOR[3]

The Westfalia Separator is another good appartus used for de-oiling of press-water in fish processing plants.

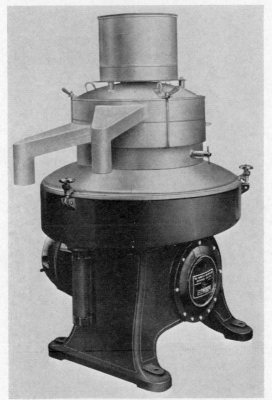

*Courtesy of The Sharples Co., Philadelphia, Pa.,
a division of Pennsalt Chemicals Corporation.*

FIG. 41.   NOZLJECTOR

SEPARATION OF FISH OILS BY SETTLING TANKS

Another method for separating fish oils from stickwater consists of
using a series of settling tanks.   Oils extracted in accordance with the most
modern technological improvements are finer, brighter, cleaner, drier and
contain less free-fatty acids than oils obtained by separation in settling
tanks.   But in seacoast countries that are not technologically far advanced,
oil of inferior grade and poor yield might be better than no oil at all.   "Half
a loaf is better than none."   Therefore, a diagram of a semi-obsolete settling system is shown in Fig. 43 and a description of such a system, as given
in "Marine Oils" Bulletin 89 (Bailey 1952) on pages 208–209, follows:

Settling systems for separating the oil from the stickwater consist of a number
of tanks set closely together in a row, with each successive tank slightly lower

_____
[3] Centrico, Englewood, N. J.

Courtesy of The Sharples Co., Philadelphia, Pa.,
a division of Pennsalt Chemicals Corporation.

FIG. 42.   SUPER-CENTRIFUGE

than the one before it so that the overflow from one can run directly into the
next.   There are usually five such tanks, each equipped with a closed steam coil
for heating its contents, and having a water inlet near the conical bottom.   The
first tank has in addition an open steam coil.   A typical settling system of a
Pacific Coast reduction plant is shown diagrammatically in Fig. 43.

The first tank (tank A) is called the "breaking tank," since the emulsion coming from the press is broken, or largely broken, in it.   The press-liquor enters the
system through the pipe E and, by means of an adjustable spout on the end of
the pipe, is delivered into the breaking tank (tank A) 12 to 18 in. below the
level of the overflow F.   In this way the surface of the liquid is kept still and
the oil has an opportunity to rise.   The overflow F is generally a shallow open
trough.   The oil, usually containing some water and solids in suspension, overflows into tank B, and the stickwater is discharged from tank A through the pipe
M.   The tanks B, C, and D are really purifying tanks, the oil passing from B to
the bottom of C, which is partially filled with hot water.   The water assists in
washing out any suspended solid particles which have not been separated in the
foots[4] recovery equipment.   The oil floated off from tank C is similarly passed
into the bottom of D, where it is again heated with hot water.   Finally it is
run into tanks T_1 and T_2 which are also equipped with closed steam coils; it is

---

[4] Suspended solids.

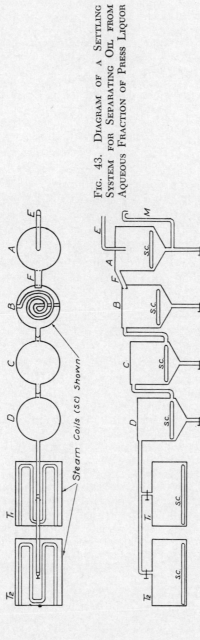

FIG. 43. DIAGRAM OF A SETTLING SYSTEM FOR SEPARATING OIL FROM AQUEOUS FRACTION OF PRESS LIQUOR

Courtesy of Fisheries Research Board of Canada, Ottawa

heated there to a high temperature to drive off any water remaining in it. From there it is pumped to storage tanks. At the end of the day's operation, water is run into tanks A, B, C, and D to float off all the oil, and after skimming this off, the valves at the bottom of each tank are opened and the tanks drained and washed out.

Heating is usually sufficient to break the emulsion of oil and stickwater which comes from the press but, if difficulty is experienced, salt is also added. This assists in breaking the emulsion.

SOLVENT EXTRACTION OF FISH-BODY OILS

Solvent extraction of fish-body oils is relatively expensive. Besides, solvent extracted oil is darker in color than oils produced by the wet reduction process regardless of the quality of the raw material. However, fish-meal prepared from oily fish and subjected to solvent extraction is lighter in color than meal prepared from the same raw material by the wet reduction process (see "Solvent Extraction of Oils," Chapter 5, for details of processes and nature of products).

DRY REDUCTION PROCESS

Fish-body oil may be recovered during the production of fish meal by the dry reduction method. It has been noted (see Chapter 11) that dry reduction is applied principally to the processing of nonoily types of fish. However, if there is enough oil in the meal, to make oil recovery feasible, it might be pressed out with a hydraulic press. Fatty types of fish such as menhaden should not be processed by the dry reduction method because the oil is darkened by the heated metal surface of the cooker-drier.

BIBLIOGRAPHY

ANON. 1945. Guide to commercial shark fishing in the Caribbean area. Fishery Leaflet 135. U. S. Fish and Wildlife Service.

ANON. 1949. Fish meal and oil. Fishing Gaz. 66, No. 6, 64–66.

BAILEY, B. E., Editor. 1952. Marine Oils, with Particular Reference to Those of Canada. Bull. 89. Fisheries Res. Board Can., Ottawa.

BALDWIN, W. H., and PARKS, L. E. 1943. The body oil from menhaden. A. Low temperature crystallization of glycerides. B. Some of the 18 and 20 carbon atom acids. Oil and Soap, 20, 6, 101–104.

BALDWIN, W. H., and PARKS L. E. 1944. The body oil from menhaden. U. S. Fish and Wildlife Service, Fishery Leaflet No. 63.

BROCKLESBY, H. N., Editor. 1941. The Chemistry and Technology of Marine Oils with Particular Reference to Those of Canada. Bull. 59. Fisheries Res. Board Can., Ottawa.

BUTLER, C. 1947. Fish reduction process, U. S. Fish and Wildlife Service, Fishery Leaflet 126. Revised 1949.

CARLSON, D., et al. 1957. Palatability of chicks fed oils containing different levels of fish oils. Food Technol. 11, 615–620.

CARVER, J. H.   1957.   Commercial uses for menhaden oil.   Com. Fisheries Rev. 19, No. 4a (supplement), 3–4.

COOKE, S. R. B.   1958.   Progress on studies in utilization of fish-oil derivatives in ore flotation.   Com. Fisheries Rev. 20, No. 1, 14–19.

COOKE, S. R. B., and STANSBY, M. E.   1957.   Utilization of fish oils in ore flotation.   Com. Fisheries Rev. 19, No. 4a (supplement) 24–29.

CORNISH, R. M., ENNIS, J. L., HYRE, J. E., and WALKER, G. E., JR.   1957.   Commercial uses for menhaden oil.   U. S. Fish and Wildlife Service, Technical Leaflet No. 12.

GRUGER, E. H., JR.   1957.   Laboratory method of obtaining unsaturated fatty alcohols from fish oils.   Com. Fisheries Rev. 19, No. 8, 1–5.

GRUGER, E. H., JR.   1957.   New Products from fish oils. Com. Fisheries Rev. 19, No. 4a (supplement) 13–17, and 18–23.

HARRISON, R. W.   1931.   Market for marine animal oils in the U. S. Invest. Rept. 7, U. S. Fish and Wildlife Service.

HARRISON, R. W., ANDERSON, A. W., POTTINGER, S. R., and LEE, C. F.   1939.   Pacific salmon oil.   Invest. Rept. No. 40, U. S. Fish and Wildlife Service.

HARRISON, R. W., and POTTINGER, S. R.   1931.   Commercial production of menhaden fish oil for animal feeding.   U. S. Fish and Wildlife Service, Invest. Rept. 4.

KRASON, W. S.   1949.   Whale and fish oils.   (Iceland).   U. S. Fish and Wildlife Service Fishery Leaflet No. 345.

KRAYBILL, H. F., and NILSON, H. W.   1947.   Chemical studies of lipoid extracts from menhaden fish meal.   Com. Fisheries Rev. 9, No. 9, 8–18.

LASSEN, S., BACON, E. K., and DUNN, H. J.   1949.   The digestibility of polymerized oils.   Arch. Biochem. 23, 1, 1–7.

LEE, C. F.   1958.   Report on development of fungicides from fish oils.   Com. Fisheries Rev. 20, No. 6, 20.

LOVERN, J. A.   1948.   The fishing industries of North America.   Part IV.   Fish meal and oil.   Food Manuf. 23, 323–327.

LOVERN, J. A.   1951.   The chemistry and metabolism of fats in fish.   The Biochemistry of fish Symposium No. 6, 49.   The Biochem. Soc., Cambridge, England.

LOVERN, J. A.   1958.   The nutritional significance of fish lipides.   Proc. Nutr. Soc. England and Scotland. 17, 161.

MATTEI, V., and RODDY, W.   1959.   The use of fish oils for fat-liquoring leather.   Part I. J. Am. Leather Chem. Assoc. 54, 12–27, 555–567, 640–653.

McDONALD, R. N., and GRUGER, E. H., JR.   1956.   New Products from fish oils. Polyamino fatty acids derived from fish oils.   Com. Fisheries Rev. 18, 9, 7–11.

MOSHER, W. A., DANIELS, W. H., CELESTE, J. R., and KELLEY, W. H.   1958. The unsaponifiable fraction of menhaden oil.   Com. Fisheries Rev. 20, No. 11a (supplement), 1–6.

NOTEVARP, O.   1953.   Investigations on the unsaturated fatty acids of fish fat. Symposium, 100, Chap. 10, p. 24, Swedish Institute for Food Preservation. Göteborg.

OLDFIELD, J. E., ANGLEMIER, A. F., and STANSBY, M. E.   1957.   Feeding fish oils to domestic animals.   Com. Fisheries Rev. 19, No. 4a (supplement) 11–12.

POWER, E. A.   1963.   Advance report on the fisheries of the U. S. 1962.   C. F. S. No. 3150. U. S. Fish and Wildlife Service.

PRIVETT, O. S., JORGENSEN, A. E., HOLMAN, R. T., and LUNDBERG, W. O.   1959.
The effect of concentrates of polyunsaturated acids from tuna oil upon essential fatty acid deficiency.   J. Nutr. *67*, 3, 423–432.

SANFORD, F. B., and LEE, C. F.   1960.   U. S. fish-reduction industry.   Bur.
Com. Fisheries.   Commercial Fisheries TL14.

SIMMONS, R. O.   1958.   Variation in physical and chemical characteristics of
herring, menhaden, salmon, and tuna oils.   Com. Fisheries Rev. *20*, No. 11a
(supplement), 15–17.

SMYTH, J. A.   1961.   World production and trade in fish meal and oil.   U. S.
Fish and Wildlife Service, Fishery Leaflet 507.

STANSBY, M. E.   1953.   Composition of fish.   U. S. Fish and Wildlife Service.
Fishery Leaflet 116.

STANSBY, M. E.   1956.   New products from fish oils.   Com. Fisheries Rev. *18*,
No. 8, 1–3.

STANSBY, M. E., and BUTLER, C.   1958   Bur. Com. Fisheries oil research program.   J. Am. Oil Chemists' Soc. *35*, No. 7, 8, 10–12.

STANSBY, M. E.   1959.   Possibilities of applying fish oil to the flotation of iron
ore.   U. S. Bur. Com. Fisheries, Technical Leaflet 26.

TRESSLER, D. K.   1923.   Marine Products of Commerce.   1st Edition.   Reinhold Publishing Corp., New York, N. Y.

TRESSLER, D. K.   1924.   Menhaden oil.   Fishing Gaz. *41*, 18.

TRESSLER, D. K., and LEMON, J. M.   1951.   Marine Products of Commerce.
2nd Edition. Reinhold Publishing Corp., New York, N. Y.

U. S. FISH and WILDLIFE SERVICE.   1963.   Industrial Fishery Products.   C. F. S.
No. 3454.

CHAPTER 14

Refining and Utilization of Fish Oils

REFINING

Refining of fish oils involves primarily the removal of impurities and oil degradation products, e.g., fatty acids and glycerine. Refining does not modify appreciably the chemical characteristics of the treated oils. The highly unsaturated nature of fish oils requires that special precautions be taken in refining them.

Refining consists of the removal of (a) free-fatty acids, (b) stearin, (c) colors, and (d) odors. Bailey (1952) classifies the refining of fish oils under the following four major divisions: (1) removal of free-fatty acids, (2) cold clearing, (3) bleaching, and (4) deodorization.

A brief summary of each of these refining procedures follows:

Removal of Free-Fatty Acids

Free-fatty acids may be removed from fish oils by several methods: (1) alkali refining, (2) vacuum-steam distillation, (3) esterification of the free-fatty acids, and (4) solvent separation. The most acceptable method industrially is alkali-refining. The other methods have particular advantages under special conditions.

Alkali Refining.—Alkali refining consists of the neutralization of the free fatty acids with a 7 to 18% solution of sodium hydroxide. If the oil contains more than ten per cent of free fatty acids, a stronger caustic soda solution is used. The theoretical amount of caustic is added to the oil, with slow stirring at about 68° to 75°F. This low temperature is maintained during neutralization in order to bring about a reaction between the caustic soda and the free-fatty acids, rather than a saponification of the oil.

Rapid stirring would cause emulsification of the soapstock with the oil. After the specified amount of alkali has been added, stirring is stopped until the soapstock is settled, usually requiring overnight storage. Heating to about 120°F., and adding some salt brine improves efficiency of the separation. After settling out is completed, the soapstock is drawn off and the refined oil is washed first with a salt brine and then several times with hot water.

In general, optimum conditions for alkali refining involve the use of fairly high concentrations of caustic soda, low temperature, and slow stirring (Bailey 1952). These conditions would tend to "grain out" the soap, including all the water, when neutrality is reached, and would also simultaneously reduce the amount of neutral oil in the soap. Similarly, the formation of slow-breaking emulsions are avoided. Furthermore, the adsorbent properties of the soap formed usually removes coloring matter and the finely dispersed proteinaceous particles.

Sodium carbonate (soda ash) can be used as a substitute for sodium hydroxide (caustic soda), with the disadvantage of procuring less decolorization, but obtaining a higher yield of neutral oil. Oil heated to 176°F. is slowly added, with stirring, to the boiling soda ash solution.

Heating may be accomplished by means of either open or closed steam coils. In the closed kettles, heating is continued until the soap gets sufficiently concentrated and rises to the top of the oil. In the open kettles, emulsification of the sodium soaps is prevented by the addition of sodium chloride. The use of closed kettles is preferred because it produces larger yields of neutral oils.

Slaked lime is not as efficient a decolorizer as sodium hydroxide, but it is inexpensive and it neutralizes the free-fatty acids. A thick lime cream is added to the oil and heated in closed steam kettles until sufficiently concentrated. Subsequently, the calcium soaps are filtered out. The soap formed has adsorbent properties which brings about a partial decolorization of the oil. The necessary precautions should be taken to reduce the vitamin A adsorption on the soap.

The removal of the last traces of dispersed soap is not accomplished by merely washing the alkali-refined oil with hot water. It is better to centrifuge it first, then follow with the addition of filter-aids such as asbestos fiber or diatomaceous earth and filtering the unwashed oil through filter presses containing special filter paper.

Vacuum-Steam Distillation.—This method is being used primarily for deodorization of industrial fish oils, during which process some free-fatty acids are also removed to reduce their concentration to 0.25%. This reduction in free-fatty acid content may be sufficient. For edible oils, alkali refining is preferred.

Esterification.—Esterification involves the chemical reaction between free-fatty acids and alcohols. If esterification is accomplished with methyl or ethyl alcohol, the esters can be removed by vacuum distillation. If a poly-hydroxy alcohol such as glycerin is the esterifying substance, the ester is left in the oil.

The ester interchange method is used for forming glycerides or esters of free-fatty acids in oils. This interchange is carried out by heating the oil with a calculated amount of another oil or fat that contains low-molecular-weight fatty acids, such as palm oil, which can be steam distilled. After the ester-interchange occurs, the liberated low-molecular-weight fatty acids are removed by steam distillation.

Solvent Separation.—Because some solvents such as alcohol and dilute acetone dissolve more free-fatty acids than neutral oil, such solvents have been utilized for the removal of free-fatty acids from oil.

Cold Clearing or Destearination

The separation and removal of the solid glyceride component from an oil on cooling, is referred to as "destearination" or "cold-clearing." The solid glyceride portion which separates from the clear cooled oil is called "stearin." This method of clarification has a marked beneficial effect on the oil. For example, destearinated oil does not cloud even during cold weather. Destearinated oils are preferred for fast drying paints. "Stearin," however, is preferable for hydrogenation because it requires less hydrogen.

Prevention of Clouding Without Stearin Removal.—Attempts have been made to prevent clouding or stearin formation during the cold weather without stearin removal, and thus maintaining the original yield of glycerides. Clayton *et al.* (1937) states that the addition of 0.1 to 0.5% of blown cacao butter to olive oil, prevents clouding. Clayton and some of his co-workers found that a sample of olive oil containing one per cent of blown cacao butter remained clear and readily pourable for at least four years at from 35° to 39°F., while a control sample set solid in a few hours. Parkin, *et al.* (1947) developed a procedure designed to solve this problem.

Bleaching

Discoloration of fish oils is due to deteriorative changes brought about by either oxidation, faulty production methods, overheating of oil especially if it is in contact with rusty iron, microbial or enzymatic activities, or a combination thereof. It manifests itself in reddening or darkening of the oil. The new colorations supplement the naturally occurring pigments, namely, carotene, xanthophyll, chlorophyll, fucoxanthin, and astacin. For the medicinal grade, cod liver oil should have a light straw color. For industrial purposes the color is of little importance.

Bleaching of discolored oils can be brought about by either physical or chemical methods.

Physical Methods.—Physical methods for the removal of colors are based on treating the oil with colloidally dispersed natural or activated clay or carbon particles which have an adsorptive capacity on the coloring matters in the oil. After the added particles have performed their function, under the specified conditions of temperature, time, and concentration, they are removed by filtration. Fuller's earth, bentonite, and other clays are used extensively either activated or in their natural state.

Bleaching fish oils on a large scale is ordinarily carried out by heating the oil with three per cent of an activated earth at 200° to 230°F., until it is decolorized. It is recommended that a ratio of from 1:20 to 1:10 of carbon to earth be used to improve efficiency of bleaching.

Simultaneously the loss of oil through its retention on the earth is considerably reduced. Oil should be free of soap or alkali before it is subjected to bleaching because their presence decreases efficiency of bleaching. Also the presence of soap during bleaching increases the free-fatty acid content.

The following are some of the United States patents pertaining to physical methods of bleaching or decolorizing of oils: 1,776,990, W. S. Baylis, 1930; 1,819,496, W. S. Baylis, 1931; 1,980,569, D. S. Belden and W. Kelley, 1934; 2,110,789, B. Clayton *et al.* 1938; and 2,428,082, R. R. King *et al.* 1947.

Chemical Methods.—Decolorization of oils could be carried out with the aid of oxidizing or reducing agents (Hampel 1947; Rollhaus et al. 1932). Oxidizing agents involve the use of oxygen, hydrogen peroxide, organic peroxides, dichromates, chromates, permanganates, hypochlorites, and other compounds. Reducing agents include hydrogen and zinc dust.

It is essential to control carefully such chemical reactions, particularly when applied to unsaturated oils, because they are very likely to attack the oil as well as the pigments. With vitamin A bearing oils, it is very risky to apply the chemical method since it tends to reduce the vitamin A potency.

Deodorization

The oxidation products of the highly unsaturated fatty acids of fish oils, whether free or combined in the triglycerides, are generally regarded as the causative agents of the characteristic fishy odors of fish oils. One method to alleviate, but not entirely to eradicate, this undesirable condition, consists of subjecting the oil to a vacuum-steam distillation at a relatively high temperature.

Hydrogenation of fish oils that are free from non-oil fishy material is another method for reducing fishy odors. Ebisawa (1931) states that by adding to fish oils about five per cent calcium hydroxide (slaked lime) and five per cent calcium oxide (quicklime), agitating and filtering, the oil becomes simultaneously deodorized, decolorized, stabilized, and also partially alkali refined.

Processing of Fish Oils

Processing of fish oils involves a change in the chemical characteristics of fish oils rendering them useful for industrial purposes. A discussion of this subject is beyond the scope of this book.

To indicate the range of subjects that processing of fish oils embraces, the topical outline on this subject as given by Bailey (1952) follows: (1) hydrolysis and saponification, (2) hydrogenation, (3) oxidation, (4) bodying oils with heat, (5) sulfation and sulfonation, (6) sulfurization, and (7) fractionation.

UTILIZATION OF FISH OILS

Fish oils are used extensively for industrial and nutritional purposes. In industry, fish oils might be used either directly as raw or refined oils, or they might be utilized in their conversion products such as soaps, paints, etc. The nutritional uses of fish oils (Bailey 1952) are as follows: human foods, medicine, animal feeding, vitamins A and D stabilized on dry carriers, and water dispersions of vitamins A and D. A further summary and discussion of these topics follow:

Fish Oils in Nutrition

Human Foods.—Oils utilized for human consumption can be used in the following four ways: canning oils, margarine, cooking fats, and shortening. The following is an elaboration of these topics:

Canning Oils.—Salmon oil is sometimes added to salmon during canning when the salmon is low in oil content. The fortifying oil is usually extracted from the same species of fresh salmon trimmings such as heads, tails, and fins.

In Norway, a slightly polymerized herring oil has been substituted for olive oil in canning sardines. The limited polymerization stabilizes the oil against rancidity and it also slightly increases its viscosity and elevates its cloud point.

Briefly, the herring oil is cold cleared, then alkali refined and filtered with a filter aid. It is next polymerized at 535° to 572°F. for 8 to 12 hr. Finally, it is deodorized by treating it under vacuum with superheated steam. The availability of vegetable oils for use in canning has almost entirely superseded the Norwegian process.

Margarine Production.—Unsaturated fish oils are sufficiently hydrogenated to remove the fish odor and flavor so that they may be exported for use in margarine production.

Cooking fats, used for ordinary and deep-fat frying, must have a high decomposition temperature. This is expressed in terms of a "smoke point" which should be above 375°F. If the "smoke point" is lower than 375°F., the fat decomposes and emits irritating fumes. Hydrogenation of fish oil raises its "smoke point," eliminates its characteristic fishy odor and flavor, and renders the oil suitable for deep-fat frying. This use in the United States is prohibited by regulation of the Food and Drug Administration.

Shortening.—Hydrogenated fats and oils originating from fish or vegetables have largely replaced lard for use as shortening in the baking industry. Fish oils, however, are not permitted in shortening production in the United States.

Medical Use.—It has been well established that vitamins A and D are essential for the proper functioning of the human body. For many years cod liver oil was the common source for medicinal vitamins A and D, but since 1930 halibut liver oil has come into use because its vitamin A potency is much higher than that of cod liver oil.

Although cod liver oil is lower in vitamin A potency than halibut liver oil, the use of cod liver oil is preferred primarily because its naturally balanced ratio between vitamins A and D potencies is best suited for human consumption. Oil concentrates are used in margarine production and other food or medicinal preparations.

Feeding Oils.—The vitamins A and D potencies of animal and poultry feeds have been supplemented with a crude grade of cod liver oil or pilchard oil. Recently "base oils," i.e., oils that are used principally as carriers of vitamins A and D, such as herring, salmon, and pilchard oils are blended with synthetic vitamin D_3 and dogfish liver oil, which is high in vitamin A, to produce feeding oils which are subsequently blended into mixed feeds. The original vitamin A potencies of the "base-oil" are merely relied on as factors of safety.

With the advent of synthetic vitamins, the use of fish liver oils in the United States dropped markedly. In developing countries, that do not have facilities for synthesizing vitamins, fish liver oils could be used economically to supplement animal and poultry feeds.

Vitamins A and D Stabilized on Dry Carriers.—Some feeding oil producers blend their vitamin A and D oils with a dry carrier instead of a "base oil." These "dry vitamin A and D" premixes are blended directly with the feeds and are presumably more stable than substances in which a "base oil" is used as the carrier.

Buxton and Konen (1946) describe a method of stabilizing vitamins A and D in a dry premix as follows: a concentrate of vitamins A and D is blended with a crude vegetable oil and this blend is further admixed with a vegetable substance that has a high affinity for fats, such as wheat germ press-cake flour, dried distillers grain solubles, and linseed oil press-cake. This blend should not contain more than 30% of fatty material. The vegetable oil used should be high in antioxidants, but with a low iodine value.

Water Dispersions of Vitamins A and D.—Another method for incorporating vitamins A and D into mixed feeds is by preparing an aqueous dispersion of these vitamins and then blending it with the feed. In this form the vitamins are more efficiently absorbed by the body and, therefore, are more effective than when oil is used as the carrier.

Other advantages to using aqueous dispersion of vitamins A and D are that a base oil is not required, shipping costs are reduced because the vitamins can be shipped in concentrated form, and, prior to their use, diluted in water. The main drawback to using an aqueous dispersion of vitamins A and D is that the dry feed is dusty, while there is much less dustiness when using feeding oils for blending the vitamins.

The following are some of the United States patents pertaining to water-dispersible preparations of vitamins A and D: 2,296,291, N. A. Milas, 1942; 2,276,531, Wechsler and Dumbrow, 1942; 2,311,554, Lipsius, 1943; 2,-321,400, Lubarsky, 1943; and 2,395,067, Richardson, 1946.

Fish Oils in Industry.—The industrial uses of fish oils generally include soaps and other detergents, paints and varnishes, floor coverings and oil-cloth, oiled fabrics, printing inks, rubber manufacture, lubricants, metal treating oils, leather, insecticides, alkyd resins, and cosmetics.

A discussion of these uses is beyond the scope of this book.

BIBLIOGRAPHY

BAILEY, B. E. Editor. 1952. Marine Oils with Particular Reference to Those of Canada. Bull. No. 89. Fisheries Res. Board Can., Ottawa.

BAYLIS, W. S. 1930. Preparing activated adsorptive clay. U. S. Pat. 1,776,-990. Sept. 30.

BAYLIS, W. S. 1931. Activated clay and method of producing same. U. S. Pat. 1,819,496. Aug. 18.

BELDEN, D. S. and KELLEY, W. 1934. Preparing absorbent low in salts and free from acids. U. S. Pat. 1,980,569. Nov. 13.

BIRD, H. R. 1944. Comparison of response of turkey poults and of chicks to different forms of vitamin D. J. Nutr. 27, 377–383.

BOUCHER, R. V. 1944. Efficacy of vitamin D from different sources for turkeys. J. Nutr. 27, 403–413.

BRADSHAW, G. B., and MEULY, W. C. 1946. Refining fats. U. S. Pat. 2,398,-492. Apr. 16.

BRIOD, A. E., and DUMBROW, B. A. 1942. Vitamin food products and producing the same. U. S. Pat. 2,283,531. May 19.

BRIOD, A. E., and BUXTON, L. O. 1947. Producing dry food products. U. S. Pat. 2,427,520. Sept. 16.

BROCKLESBY, H. N., and MOORE, L. P. 1933. Studies in fish oils. II. The decolorization of pilchard oil. Contrib. Can. Biol. Fisheries 7, 413–424.

BROCKLESBY, H. N., and KUCHEL, C. C. 1938. Adsorption of vitamin A from oils by soaps formed in situ. J. Fisheries Res. Board Can. 4, 174–183.

BURGHARDT, O. 1931. Activated bleaching clays. Ind. Eng. Chem. 23, 800–802.

BUXTON, L. O., and KONEN, H. J. 1946. Stable vitamin containing products. U. S. Pat. 2,401,293. June 4.

CHALMERS, W., and BIELY, J. 1947. Pilchard oil as a source of vitamins A and D. Poultry Sci. 26, 535–536.

CLAYTON, W. S., BACK, S., MORSE, J. F., and JOHNSON, R. I.   1937.   Treatment of olive oil to prevent stearin coming down at low temperature.   U. S. Pat. 2,097,720.   Nov. 2.

CLAYTON, B., and THURMAN, B. H.   1938.   Bleaching oils.   U. S. Pat. 2,110,-789.   Mar. 8.

COOKE, S. R. B., and STANSBY, M. E.   1957.   Utilization of fish oils in ore flotation.   Com. Fisheries Rev. 19, No. 4a (supplement) 24–29.

COOKE, S. R. B.   1958.   Progress on studies in utilization of fish-oil derivatives in ore flotation.   Com. Fisheries Rev. 20, No. 1, 14–19.

CORNISH, R. M., ENNIS, J. L., HYRE, J. E., and WALKER, G. B. JR.   1957.   Commercial uses for menhaden oil.   U. S. Fish and Wildlife Service, Technical Leaflet No. 12.

DRUMMOND, J. C., and HILDITCH, T. P.   1930.   The Relative Value of Cod Liver Oils from Various Sources.   H. M. Stationery Office.   London, Gr. Brit. Empire Market Bd. Rept. 35, 1–129.

EBISAWA, G.   1931.   Purification of fish oils.   Japan.   Pat. 91,076.   Apr. 15.

ECKEY, E. W., and LUTTON, E. S.   1941.   Improving salad oils.   U. S. Pat. 2,-266,591.   Dec. 16.

FRITZ, J. C., ARCHER, W., and BARKER, D.   1941.   Vitamin D requirements of ducklings.   Poultry Sci. 20, 151–154.

GRUGER, E. H., JR.   1957.   Laboratory method of obtaining unsaturated fatty alcohols from fish oils.   Com. Fisheries Rev. 19, No. 8, 1–5.

GRUGER, E. H., JR.   1957.   New products from fish oils.   Com. Fisheries Rev. 19, No. 4a (supplement) 13–17, and 18–23.

GUILBERT, H. R., MILLER, R. F., and HUGHES, E. H.   1937.   Minimum vitamin A and carotene requirement of cattle, sheep and swine.   J. Nutr. 13, 543–564.

HAMPEL, C. A.   1947.   Bleaching.   U. S. Pat. 2,433,661-2.   Dec. 30.

HARRISON, R. W., and POTTINGER, S. R.   1931.   Commercial production of menhaden fish oil for animal feeding.   U. S. Fish and Wildlife Service, Invest. Rept. 4.

HARRISON, R. W.   1931.   Market for marine animal oils in the U. S.   U. S. Fish and Wildlife Service, Invest. Rept. 7.

HART, G. H., and GUILBERT, H. R.   1933.   Vitamin A deficiency as related to reproduction in range cattle.   Calif. Agr. Expt. Sta. Bull. 560, 3–30.

HAUGE, S. M., HILTON, J. H., and WILBUR, J. W.   1937.   Vitamin A suppressing factors in soybeans.   Purdue Agr. Expt. Sta. Rept. of the Director, 8–9, 40.

HILTON, J. H., WILBUR, J. W., and HAUGE, S. M.   1944.   Producing milk rich in vitamin A.   J. Dairy Sci. 27, 631–632.

HOLMES, A. D., TRIPP, F., and SATTERFIELD, G. H.   1938.   The vitamin A reserve of fur-bearing animals.   Am. J. Physiol. 123, 693–700.

JOHNSON, D. W., and PALMER, L. S.   1941.   Meeting the vitamin D requirement of pigs with alfalfa hay and winter sunshine.   J. Agr. Res. 63, 639–648.

KING, R. R., PACK, S. E., and WHARTON, F. W.   1947.   Oil bleaching process and apparatus.   U. S. Pat. 2,428,082.   Sept. 30.

LEE, C. F.   1958.   Report on development of fungicides from fish oils.   Com. Fisheries Rev. 20, No. 6, 20.

LIPSIUS, S. T.   1943.   Water-dispersible fat-soluble vitamin composition and preparing the same.   U. S. Pat. 2,311,554.   Feb. 16.

Lloyd, E. A., and Biely, J. 1947. Practical Poultry Feeding. U. S. Dept. Agr. Bull., No. 107, B. C.

Lubarsky, G. H. 1943. Vitamin containing composition and making the same. U. S. Pat. 2,321,400. June 8.

Mattei, V., and Roddy, W. 1959. The use of fish oils for fat-liquoring leather. Part I. J. Am. Leather Chem. Assoc. 54, 12–27, 555–567, 640–653.

McDonald, R. N., and Gruger, E. H., Jr. 1956. New products from fish oils. Polyamino fatty acids derived from fish oils. Com. Fisheries Rev. 18, 9, 7–11.

Milas, N. A. 1942. Water soluble derivative of vitamin D. U. S. Pat. 2,296,-291. Sept. 22.

Moore, L. C., and Norman, A. C. 1938. Deodorizing and bleaching oils. U. S. Pat. 2,122,260. June 28.

Musher, S. 1946. Preserving vitamin containing oils. U. S. Pat. 2,410,455. Nov. 5.

Oldfield, J. E., Anglemier, A. F., and Stansby, M. E. 1957. Feeding fish oils to domestic animals. Com. Fisheries Rev. 19, No. 4a (supplement) 11–12.

Parkin, F. P., and Walker, G. N. 1947. Winterizing vegetable oils. U. S. Pat. 2,425,001. Aug. 5.

Remington, R. E. 1938. The Weston-Levine Vitamin Chart. Ind. Eng. Chem. News Ed. 16, 234–235.

Richardson, A. C. 1946. Proportioning vitamin carrying mediums in food products. U. S. Pat. 2,395,067. Feb. 19.

Rollhaus, P. E., and Stoddard, W. B. 1932. Bleaching methods and agents. U. S. Pat. 1,854,764. Apr. 19.

Royce, H. D. 1947. Improvement in winter vegetable oil. U. S. Pat. 2,418,-668. Apr. 8.

Sebrell, W. H. Jr., and Harris, R. S. 1954. The Vitamins, Chemistry, Physiology, Pathology. Three volumes. Academic Press, New York.

Smith, S. E. 1942. Minimum vitamin A requirement of the fox. J. Nutr. 24, 97–107.

Smyth, J. A. 1961. World production and trade in fish meal and oil. Fishery Leaflet 116. U. S. Fish and Wildlife Service.

Stansby, M. E. 1956. New products from fish oils. Com. Fisheries Rev. 18, No. 8, 1–3.

Stansby, M. E. 1959. Possibilities of applying fish oil to the flotation of iron ore. U. S. Bur. Com. Fisheries, Technical Leaflet 26.

Thomssen, E. G., and Kemp, C. R. 1937. Modern Soap Making. MacNair-Dorland Co., New York.

Wechsler, R., and Dumbrow, B. A. 1942. Water-dispersible vitamin composition. U. S. Pat. 2,276,531. Mar. 17.

Wheeler, H. H. 1945. Effect of high vitamin A in the diet of domestic and non-domestic animals. Nature, 156, 238.

Wurster, O. H., and Stockmann, G. J. 1942. Processing Oils and Fats. Wurster and Sanger, Inc., Chicago.

CHAPTER 15

Production of Fish Albumin, Peptones, and Amino Acids

FISH ALBUMIN

The proteinaceous fraction of scrap or of fillets of cod, haddock, shark, or similar fishes contain 16 to 22% fish albumin.

Fish albumin is comparable in its physical and chemical properties to egg albumin or to any egg-white substitute. It is also noteworthy that proteins obtainable from fish waste constitute the cheapest source of raw materials from which egg-white substitutes can be derived as compared to other proteinaceous sources such as milk, wheat, peanuts, or soybeans, that might be employed for the production of egg-white substitutes.

The manufacture of egg albumin from the white of eggs is relatively expensive since it requires 150 eggs to produce one pound of egg albumin.

MANUFACTURE OF FISH ALBUMIN

U. S. Fish and Wildlife Service (1946) gives the following procedure for the production of albumin from fish protein using either fillets or preferably the proteinaceous residue obtainable from fish scrap or fish waste.

Cod or haddock or other similar types of fish that are low in fat, as well as sharks, may be used as the raw material. Fresh stock yields a pure white and superior product, whereas, partially decomposed stock yields a yellow and inferior product with a salty taste and fishy aroma. The latter product, nevertheless, can be used for technical purposes.

DETAILED PROCEDURE FOR THE MANUFACTURE OF FISH ALBUMIN

The fish protein is first minced and then heated with stirring at 160° to 176°F., for one hour in an aqueous solution, containing 0.5% acetic acid. This produces partial hydrolysis and extracts mainly the connective tissues. It is then washed in cold water in a rotating perforated drum to remove the digested proteins and some of the acid. The residue is partially concentrated by pressing, leaving not more than 40% water in the press-cake.

The press-cake is broken up and is subjected to a continuous oil extraction for 6 to 8 hours, using either ethyl alcohol or trichlorethylene. The fat-free material is dried in 300-kg. lots, under vacuum, in a steam-jacketed drier for 2 to 3 hours at a temperature in the material of about 122°F. This dried insoluble material constitutes the technical grade of fish albumin.

To produce the pure food and pharmaceutical grades of fish albumin, the finely ground insoluble material is digested in a caustic soda solution, using 500 liters of water with 100 kg. of dry protein to which 6 to 8 gm. of caustic soda are added per 100 gm. of protein. Digestion is carried out for about one hour at 86°F., followed by another hour at from 176° to 194°F.

The progress of the digestion is followed by means of viscosity tests, under specified conditions.

After the caustic digestion is completed, the digest is neutralized to pH of 7 with acetic or lactic acid. The former is preferable since it leaves a nonhygroscopic product, although lactic acid yields a better flavored product.

Finally, the neutralized fluid is spray-dried, in air at 176°F. The air entering the drying chamber is at temperature of from 257° to 302°F.

The edible grade of fish albumin consists mostly of polypeptides with little or no free amino acids. Being 100% digestible, it has nutritional value although its amino acids variety is less than that of the original material. It can be used for all purposes for which egg-albumin is used.

EQUIPMENT REQUIRED FOR PRODUCING FISH ALBUMIN

The following equipment has been used to produce fish albumin, according to U. S. Fish and Wildlife Service (1946): (a) a steam-jacketed cooking tank with stirring apparatus and outlet to a perforated washing drum, (b) a perforated rotating washing drum wherein a flow of cold water frees the protein from acetic acid, hydrolysis products of the connective tissue, and extractives, (c) a sieve-bottomed reservoir for the washed material, (d) a hydraulic press which reduces the water content to 40%, (e) two continuous extractors for treatment with alcohol or trichloroethylene, (f) a steam-jacketed vacuum drier for recovery of solvents and drying of material in batches of 300 kg., (g) a grinding mill where the dried material is reduced to a fine powder for treatment with alkali, (h) steam-heated digestion tanks where the product in powdered form is digested and subsequently neutralized by acetic or lactic acid, and (i) a spray drying tower.

USES OF FISH ALBUMIN

Fish albumin has a wide range of useful applications in food and pharmaceutical products as whipping, suspending, or stabilizing agents. The technical grade, which is less pure, performs similar functions in certain industrial products. Its uses in the food industry includes its incorporation into the following products: ice cream, soup powders, puddings, confectionery, bakery products, mayonnaise, custard powder, and other similar items. The technical, or less refined grade of fish albumin has industrial uses in the manufacture of the following products: paints and varnishes, textiles, paper, synthetic resins, leather, lacquer, foam extinguishers, laundry services, cosmetics, and soap.

Technical Grade of Fish Albumin as a Stabilizer in the Foam-Rubber Industry

The technical grade of fish albumin could be used as a stabilizer in the foam-rubber industry. It acts as a protective colloid for the rubber ingredients. Only a small quantity of stabilizer is used in that industry, but large quantities of albumin could be consumed in the foam-rubber industry for the manufacture of pillows, mattresses, and other products. It must, however, compete in price with gelatin, glue, technical casein, or soybean proteins (Omansky 1964).

Requirements of a Protein Stabilizer in Rubber

A protein stabilizer must fulfill the following specifications (Omansky 1964) before it can be used in the rubber industry: (a) it must be odorless, retaining no fishy odor, (b) it should contain no copper or manganese, and (c) it must be dispersible in cold water. It could become dissolved or dispersed in an aqueous solution of ammonia or borax, forming a water-soluble dispersion.

Formulas for the Use of Fish Albumin in the Baking Industry

U. S. Fish and Wildlife Service (1946) gives formulas for the use of fish albumin in the manufacture of pastries. The following compositions and directions are given as being illustrative of the fish albumin used in that industry:

Pastry Dough

Without egg and fat
    100 gm. fish albumin (dry powder)⎫
    1,250 gm. sugar   ⎬ beaten together
    2,000 gm. (2 liters) water
    5,000 gm. flour   ⎭
    150 gm. ammonium carbonate, pinch salt, egg coloring and flavoring.
Mix flour and ammonium carbonate and proceed accordingly in the usual way.

Fat-Free Puff Pastry

      80 gm. fish albumin (dry powder)⎫
  2,000 gm. sugar
    300 gm. full egg (or 6 eggs) ⎬ beaten together
  1,200 gm. water
  5,000 gm. flour   ⎭

about $1^1/_2$ liters skimmilk or water
  120 gm. baking powder
  2,500 gm. fruit, egg coloring, flavoring, pinch salt
Directions: Flour, skimmilk, and other ingredients are beaten together.

Whipped Cream

With flour, without gelatin for filling-garnishing
    3 liters water or skim milk
500 gm. sugar
  40 gm. fish albumin (dry powder)
500 gm. flour
pinch salt
2 liters of water or skimmilk to be brought to boil
Mix the 500 gm. sugar, 50 gm. dry powder, and 500 gm. flour in the remaining liter water. This is added to the boiling water and mixed and allowed to boil vigorously and made to the desired volume. To the cream, any desired flavor may be added.

COMPARISON BETWEEN FISH ALBUMIN AND HYDROPHILIC COLLOIDS EXTRACTED FROM SEA PLANTS

Fish albumin has certain advantages as a stabilizer when compared to Irish moss and other similar sea plants in a number of instances, especially since fish albumins inherently possess nutritious properties and are readily digestible. The sea plant extractives belong to the complex polysaccharide group which, though they like the fish albumins have stabilizing, whipping, and suspending properties, are not readily digested and assimilated by humans. In food and pharmaceutical products requiring whipping, suspending, or stabilizing properties, fish albumin might be preferable to the hydrophilic colloidal extractives from sea plants.

PEPTONES

The hydrolysis or breakdown of proteins takes place in several stages, with each stage resulting in a molecule which is smaller than the one immediately preceding it. The intermediate hydrolytic products of proteins are generally classified as proteoses, peptones, polypeptides, and amino acids (Hawk et al. 1949).

The peptones, which are partially hydrolyzed proteins, differ somewhat in their properties from the complete proteins. For instance, peptones are soluble in water and are not heat coagulable. These properties render them particularly suitable for use in bacteriological culture media, especially when they are derived from complete proteins, i.e., proteins that contain all of the amino acids (Dunn 1964).

Peptones are particularly desirable in the cultivation of pathogenic bacteria, which generally require the partially hydrolyzed products of a complete protein. For bacteriological purposes, peptones are ordinarily prepared by the careful partial hydrolysis of meat, casein, or vegetable protein.

The Difco Laboratories, Inc. (1953) records, in its Difco Manual, the history of the use of peptone for the cultivation of microorganisms as follows: "Because of its [peptone's] content of amino acids and of other nitrogenous compounds which are readily utilized by bacteria, peptone soon became one of the most important constituents of culture media, as it still remains."

Fish proteins, especially fish muscle proteins, contain all of the amino acids in a favorable balance (see Chapter 11: Fish-Meal Production). Furthermore, fish also supply their own active proteolytic enzymes, i.e., the pyloric caeca of fish contain trypsin, and the stomachs of fish contain pepsin, both enzymes being active under their two different optimum pH values of 8.5 and 2.0, respectively. Consequently, fish peptones have been prepared and evaluated for their efficiency as bacteriological culture media.

PROCEDURES FOR THE PREPARATION OF PEPTONES

Peptones were prepared by Tarr and Deas (1948) from the flesh of lingcod, grey cod, starry flounder, and chum salmon, and were compared with three commercial preparations. The preliminary procedure applicable to the four different hydrolytic methods which Tarr and Deas evaluated, consisted of comminuting fish flesh and diluting each batch with an equal weight of water. The fish proteins were then hydrolyzed by one of the following four methods: (1) peptic enzyme hydrolysis, (2) tryptic enzyme hydrolysis, (3) acid hydrolysis, or (4) alkali hydrolysis.

A detailed procedure for each of the four methods of hydrolysis follows.

Peptic Enzyme Hydrolysis

The aqueous fish flesh suspension is first heated for from 5 to 10 minutes at 212°F. to kill the vegetative cells and is cooled to 98°F. The suspension is acidified to pH 2.0 with dilute hydrochloric acid and treated with comminuted fish intestinal mucosa which contain peptic enzymes (Johnston 1941). The suspension is then partially hydrolyzed through the peptone stage requiring at least two weeks incubation at 98°F.

Dassow (1964) points out that "in much seine-caught salmon, there is a reduced amount of the peptic enzyme in the viscera simply because the salmon have quit feeding several weeks previously and the digestive system has withered away to little or nothing. The salmon, of course, is soon to die and has little further need of digestive enzymes."

Tryptic Enzyme Hydrolysis

The aqueous fish flesh suspension is heated to 212°F. to kill the vegetative cells and is cooled to 98°F. The suspension is continuously maintained at pH 8.5 with a dilute lye solution, and is treated with comminuted pyloric caeca which contain tryptic enzymes. It is partially hydrolyzed through the peptone stage during its incubation at 98°F. for several days or several weeks. The suspension is preserved by adding some toluene and occasionally shaking it.

Acid Hydrolysis

The suspension is treated with hydrochloric or sulfuric acid and partially hydrolyzed through the peptone stage under steam pressure, at 250°F., for approximately five hours.

Alkali Hydrolysis

The hydrolysis is carried out in the same manner as in acid hydrolysis except that dilute lye is substituted for the acid. The hydrolyzed suspensions are filtered to remove residual solid material. Filtrates are neutralized. In the last two methods, residual lye or hydrochloric acid is removed by ion-exchange resins. The neutralized solutions are concentrated at a temperature not exceeding 212°F., and dried under a partial vacuum.

The powdered products, which range in color from a pale brown to a dark brown, resemble commercial peptones in odor and appearance. Most peptones are water soluble.

COMPARISON BETWEEN ACID, ALKALI, AND ENZYMATIC HYDROLYSES

A comparison of the end-products obtained from acid, alkali, and enzymatic hydrolyses indicates the following differences (Hawk *et al.* 1949):

Acid hydrolysis partially decomposes certain amino acids and completely destroys tryptophan, especially if the protein contains carbohydrate.

Alkali hydrolysis destroys, either partially or completely, the amino acids, cysteine, cystine, and arginine. In addition, all the amino acids lose their optical activity.

Enzymatic hydrolysis is relatively mild, i.e., none of the amino acids is destroyed. The hydrolysis is generally incomplete and it is time-consuming. It is also more costly than either acid or alkali hydrolysis.

EVALUATION OF FISH PEPTONES AS CONSTITUENTS OF BACTERIOLOGICAL CULTURE MEDIA

Evaluations of the various fish peptones as constituents of bacteriological culture media have been made, using strains of *Streptococcus haemolyticus* and *Clostridium botulinum* as the test organisms. The results indicated that the enzymatic hydrolyzed peptones were as good as, and sometimes even better than, three well-known commercial products for supporting bacterial growth but that the acid or alkali-hydrolyzed fish peptones proved to be inferior. Consequently, fish muscle proteins can yield peptones suitable for use as bacteriological culture media (Tarr and Deas 1948 and 1949).

Although a potential for the manufacture of peptones from fish has been shown, up to this time (1965), these peptones have not been standardized and utilized for bacteriological culture media in the United States possibly because of economic infeasibility.

AMINO ACIDS FROM FISH PROTEINS

Amino acids form the building blocks of the protein molecule. The nutritional value of a protein depends on the number and kind of amino acids that the protein contains. A high-quality protein contains all of the ten essential amino acids as well as nonessential ones in suitable proportions, and in readily digestible and assimilable form (Block and Bolling 1945).

Amino Acids in Fish

Fish proteins are high in nutritive value (Lanham and Lemon 1938). They contain all of the essential amino acids in a balanced amount and are readily digestible and assimilable. Fish proteins also contain the nonessential amino acids. In fact, naturally occurring amino acids are processed from residues of tuna and mackerel canning operations.

Table 21 indicates that the amino acid content of haddock compares favorably with that of other animal proteins such as thin beef carcass, cottage cheese, and eggs (Orr and Watt 1957).

Fish protein, therefore, can be used as a good raw material in amino acid preparation.

GENERAL METHOD OF PREPARING AMINO ACIDS

Hydrolysis

Amino acids can be prepared by hydrolyzing proteins with acids, alkalis, or enzymes under specified temperature and pH conditions. On hydrolysis the protein yields the following intermediate degradation products: proteoses, peptone, polypeptides and, finally, amino acids.

Each method of proteolysis has certain limitations. For a further discussion on this subject see section on Peptones, in this chapter.

TABLE 21

COMPARISON OF PER CENT PROTEIN AND AMINO ACID CONTENT (IN GRAMS PER 100 GM. EDIBLE
PORTION) OF FISH WITH THOSE OF OTHER ANIMAL PROTEINS AND PLANT PROTEINS   (ORR AND
WATT 1957)

Item → % Protein → Amino Acids	Haddock 18.2	Thin Beef Carcass 18.8	Cottage Cheese 17.0	Eggs (Chickens) 12.8	Pea Beans 21.4	Wheat Flour (White) 10.5
Tryptophan	0.181	0.220	0.179	0.211	0.199	0.129
Threonine	0.789	0.830	0.794	0.637	0.928	0.302
Isoleucine	0.923	0.984	0.989	0.850	1.216	0.483
Leucine	1.374	1.540	1.826	1.126	1.839	0.809
Lysine	1.596	1.642	1.428	0.819	1.589	0.239
Methionine	0.530	0.466	0.469	0.401	0.216	0.138
Phenylalanine	0.676	0.773	0.917	0.739	1.181	0.577
Valine	0.970	1.044	0.978	0.950	1.298	0.453
Arginine	1.025	1.212	0.802	0.840	1.287	0.466
Histidine	...	0.653	0.549	0.307	0.609	0.210

Table Courtesy U. S. Dept. of Agriculture.

Whenever amino acids are prepared for intravenous or parenteral injection, they must be free from pyrogens, or any partially hydrolyzed proteins which would cause a very severe immunological reaction (Miller 1964).

USES OF AMINO ACIDS

Amino acids and their salts could be administered to patients who suffer from gastrointestinal disorders, or who have been confined and underfed for a prolonged period as in prison camps, or have severe burns or fractures, in which case, natural proteins cannot be consumed. It is best to administer them by intravenous or parenteral injection, since pure amino acids have a disagreeable taste, when taken orally.

Healthy individuals need not take amino acids because the digestive tract has an abundance of proteolytic enzymes to carry out the natural hydrolysis (Beaser 1964).

GENERAL REMARKS ON FISH PROTEINS

Orr and Watt (1957) have summarized all analytical data available up to 1957, giving the per cent protein and the amino acid content of foods, based on 100 gm. of edible portion. These tables indicate the existence of a species variability in the amino acid content of fish, as well as in protein content. Mancuso (1964), has shown a method for identifying fish of various species by disc electrophoresis. This method is based on the fact that fish of various species differ sharply in total protein content and distribution of their protein fractions, which differences are readily shown by disc electrophoresis. Thompson (1964) pointed out that it would be useful to discuss the variations in the amino acid content and in the digestibility of the proteins of the various species of fish. She also stated that it would be useful to point out the ability of fish products to satisfy the amino acid requirements of man, fowl, ruminants, and mink. However, a discussion of these fascinating nutritional aspects of fish proteins is beyond the scope of this volume.

The main point to be made in presenting the section on "Amino Acids from Fish Protein" is to indicate that fish protein can be used as a source in the production of both the essential and the nonessential amino acids.

It is worthy of note that the three products discussed in this chapter, namely, fish albumin, peptone, and amino acids are fishery by-products with a potential adaptable especially to developing countries.

One large firm in the United States is producing peptones and peptides from fish. Fish solubles, which are relatively high in amino acids, are produced extensively in the United States to supplement poultry rations.

All of the essential and nonessential amino acids can be produced in pure form from fish. They could be used to supplement synthetic amino acids. In the United States, however, it is more economical to produce amino acids from casein or from soybean protein than to produce them from fish. This may not be true in developing countries.

BIBLIOGRAPHY

ANON. 1948. Pilot plant for fish albumin. Fisheries Newsletter 7, No. 3, 23–25.

BEASER, S. B. 1964. Personal communication. Boston, Mass.

BLOCK, R. J., and Bolling, D. 1945. The Amino Acid Composition of Proteins and Foods. Charles C. Thomas, Publisher. Springfield, Ill.

BORGSTROM, G. Editor. 1961–1962. Fish as Food. Volumes I and II. Academic Press, New York.

DASSOW, J. A. 1964. Personal communication. Seattle, Wash.

DEAS, C. P., and TARR, H. L. A. 1949. Amino acid composition of fishery products. J. Fisheries Res. Board Can. 7, 513–521.

DIFCO LABORATORIES INCORPORATED. 1953. Difco Manual of Dehydrated Culture Media and Reagents for Microbiological and Clinical Laboratory Procedures. 9th Edition. Detroit, Mich.

DREOSTI, G. M. 1947. Rough estimate of cost of producing fish albumin. Fishing Ind. Res. Inst., Progr. Rept. No. 3, Cape Town, Union of South Africa.

DUNN, C. G. 1964. Personal communication. Cambridge, Mass.

ELMAN, R. 1946. Amino acid mixtures. J. Am. Pharm. Assoc., Pract. Edition 7, No. 1, 13–20.

FROBISHER, M. 1953. Fundamentals of Microbiology. 5th Edition. Saunders, Philadelphia.

GORTNER, R. A., JR., and GORTNER, W. A. 1950. Outlines of Biochemistry. 3rd Edition. John Wiley and Sons, New York.

HAWK, P. B., OSER, B. L., and SUMMERSON, W. H. 1949. Practical Physiological Chemistry. 12th Edition. The Blakiston Co., Philadelphia.

JOHNSTON, W. W.   1941.   Tryptic enzymes from certain commercial fishes.   J. Fisheries Res. Board Can. 5, No. 3, 217–226.

LANDGRAF, R. G., JR.   1953.   Technical Note No. 27.   Alaska pollack: proximate composition; amino acid, thiamin and riboflavin content; use as mink feed.   Com. Fisheries Rev. 15, No. 7, 20–22 (Sep. No. 354).

LANHAM, W. B., JR., and LEMON, J. M.   1938.   Nutritive value for growth of some proteins of fishery products.   Food Research 3, 549–553.

MANCUSO, V. M.   1964.   Protein typing of some authentic fish species by disk electrophoresis.   J. Assoc. Off. Agr. Chemists 47, 841–844.

MEISTER, A.   1957.   Biochemistry of the Amino Acids.   Academic Press, New York.

MILLER, S. A.   1964.   Personal communication.   Boston, Mass.

OMANSKY, M.   1964.   Personal communication.   Cambridge, Mass.

ORR, M. L., and WATT, B. K.   1957.   Amino acid content of foods.   Home Economics Research Report No. 4.   U. S. Dept. Agr., Washington, D. C.

PATTON, A. R.   1946.   Proteins and amino acids in animal nutrition.   Flour and Feed 46, 12, and 22.

POTTINGER, S. R., and BALDWIN W. H.   1946.   The content of certain amino acids in seafoods.   Com. Fisheries Rev. 8, No. 8, 5–9 (Sep. No. 145.)

ROSE, W. C.   1937.   The nutritive significance of the amino acids and certain related compounds.   Science 86, 298–300.

SEAGRAN, H. L.   1953.   Amino acids content in salmon roe.   Com. Fisheries Rev. 15, No. 3, 31–34.   Tech. Note No. 25 (Sep 346.)

SHENSTONE, F. S.   1953.   Egg white and yolk substitutes.   Wiking Eiweiss. Food Preserv. Quart. 13, No. 3, 45–50.

STANSBY, M. E.   1953.   Composition of fish.   U. S. Fish and Wildlife Service, Fishery Leaflet 116.

STANSBY, M. E., et al.   1953.   Utilization of Alaska salmon cannery waste. U. S. Fish and Wildlife Service, Special Scientific Report: Fisheries No. 109.

SYKES, G.   Editor.   1956.   Constituents of Bacteriological culture media; a review of information available on methods of manufacture, prepared by the Standardization Subcommittee of the Society for General Microbiology. Cambridge University Press.

TARR, H. L. A., and DEAS, C. P.   1948.   The utilization of fish wastes.   Bacteriological peptones from fish.   Fisheries Res. Board Can., Progr. Rept. Pacific Coast Sta. No. 75, 43–45.   Vancouver, B. C.

TARR, H. L. A., and DEAS, C. P.   1949.   Bacteriological peptones from fish flesh.   J. Fisheries Res. Board Can. 7, No. 9, 552–560.

THOMPSON, M.   1964.   Personal communication.   Pascagoula, Miss.

U. S. FISH and WILDLIFE SERVICE,   1946.   Fishery Leaflet 210.   Certain aspects of the German fishing industry.   Report V. Wiking Eiweiss.

CHAPTER 16

Animal Feed

INTRODUCTION

The use of trash fish or industrial fish, fish scrap, and shrimp waste is not limited to the production of fish-meal and fish oil which are used as supplements to poultry feed rations. These nutritionally valuable and low-cost raw materials also have wide application in the broad field of animal feeding. They are utilized extensively in pet food formulations, particularly in cat food, and on fur farms, especially in mink feed. Fish liquefied and preserved with urea (Brody 1955A) constitutes another good supplement to animal feed.

The term fish scrap as used here refers to the entire waste portion of fish that remains after filleting. It embraces the entire skeletal structure of the fish, including head, tail, some skin, and the flesh adhering to the various bony structures, which escaped the filleting knife, but excluding the viscera. The flesh includes muscle tissue, cartilaginous connective tissue, and the other types of specialized proteinaceous tissues that adhere to the bony structure.

The extensive utilization of these nutritious and low-cost raw materials as animal feed supplements constitutes an economic advantage to the entire fishery industry (see Chapter 11).

For an excellent summary on the nutritive properties of fish, the reader is referred to two authoritative volumes edited by Borgstrom (1961–1962).

Pet Food

In the United States there are about 26,000,000 dogs and 29,000,000 cats. The total canine population is increasing approximately six times faster than the human population. Accordingly, most, if not all, canned or dry pet foods are very carefully compounded by the various manufacturers with the view of furnishing a ration which is nutritionally balanced.

The 1964 pet food business in the United States is estimated to be worth one-half billion dollars (*Boston Traveler*, 12/21/64, p.1).

In 1958, over 3,000,000,000 lb. of animal feed were prepared. Most of it was consumed by cats and dogs (Jones 1960). It is generally believed that cats relish a fish diet, while dogs prefer mostly meat, but there are many exceptions to this rule. In accordance with this general dietary preference, some pet food canners pack fish exclusively for cats and meat for dogs. Some manufacturers add limited amounts of cereal grains, such as soybean meal or corn meal, to various pet food formulations to reduce the raw material cost and to improve consistency, or body, of the canned product (Spiegel 1964). Whole trash fish or fish waste obtained from filleting or canning plants are used extensively in the various pet food formulations to supplant or to supplement high quality protein at a relatively low cost.

Canning of Pet Food

Preliminary Considerations.—Principles and procedures of canning foods for human consumption are applicable to the canning of pet food. The first essential in the manufacture of an acceptable canned product is to use fresh and wholesome ingredients.

The canning of decomposed raw ingredients would result in a low-quality pet food, which would be readily detected and rejected by pets. Cleanliness of a pet food processing plant should be maintained to the same degree as that of a cannery of human food (Usen 1964).

General Canning Procedure.—Fish and meat by-products are first coarsely ground. The fish is heated in a continuous pre-cooker with jets of live steam (Fig. 44) and is ground to a uniform consistency. Fish may

Courtesy of Usen Canning Co., Woburn, Mass.

FIG. 44.   CONTINUOUS PRE-COOKER

be canned directly as a whole fish pet food or specific amounts of supplementary ingredients may be admixed with it, such as ground meat or cereal grains with added vitamins and minerals, to produce a balanced pet food, using a ribbon type blender for batch mixing (Fig. 45).

The pet food mixture is filled into cans while hot. It is next sealed and transferred into a retort for processing. The temperature and time of retorting vary with the sizes of the cans.   Immediately after completion of processing, the cans are cooled to an average temperature of approximately 100°F., at which temperature drying of the cans is facilitated.   They are then labeled and cased in corrugated cardboard boxes (Usen 1964).

Not all pet food canning plants are of the continuous type.   Some plants operate in batch-wise manner.   Both types of plants use essentially the same processes, i.e., grinding, cooking, blending, filling, retorting, cooling, and packaging for shipment.

Courtesy of Usen Canning Co., Woburn, Mass.

FIG. 45.   RIBBON TYPE BLENDER FOR BATCH MIXING

Dehydration of Pet Food

There is another form of pet food, viz., dehydrated.   It is generally prepared by blending fish meal, cereal grains, and nutritional supplements, e.g., vitamins and minerals.   This dry mixture is steamed to moisten it somewhat, then extruded into a pallet shape.   This product is very stable because of its low moisture content.   It is a very popular type of pet food (Spiegel 1964).

Typical Composition and Analysis of Canned Pet Food.—A typical commercial pack of canned pet food may contain the following ingredients: fresh fish, meat and meat products, ground corn, soy grits, cracked wheat, cracked barley, ground bone, salt, and sufficient water for processing. Some foods have added vitamins.   A typical pack may have the following approximate composition: protein, 10 to 15%; crude fat, 2 to 8%; crude fiber, 1%; ash, 4% maximum; salt, 1% maximum; water, 74% maximum.

MINK FEED

The offal obtained from filleting bottom fish has been used successfully in feeding mink. In the Pacific Northwest, where mink farming has become an important industry, as much as 70% of mink feed consists of fish.

Processing of Fish for Mink Feed

Minks are very sensitive to changes in their diet. Therefore, only fresh fish waste, low in fat content, can be used safely. When whole fish are used, such as trash fish, they must first be washed thoroughly. The fish are then comminuted, dispensed in paper bags, frozen, preferably to $-40°F.$, and stored at $-10°$ to $0°F.$, for subsequent use.

The raw fish used for mink feed should not be of a species that has thiaminase, i.e., the enzyme that destroys thiamin (Lee 1948). In the absence of thiamin in fish, the minks may develop Chastek's paralysis (Sanford 1957). Furthermore, the fish should not contain any more than eight per cent fat and preferably less. A high content of polyunsaturated fatty acids in the raw fish may cause "yellow fat disease." (Lalor et al. 1951).

SWINE FEED

A good initial growth of swine has been obtained in Denmark when feeding fish offal. Care must be taken to stop feeding fish six to eight weeks before slaughtering to avoid residual fish flavor in the meat.

UREA TREATED FISH AS A FEED SUPPLEMENT

Brody (1955A) described a new method for simultaneously solubilizing and preserving fish entrails, fish offal, or whole fish with the aid of urea. It is especially effective on the soft animal tissues of fish, poultry, or mammals. However, it is not effective on a few hard parts such as the skeleton and eyeballs of fish and the stomach of poultry and mammals.

One of the important features of this patented process is the fact that the solubilization of the proteinaceous material is carried out at room temperature. Also, it does not involve the use of expensive equipment. Furthermore, in the solubilized form, the product can be readily admixed with other ingredients.

Only during evaporation does the temperature of the product rise to a maximum of about $140°F.$, for a very short period of time. The solubilized fish can be concentrated to about 65% solids. In this high concentration it retains a fluid consistency and is well preserved so that it may be kept at room temperature for several years, without showing any signs of deterioration. In addition, because the temperature of the material throughout the process is low, any proteinaceous material treated in this manner would tend to have its original nutritional value affected very little.

The urea solubilized fish product cannot be dried in the liquefied form. In order to be able to dry it, the urea is converted to yeast, by diluting the solubilized product sufficiently with water and by setting up conditions favorable to a fish-molasses-yeast and urea fermentation (Brody 1955B).

BIBLIOGRAPHY

BELL, J. M., and THOMPSON, C. 1951. Freshwater fish as an ingredient of mink rations. Bull. 92, Fisheries Res. Board Can., Ottawa.

BORGSTROM, G., and HEIGHWAY, A. J. Editors. 1961. Atlantic Ocean Fisheries. Fishing News (Books) Ltd., London.

BORGSTROM, G. Editor. 1961–1962. Fish as Food. Volumes I and II. Academic Press, New York.

BRODY, J. 1955A. Treatment of proteinaceous materials. U. S. Pat. 2,717,835. Sept. 13.

BRODY, J. 1955B. Process of converting urea. U. S. Pat. 2,717,836. Sept. 13.

BUTLER, C. 1945. Survey of available and potential fish waste for reduction in Washington and Oregon. Fishery Market News 7, 2, 8–15 (Sep. No. 91.)

CRAVEN, H. J. 1953. Alaska salmon potential. National Fisheries Yearbook, 107–108, 113.

DUNN, C. G. 1964. Personal communication. Cambridge, Mass.

FELLERS, C. R., LEMACK, N. I., and LIVINGSTON, G. E. 1958. Chemical and enzymic hydrolysis of fish scales. Com. Fisheries Rev. 20, No. 8, 1–3 (Sep. No. 517).

HEEN, E., and KREUZER, R. Editors. 1962. Fish in Nutrition. Fishing News (Books) Ltd., London.

JONES, W. G. 1960. Fishery resources for animal food. Fishery Leaflet 501. U. S. Fish and Wildlife Service. (A collection of reprints from Petfood Industry.)

LALOR, R. J., LEOSCHKE, W. L., and ELVEHJEM, C. A. 1951. Yellow fat in mink. J. Nutr. 45, No. 2, 183–188.

LANDGRAF, Jr., R. G., MIYAUCHI, D. T., and STANSBY, M. E. 1951. Utilization of Alaska salmon cannery waste as a source of feed for hatchery fish. Com. Fisheries Rev. 13, 11A (November Supplement), 26–33 (Sep. No. 298).

LANDGRAF, JR., R. G. 1953. Alaska pollack: proximate composition; amino acid, thiamin, and riboflavin content; use as mink feed. Com. Fisheries Rev. 15, No. 7, 20–22 (Sep. No. 354).

LEE, C. F. 1948. Thiaminase in fishery products: a review. Com. Fisheries Rev. 10, No. 4, 7–17 (Sep. No. 202).

LEEKLEY, J. R., LANDGRAF, JR., R. G., BJORK, J. E., and HAGEVIG, W. A. 1952. Salmon cannery waste for mink feed. U. S. Fish and Wildlife Service, Fishery Leaflet No. 405.

MORRISON, F. B. 1956. Feeds and Feeding. 22nd Edition. Morrison, Ithaca, N. Y.

NATIONAL RESEARCH COUNCIL. 1944–1945. Bulletin Series. Recommended Nutrient Allowances for Domestic Animals: I. Poultry; II. Swine; III. Dairy Cattle; IV. Beef Cattle; V. Sheep. Washington, D. C.

NIELSEN, K. H. 1955. Feeding mackerel and herring to mink kits. Dansk Pel-soyraul *18*, 223–225.

SANFORD, F. B. 1950A. Utilization of fishery by-products in Washington and Oregon. U. S. Fish and Wildlife Service, Fishery Leaflet No. 370.

SANFORD, F. B. 1957A. Utilization of fish waste in northern Oregon for mink feed. Com. Fisheries Rev. *19*, No. 12, 40–47 (Sep. No. 496).

SANFORD, F. B. 1957B. Fish hatchery food from anchovies caught near Santa Barbara, Calif. Com. Fisheries Rev. *19*, No. 2, 16–19 (Sep. No. 471).

SPIEGEL, L. S. 1964. Personal communication. Boston, Mass.

STANSBY, M. E., *et al.* 1953. Utilization of Alaskan salmon cannery waste. Special Scientific Report: Fisheries No. 109. U. S. Fish and Wildlife Service.

U. S. DEPT. of AGRICULTURE. 1937. Food and Life (Yearbook of Agriculture).

USEN, R. D. 1964. Personal communication. Boston, Mass.

WATT, P. R. 1952A. The feeding of marine fishes to mink. National Fur News *24*, No. 6, 12–13, 25.

WIGUTOFF, N. B. 1952. Potential markets for Alaska salmon cannery waste. Com. Fisheries Rev. *14*, No. 8, 5–12 (Sep. No. 320).

WHITEHAIR, C. K., SCHAEFER, A. E., and ELVEHJEM, C. A. 1949. Nutritional deficiencies in mink with special reference to hemorrhagic gastroenteritis "yellow fat" and anemia. J. Am. Vet. Med. Assoc. *115*, 54–58.

CHAPTER 17

Plant Food

INTRODUCTION

Plant foods, more popularly known as fertilizers, are nutrients which are added to soil to increase the quantity and quality of crops. Continued cultivation of vegetables, fruits, or any other form of plant life without the addition of adequate plant food to the soil, will deplete the soil of its natural fertility, or mineral content, and will result in a low yield and in poor quality crops.

From the earliest days of recorded agricultural history up to about the middle of the nineteenth century, farmers used to fertilize their soil with organic matter such as manure or ground up bones. They were aware of the fact, without knowing the reason, that when these materials were added to the soil, a better and more profitable crop yield was obtained.

Fish offal or trash fish can be converted into a fertilizer by digesting it with sulfuric acid. This process, developed in Japan, reduces the fish odor, converts some of the fish protein into ammonium sulfate, and renders the bone phosphate absorbable by plants.

ORGANIC FARMING OR GARDENING

The essence of organic farming or gardening consists of the utilization of naturally occurring organic materials (Fig. 46) instead of chemical fertilizers, to maintain fertility of the soil. A classical example is the practice of the North American Indians for obtaining a larger corn crop yield by "planting a fish in every hill of corn." Organic farming has a very limited but definite following at the present time. As an example of this, the use of liquid fish fertilizers is becoming more and more popular. They are, however, relatively low in nitrogen content.

Nitrogen is an essential element in a fertilizer, for boosting plant growth and development. Nitrogen, along with magnesium is mainly responsible for the green color in foliage (Bear 1938).

ENRICHING NITROGEN CONTENT OF PROTEINACEOUS MATERIAL WITH UREA

When a high organic nitrogen content is required in an organic fertilizer, proteinaceous material can be enriched by solubilizing it with urea in accordance with a patented process (Brody 1955A, See Chapter 16). In the concentrated form a fish-urea blend is well preserved for several years.

Courtesy of International Minerals and Chemical Corp., Woburn, Mass.

FIG. 46. BAGGING MELLO-GREEN

An organic fertilizer at IMC's Woburn plant

A number of advantages are gained by using this fertilizer. These advantages are enumerated in the following section.

ADVANTAGES OF USING LIQUEFIED PROTEINACEOUS MATERIALS AS FERTILIZERS WHEN SOLUBILIZED WITH UREA

When proteinaceous offal is liquefied with the aid of urea (.Brody 1955A, see Chapter 16), the resulting fluid fertilizer does not leach out nearly as readily as when inorganic salts such as ammonium sulfate or sodium nitrate are used to supply nitrogen. This is true because the liquefied protein molecules are still in their original protein or proteose stages but not in the peptone, polypeptide, or amino acid stages. The large size of these molecular aggregates retards their loss of nitrogen by leaching.

Liquefied proteinaceous material, being an organic compound must undergo several hydrolytic changes by the soil bacteria before it becomes available to plants. This organic fertilizer, therefore, tends to liberate nitrogen gradually, thus making it available to the plants through most of the growing season. In this way, crops may be furnished with a supply of available nitrogen, with one application, during most of the growing period.

Because of the fact that urea tends to furnish available nitrogen to plants faster than proteinaceous material, the addition of urea results in a better balance of the available nitrogen supply than is obtained from proteinaceous material alone. First, available nitrogen is supplied by the urea and subsequently it is furnished by the gradually hydrolyzed liquid proteinaceous material.

Advocates of organic farming say that organic fertilizer contains most of the trace elements in soluble form. Liquefied proteinaceous material could be used either as a "top dressing" or "side dressing"; or it could be incorporated in a liquid fertilizer to furnish liquid organic nitrogen, phosphorus, and potassium.

At the beginning of the vegetable planting season, or even before planting, especially in sandy soils, a *complete fertilizer,* containing nitrogen, phosphorus, potassium, and magnesium, is applied to the soil. During the growing season, several additions of nitrogen are made. These nitrogen applications are referred to as *top-dressings* or *side-dressings* which are ordinarily supplied as ammonium sulfate, sodium nitrate, ammonium nitrate, or potassium nitrate. These extra nitrogen applications during the growing season are essential since they supplement the original inorganic nitrogen content of the *complete fertilizer* which has been lost by leaching.

Urea-solubilized fish offal does not have strong characteristic fish odor, does not change the quality of the soil, is not readily leachable from the soil by excessive moisture, and is absorbed by plants at a lower rate than inorganic fertilizers.

In addition to the above mentioned advantages, all the favorable points enumerated in the next section under the heading, "Advantages in Using Liquid Fertilizers," apply here as well.

ADVANTAGES OF USING LIQUID FERTILIZERS

There are a number of advantages in using liquid fertilizers in contrast to dry fertilizers. They are as follows: (1) liquid fertilizers are relatively easier to apply and require less labor to handle than dry fertilizers, (2) a more uniform distribution of fertilizer can be obtained when efficient dispersing machinery is used, (3) fertilization and watering can be carried out simultaneously, and (4) liquid fertilizers cannot be blown away by strong winds as dry fertilizers can be.

COMMERCIAL FERTILIZERS

With the development of inorganic chemistry and particularly with von Liebig's extensive research in agricultural chemistry about the middle of the nineteenth century, the use of inorganic compounds as fertilizers was established. These compounds furnish the three elements which are of *primary* importance to plants; namely, nitrogen, phosphorus, and potassium, abbreviated NPK. Calcium, magnesium, and sulfur are known as the *secondary* elements. *Trace* elements consists of iron, zinc, manganese, copper, boron, and molybdenum. It is essential that all these elements should be used in their proper form and proportion in order to produce the best crops.

Commerical fertilizers can be produced in highly concentrated forms, particularly the mixed fertilizers which contain all of the three major elements, NPK, in one homogeneous mixture. The percentage of each of the three major nutrients must be declared on the label. Thus a ratio of 5-10-5 on the label refers to 5% nitrogen expressed as nitrogen, (N); 10% phosphorus expressed as phosphorus pentoxide, (P_2O_5); and 5 % potassium expressed as potassium oxide, (K_2O). Trace elements are usually incorporated in the mixed fertilizers.

It is not compulsory to declare the addition of trace elements, but if a declaration is made, the amounts added must be declared.

QUANTITIES OF COMMERCIAL FERTILIZERS CONSUMED IN THE UNITED STATES AND AVERAGE PLANT FOOD CONTENT

The quantities of commercial fertilizers consumed in the United States during 1940, 1950, 1955, and 1961 and the average plant food content are shown in Table 22.

TABLE 22

QUANTITIES OF COMMERCIAL FERTILIZERS CONSUMED IN THE UNITED STATES (1940–1961) AND AVERAGE PLANT FOOD CONTENT. ALL FERTILIZERS

Year	Quantity, 1,000 tons	Nitrogen, %	Phosphoric Oxide, %	Potassium, %
1940	9,360	4.8	10.4	4.9
1950	20,991	5.9	10.0	6.6
1955	22,194	8.7	10.1	8.4
1956	22,709	9.4	10.1	8.5
1957	22,516	10.1	10.2	8.6
1958	25,308	10.6	10.1	8.7
1959	24,877	11.0	10.3	8.7
1960	25,567	11.8	10.3	8.5
1961 (Prel)	26,624	12.7	10.4	8.5

Table courtesy of U. S. Department of Agriculture, Economic Research Service.

CONCLUDING REMARKS

There is a place for liquid organic fertilizer in home horticulture, floriculture, and vegetable greenhouse production. It is particularly suited for general farming in areas of high rainfall because of its resistance to leaching (Young 1964).

BIBLIOGRAPHY

ALLISON, F. E. 1931. Forms of nitrogen assimilated by plants. Quart. Rev. Biol. 6, 313.

ANDREWS, W. B. 1947. The Response of Crops and Soils to Fertilizers and Manures. 3rd Edition. W. B. Andrews, State College, Mississippi.

BEAR, F. E. 1938. Theory and Practice in the Use of Fertilizers. 2nd Edition. John Wiley and Sons, New York.

BRODY, J. 1955A. Treatment of proteinaceous materials. U. S. Pat. 2,717,835. Sept. 13.

BRODY, J. 1955B. Process of converting urea. U. S. Pat. 2,717,836. Sept. 13.

COLLINGS, G. H. 1941. Commercial Fertilizers. 3rd Edition. The Blakiston Co., Philadelphia.

EASEY, B. 1952. Practical Organic Gardening. 1st Edition. Faber and Faber Ltd., London.

GUSTAFSON, A. F. 1939. Handbook of Fertilizers. Their Sources, Make Up, Effects and Use. 3rd Edition. Orange Judd Publishing Co., Inc., New York.

HARTWELL, B. L. 1932. The influence of fertilizers on crop quality. Proc. Nat. Fertilizer Assoc. Section II.

JOHNSON, T. C. 1924. Effects of organic matter in maintaining soil fertility for truck crop production. Proc. Am. Soc. Hort. Sci., 277.

LAUGHLIN, C. S. 1954. Fertilize Soil from the Sea. Perpetua Press. Portland, Me.

MERZ, A. R. 1940. Selecting fertilizers. U.S. Dept. Agr. Circ. 487.

PIERRE, W. H. 1931. Effect of nitrogenous fertilizers on soil acidity. Ind. Eng. Chem. 23, 1440.

REHLING, C. J., and TRUOG, E. 1939. Activated sludge. Ind. Eng. Chem. 11, 281.

RODALE, J. I. 1948. The Organic Front. Rodale Press. Emmaus, Pa.

RODALE PRESS. Organic Farming and Gardening. A monthly magazine. Rodale Press, Emmaus, Pa.

ROSS, W. H., and MEHRING, A. L. 1938. Mixed fertilizers. U.S. Dept. Agr. Yearbook.

SHEAR, M. J., WASHBURN, M., and KRAMER, B. 1929. Composition of bone. J. Biol. Chem. 83, 697.

CHAPTER 13

Fish Protein Concentrate (Fish Flour)

INTRODUCTION

The biblical admonition: "not by bread alone doth man live" (Deuteronomy, Chapter 8,) has a literal as well as a philosophical meaning. It strikes the keynote of the entire problem of enrichment of bread and cereals with a high-quality protein concentrate which is adequately rich in lysine.

Actually, from a nutritional standpoint, man cannot easily survive on a bread diet or on a diet consisting mostly of cereal grains because all cereal grains are low in content and quality of protein (Scrimshaw and Bressani 1960). They are particularly low in lysine, an essential amino acid (Harris 1964).

Lysine is "essential" because it cannot be synthesized by the body and it must be supplied either by the consumption of an animal protein or a balanced vegetable protein. A practical way to supplement this nutritional deficiency is by eating meat, fish, eggs, and dairy products which supply high-quality proteins. But approximately two billion people, out of a world population of about three billion, cannot afford to buy these nutritious but expensive products (U. S. Fish and Wildlife Service, Report No. 3). Nor is there enough of these foods available to feed the exploding world population.

The problem, therefore, resolves itself simply to the finding of an inexpensive way to fortify or to supplement bread and all other bakery products, as well as the cereal grains, with an inexpensive high-quality protein that is properly preserved and stabilized to retain its nutritive quality and that will correct the amino acid imbalance in the diet and will particularly supply the necessary lysine and methionine of which there is a serious shortage.

Levin (1964) says that fish protein concentrate, popularly known as fish flour, when correctly processed, meets the desired requirements and that no other dry animal protein in commercial form meets these requirements except, perhaps, nonfat milk powder. Eggs and whole milk powder are not stable.

Levin further stated that, while lysine is significant in cereal fortification, fish is marginal in methionine. Thus, cereals rich in methionine and low in lysine supplement fish flour, low in methionine, and rich in lysine.

The absence of such nutritional supplementation leads to malnutrition which is the forerunner of a combination of ill-effects that manifest them-

209

selves adversely in physical, mental, political, and social ways (Pariser 1962).

To overcome the world shortage of high-quality proteins, particularly among the growing children of the poor inhabitants of Central American countries and Panama who use largely a starchy diet, Incap, the Institute of Nutrition of Central America and Panama, was established in 1949. Its formation was first proposed by Dr. Robert S. Harris, professor of nutrition at M.I.T. INCAP is a research cooperative among Costa Rica, El Salvador, Guatemala, Honduras, Nicaragua, and Panama. The Director of INCAP for 12 years was Dr. Nevin S. Scrimshaw, who is now head of the Department of Nutrition and Food Science at M.I.T.

Scrimshaw and Bressani (1960) succeeded in efforts to overcome this critical nutritional deficiency by developing vegetable combinations of high protein value with a balanced amino acid content, at low cost, using inexpensive vegetables that are indigenous to Central America. These vegetable mixtures were named Incaparina and have been accepted by the people of Guatemala. They are most suitable for children one to five years of age who, after weaning, are not given an adequate protein diet.

These vegetable mixtures prevent kwashiorkor, a children's disease resulting from severe protein malnutrition. Scrimshaw's basic research has set a precedent in showing the way to relieve this type of malnutrition the world over, by utilizing similar combinations prepared from vegetables indigenous to the various parts of the globe, at low cost, but high in nutritive value. Thus, he has helped immeasurably to advance the frontiers of this essential phase in nutrition.

Gaining flavor acceptance of an Incaparina-type of product in other countries of Central America, and in various parts of the globe that might be using local materials, constitutes a baffling problem for each individual locality. People generally eat what they like, but not what is good for them. Therefore considerable effort and technological know-how has to be applied to each new Incaparina-type product before it becomes locally acceptable.

While these developments constitute a great forward stride toward solving the serious problem of high-quality protein shortage, nutritionists and food technologists, ever mindful of the skyrocketing increase in world population, must look for other sources of high-quality proteins to make up for this global dietary deficiency.

The limitation of the earth's production of vegetable proteins might be evaluated more accurately in the light of the following statistics: approximately 30% of the earth's surface is land, occupying about $33^{1}/_{2}$ billion acres. Of this land total only four billion acres are available as potential crop land of which 80% is already under cultivation.

If the remaining 20% of tillable soil were utilized to its maximum yield, it would supply at best, enough food for the entire present world population, without regard for the exceedingly large anticipated increase in population (U. S. Fish and Wildlife Service, Report No. 3).

The world population, at its present rate of growth, will double by the year 2000. Consequently, it is essential to proceed with "full steam ahead," in further alleviating the world shortage of high-quality proteins by exploiting every possible source of a balanced animal protein, for example, by utilizing fish proteins which have, in addition to a high lysine content, a favorable balance of all other amino acids plus vitamins and minerals and which are readily digestible.

Any of the thousands of fish species that exist under the 70% of the globe's surface occupied by various bodies of water could be used as a source of complete protein supplementation. With proper management in the prevention of over-fishing any one area, the supply of fish in the ponds, lakes, rivers, and oceans would be as inexhaustible as the supply of energy from the sun, which propagates life in the waters as well as on land. Accordingly, over 23 seacoast countries have attempted to solve the basic problems connected with the production of a dehydrated fish protein concentrate, that would supplement vegetable proteins. (U. S. Fish and Wildlife Service, Report No. 1).

Levin (1964) stated that dehydration alone will not stabilize fish. The concentrate must be defatted. In fact, it has been found that phosphatides must be removed, or reversion will occur. This has been a difficulty with many methods that appear sound. For example, heptane, a nonpolar solvent, removes the glycerides but it takes many washes of alcohol to remove the phosphatides which heptane does not remove; thus, the use of heptane is unsuccessful in the first step of making fish flour.

The VioBin Corp., Monticello, Ill., uses a polar solvent that removes the phosphatides and thus the amines and associated substances, which are responsible for fishy taste in the meal after the oil is removed, can be eliminated with a few washes with alcohol (Levin 1964).

AVAILABILITY OF FISH

Marine biologists estimate conservatively that the seas could supply 500 billion pounds of fish annually (U. S. Fish and Wildlife Service, Report No. 2). Actually, only about 15% of this potential is being harvested from the various bodies of water. U. S. fishermen could harvest over 12 billion pounds of fish annually and still not exhaust the supply in our surrounding waters (U. S. Fish and Wildlife Service, Report No. 5). This quantity of fish is two and one-half times the current U. S. harvest.

The various bodies of water could supply high-quality animal protein in the form of fish protein concentrate to feed some of the expanding world population. Protein is sadly lacking in the diet of the many developing countries in Asia, Africa, and South America because of their rapid population growth (Pariser 1962). Even in the United States and Canada, and in most of the European countries, where the supply of meat, fish, eggs, and dairy products is relatively abundant, fish protein concentrates could be used to enrich bread, cereal grains, infant and geriatric foods.

PROCEDURES FOR THE MANUFACTURE OF FISH PROTEIN CONCENTRATES

A number of procedures have been developed for the manufacture of fish protein concentrate, each based upon a somewhat different principle. The outstanding contribution to this development was made by the Vio-Bin Corporation of Monticello, Illinois (U. S. Fish and Wildlife Service, Report No. 1). The pioneering efforts of Levin (1959) resulted in the successful Azeotropic Solvent Process for fish flour, or fish protein concentrate. Fish meal manufacture was then developed and put into large scale operation.

As recently as August 1963, the VioBin Corp. was still the only firm in the world that produced fish flour commercially from whole fish. The VioBin Corp. carried out many experiments in the United States and in other countries, proving the efficiency of their process and demonstrating the high quality of their products. The fact was conclusively demonstrated that it is possible to produce a highly nutritious and stable protein concentrate from whole fish, on a large scale, at low cost. Accordingly, a brief description of the VioBin process and a discussion of its salient features follows.

The VioBin Process

Description of Process.—The VioBin process is a low-temperature azeotropic dehydration-extraction procedure carried out with the aid of ethylene dichloride, which is a water-immiscible fat solvent. The process is essentially as follows (Levin 1964): The raw fish is first mechanically ground into small particles and suspended in ethylene dichloride.

The entire mixture is put into a solvent cooker and heated to boiling by indirect steam. A constant boiling mixture is formed with the solvent. The azeotropic distillation temperature is 160°F., at atmospheric pressure. The solvent itself boils at 181°F., and water at 212°F. The azeotrope boils below both boiling points, namely 160°F.

The azeotropic distillation removes the water in vapor form and dissolves the oil simultaneously. The miscella, i.e., the oil-solvent solution, is removed from the vessel continuously while the dehydrated defatted meal is removed for desolventizing. The phosphatides also are removed by the azeotropic distillation.

This product is nondeodorized fish flour. The VioBin Corp. is making 6,500 tons of it annually and selling almost all of it for animal feed. The amines and associated compounds that give the defatted product a fishy taste are extracted with methyl alcohol.

Basic Requirements for Manufacturing Fish Meal by the VioBin Process.—In order to produce a stable and standard fish meal that would retain all chemical and biological values of the fish from which it is produced, Levin (1959) suggests adherence to the following basic requirements: (1) the entire fish, including the solubles, should be processed, (2) low temperatures must be used in defatting and drying the fish, so as not to adversely affect the finished product, and (3) standardization of fish meal must be made, first, on the basis of biological value, using an animal assay for determining protein quality and, second, a biological determination for the unidentified growth factors.

The Advantages Derived from the VioBin Process may be summarized as follows (Levin 1963): (1) the azeotropic solvent method yields a fish flour for human consumption or fish meal for animal feed which is stable and uniform in quality, (2) this is a contained chemical process that produces no pollution of the air or water, (3) the original nutritive value of the whole fish is retained in the fish flour or fish meal because of the retention of the soluble solids together with their inherent nutrients and growth factors, removed in processes for making conventional fish meal, therefore, the finished product retains its original high biologic value—digestibility as well as APF (animal protein factors), (4) defatted fish meal has no fish oil, therefore,it does not impart any fishy flavor to eggs, meat, or milk, when the meal is added to poultry or animal feeds, (5) fish flour may be produced by the VioBin process either completely deodorized, partially deodorized, or it might retain the fishy odor and flavor, whenever deodorization is not necessary,[1] (6) Up to 5% of nondeodorized fish flour can be added to certain foods without imparting detectable fish odors, (7) "reversion" of fishy flavor does not occur in VioBin fish flour, (8) ethylene dichloride is nontoxic and traces are innocuous to health,[2] (9) defatted

[1] It is important to note that deodorization is necessary only in Latin America and in other parts of the world where the fish taste would be rejected. By far, the greatest number of human beings who now need and will continue to need fish flour do not object and, in some instances, desire the fish taste.

[2] This is based on a statement from the National Academy of Sciences: "The problem of solvent residues from ethylene dichloride or petroleum fractions was considered not to be of concern but the use of other chlorinated solvents may be of concern." See October 29, 1962: "Report of Temporary Committee on Questions Submitted by Secretary of Interior Concerning Fish Protein Concentrates."

whole fish is being used effectively in dry dog and cat feed rations, and is substituted for milk, in part, in calf and pig rations, (10) the source of raw material for producing fish flour or fish meal can be any species of whole fish, whether oily or nonoily. When fish offal is used as the raw material, a nutritionally low-quality protein will be produced because of the large amount of bone in the offal. The uniqueness of the VioBin process lies in the fact that it uses whole fish. No offal is used in the product to be used for human food, and (11) a stable fish oil is recovered.

Analyses of VioBin Whole Fish Flour

	Deodorized	Nondeodorized
Protein (Nx6.25),%	80.8	74
Ash,%	16.3	17.3
Moisture,%	3.6	7.2
Fat	Trace	1.5%

Comparing the analytical data of VioBin's whole fish flour with the Tentative Specifications given on pages (218, 220), it is evident that the protein content of the VioBin product exceeds by a considerable margin the minimum requirement.

Cost of Producing VioBin's Whole Fish Flour.—As recently as September 1963, whole fish flour could be made for 15 cents a pound in any country where the deodorized product is desired or at 11 cents a pound in any country in Africa or the Far East where the nondeodorized product can be used, and is preferred.

VioBin's Research In Evaluating the Nutritional Quality of their Fish Protein Concentrates.—A VioBin solvent rendering process flow chart is shown in Fig. 47.

A brief summary of a few of the tests of VioBin products follows.

Graham (1962) and his associates of Peru showed that fortifying 90% white wheat flour with 10% of VioBin's fish flour would result in a product which is equal in nutritional value to a superior type of milk product called Similac, in curing of kwashiorkor and marasmus (severe caloric undernutrition), which are known to affect literally millions of children in various parts of the world. Furthermore, this combination of wheat flour and fish flour when used with suitable amounts of oil and sugar could also serve as a substitute for mother's milk, reducing, thereby, the high infant mortality caused by a lack of breast feeding where no other suitable substitute is available. The cost would be less than one cent a day per child.

Another series of controlled tests indicated that the same effect is obtained when $7\frac{1}{2}$% fish meal is added to corn (maize).[3]

Further, a 90% rice and 10% fish flour mixture was shown to be equal in biological value to egg.[3]

---

[3] Private communications on hitherto unpublished reports (Levin 1963).

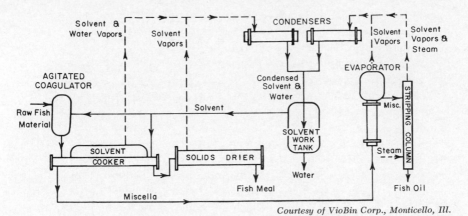

Courtesy of VioBin Corp., Monticello, Ill.

FIG. 47. VIOBIN SOLVENT RENDERING PROCESS FLOW CHART

Pretorius and Wehmeyer (1964) assessed the nutritive value of fish flours, using a VioBin product, versus dried skim milk in the treatment of convalescent kwashiorkor patients. They concluded that no differences exist between the efficacy of VioBin fish flour and that of dried skim milk in this treatment. They concluded, further, that high quality fish flour would be of considerable value in the prevention of protein malnutrition.

These tests, carried out on standard fish flour, all clearly point to the fact that this fish protein concentrate is an excellent source of a high-quality protein because it contains a favorable balance of all essential amino acids, plus minerals in their original and practically unmodified forms.

Notwithstanding the many advantages derived from the VioBin process, the Food and Drug Administration views it with disfavor on the basis of aesthetic acceptability. On the other hand, the National Academy of Sciences has gone on record as saying that whole fish flour is acceptable.[4]

Other Methods for Fish Protein Concentrate Production

A number of other procedures for the manufacture of fish protein concentrate have been developed. Two of them will be described here. They are as follows: (1) powdered fish production, and (2) production of edible fish protein (fish flour) from cod and haddock.

Each of these processes illustrates an approach which is somewhat different from that of other processes. A process described in a British

---

[4] See October 29, 1962: "Report of Temporary Committee on Questions Submitted by Secretary of Interior Concerning Fish Protein Concentrates." It states: "The committee concluded that a wholesome, safe, and nutritious product can be made from whole fish."

patent uses ethyl alcohol and acetone, while a Canadian method uses iso-propanol. These procedures are as follows.

Powdered Fish Production (Brit. Pat. 727,072).—The object is to manu-facture a tasteless and odorless powdered fish meal for human consumption by the practically complete removal of its oil content. The process is carried out in three stages: (1) pulped fish is kneaded for about 45 min. with its own weight of acetone at 122°F. and the solids are thoroughly dried under vacuum, (2) the dried fish pulp is kneaded and heated for about 45 min. with its own weight of 90% (by weight) ethyl alcohol, to disintegrate the tissues and the mixture is again dried under vacuum, and (3) fish pulp is again kneaded and boiled for about 30 min. with 90% (by weight) of ethyl alcohol, equal to half the original volume of the fish. The liquid phase is then drained off and residual traces of alcohol are re-moved by sucking warm air through the mass.

The dried fish is subsequently pulverized by passing it through a grinder and sieve. The two solvents, acetone and ethyl alcohol are re-covered by distillation. The oil is separated from the water by decanta-tion. Finally, the separated oil is further purified.

Process Using Cod and Haddock (Guttman and Vandenheuvel 1957).—This process consists of two major steps: (1) acid treatment of offal, and (2) isopropanol extraction of oil and water from press-cake.

A description of these steps follows.

(a) *Acid Treatment of Offal.*—An aqueous suspension of ground fresh offal is adjusted to pH 5.5 with polyphosphoric acid. The offal consists of trimmings taken from cod, haddock, and hake, excluding the heads.

The temperature of the mass is maintained at from 167° to 172°F. for 30 min. with mechanical stirring. It is filtered and the cake is washed with hot water. The filtrate and first washing are used to prepare soup extract. Washing is continued until filtrates are almost colorless. Washings are then discarded. The yield of 100 parts of ground offal is 43 parts of press-cake containing approximately 56% water.

(b) *Isopropanol Extraction of Oil and Water from Press-Cake.*—Iso-propanol is used to extract fat and water from the press-cake in the follow-ing two steps: (1) the press-cake is suspended in double its volume of isopropanol and is refluxed for 15 min., then the entire mass is filtered hot, yielding a filter cake and a filtrate consisting of isopropanol in which is dissolved most of the fat and water, and (2) the press-cake is washed with double its volume of hot isopropanol and the washed cake is screened, dried, and ground.

The screenings consist of coarser particles, which are principally skin and bones, comprising 35% of the original dry material. The residual iso-propanol is removed under vacuum.

The yield from 100 parts of original offal is ten parts of finished fish flour. The isopropanol is recovered by distillation and is re-used. The triglycerides, as well as the phospholipides, are extracted by the isopropanol.

It has been pointed out earlier (see page 214) that a nutritionally low-quality protein is obtained when fish offal is used as the raw material for the preparation of a fish protein concentrate.

Properties of Edible Fish Flour Produced by Guttman and Vandenheuvel (1957).—The fish flour is practically odorless and tasteless with a grayish-white to white color. It keeps well in storage. Analysis yields the following results: moisture, 2–3%; ash, 2–5% (mostly calcium phosphate); lipids (including fats), negligible; and protein, 94 to 98% (dry, ash-free basis).

This process also yields two by-products. Their yield calculated on the basis of 100 lb. of offal is approximately as follows: bone meal and skin, 5.2%; solids (soup extract) from acid washings, 3.7%.

A Chemical Method for Determining the Available Lysine Content

A chemical method (Pritchard. *et al.* 1964) can be used to measure the available, or utilizable, lysine content in animal protein concentrates, applied to livestock rations, which compares favorably, from the standpoint of time consumption, to the biological tests. This method is based upon a reaction of lysine with fluorodinitrobenzene.

M.I.T.—UNICEF Investigations of Fish Protein Concentrate Production

Extensive research on fish protein concentrate production was conducted, several years ago, at the Massachusetts Institute of Technology in the Department of Food Technology, which was then headed by the late Professor B. E. Proctor. It was a joint effort, involving the United Nations International Children's Emergency Fund (UNICEF), the Food and Agricultural Organization (FAO), and M.I.T. This study was completed in 1961.

A portion of this work was summarized by Pariser and Odland (1963). In that article is recorded their evaluations of several processing methods and equipment and results of an investigation of the effects of the processing variables on the final product.

The raw materials selected for these experiments were as follows: (1) various types of fish meal produced commercially on the eastern coast of the United States; (2) whole fresh fish obtained locally, such as cod, haddock, pollack, and mackerel; (3) fish meal produced commercially from Chilean hake (merluzza); and (4) fresh frozen and degutted merluzza.

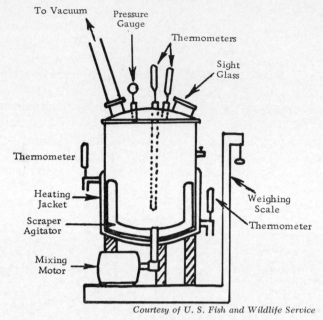

Courtesy of U. S. Fish and Wildlife Service

FIG. 48.   VACUUM DEHYDRATOR

Equipment Used in These Investigations.—The principal equipment used in evaluating several processing methods were as follows: (1) a 40-liter vacuum dehydrator (Fig. 48), used both for vacuum drying and for simultaneous dehydration and extraction, and (2) M.I.T.-UNICEF pilot plant (Fig. 49), in which was a self-contained unit, consisting of a 40-liter extraction vessel, equipped to carry out the entire operation, e.g., solvent extraction, solvent recovery, etc.

They also investigated the following dehydration methods: (1) vacuum drying in oil suspension (Fig. 50), and (2) drying by azeotropic distillation.

Tentative Specifications for Fish Protein Concentrates (Edible Fish Flour and Fish Meal)[5].—The following criteria are considered important to guarantee the quality of fish protein concentrates (edible fish flour and fish meal) for human consumption.

1. *Raw Materials:* The various types of fish protein concentrates (A, B, and C) may be prepared from the same material. This material need not be confined to fish flesh, but could include whole fish, deheaded and degutted fish, or trimmings of suitable type. In all cases, it should be in a condition fit for human consumption.

---

[5] Courtesy of the Food and Agriculture Organization of the United Nations.

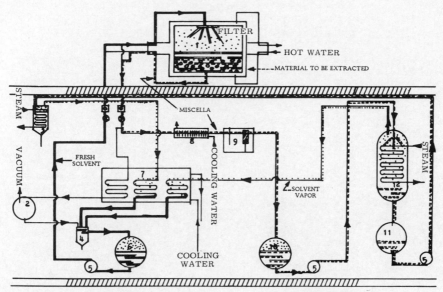

Legend: 1. Extractor, pressure jacketed, with manhole, equipped
          with two filters.
     2. Concentrator for removing solvent from extracted
          residue.
     3. Hexane/water separator.
     4. Vacuum tank.
     5. Pumps.

      6. Fresh solvent tank.
      7. Water-cooled coil condenser.
      8. Water-cooled miscella cooler.
      9. Miscella settling and filtering tank.
     10. Miscella tank.
     11. Residue receiving tank.
     12. Evaporator.

Courtesy of U. S. Fish and Wildlife Service

FIG. 49.   TYPICAL FLOW SHEET OF M.I.T.-UNICEF PILOT PLANT

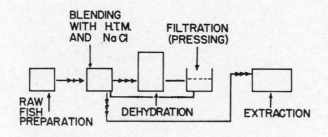

Legend:
▸▸▸ fresh fish.
——— dehydrated fresh fish.

Courtesy of U. S. Fish and Wildlife Service

FIG. 50.   FLOW DIAGRAM FOR THE HEAT-TRANSFER METHOD
OF DEHYDRATION

2. *Processing:* The processing methods which could be used to produce types A, B, and C of fish protein concentrates need not be specified in detail. However, sanitary precautions ordinarily applied in producing human food must be observed in the handling of the fish from catch to end of processing.

3. *Production Specifications:*

	Type A	Type B	Type C
(a) Protein Nx6.25			
Protein content (at 10% moisture content)	Minimum 67.5%	Minimum 65%	Minimum 60%
Pepsin digestibility	Minimum 92%	Minimum 92%	Minimum 92%
Available lysine	Minimum 6.5% of the protein	Minimum 6.5% of the protein	Minimum 6.5% of the protein
(b) Moisture	Maximum 10%	Maximum 10%	Maximum 10%
(c) Fat content	Maximum 0.75%	Maximum 3%	Maximum 10%
(d) Chloride	Maximum 1.5%	Maximum 1.5%	Maximum 2%
(e) Silica	Maximum 0.5%	Maximum 0.5%	Maximum 0.5%

4. *Odor and Taste:* Type A should have no more than a faint odor and taste: when wetted with boiling water in a closed container. No specifications can be made for types B and C since they will show a wide range of odors and flavors.

5. *Storage Stability:* Type A, after six months storage at 80°F. (27°C); and when packed in a hermetically-sealed container, should exhibit no significant deterioration as judged by the development of off-flavors or by loss in protein quality as shown by digestibility and available lysine values appreciably below the specific minima.

In types B and C the requirements are the same for protein quality, but no specification is possible for the development of off-flavors.

6. *Bacteriology:* Type A should be free from *Enterococci, Salmonella/Shigella,* coagulase-positive *Staphylococci* and clostridia, and have a total bacterial plate count at 98.6°F. of not more than 10,000 per gram.

For types B and C the same requirements would apply for *Enterococci, Salmonella/Shigella,* coagulase-positive *Staphylococci,* and pathogenic anaerobes.

7 *Safety:* No additives, preservatives, or harmful solvent residues should be present in type A. Safety tests on at least one species of animal should be done according to the requirements of the appropriate official agency of the country where the product is to be used.

Types B and C should contain no solvent residues and no substances such as antioxidants, or flavorings should be added unless permitted by the consuming country. Safety tests with animals are required as with product A.

8. *Methods of Analysis:* (a) The fat content of Types A and B should be determined by extraction for six hours with boiling ethanol or chloroform-methanol (2:1). The fat content of Type C should be determined by extraction with ethyl ether for six hours in a Soxhlet apparatus. (b) Available lysine should be determined by the method of Carpenter. (c) Prior to large-scale testing and, if accepted for mass feeding trials, at reasonable intervals thereafter, biological evaluation of protein quality would be required. The level should be specified.

Other problems remain to be dealt with when the necessary information is available. Thus there are problems of dispersability, grittiness, and volatility, particularly for products of Type A. There are problems of packaging. The suggestions above have been made in an effort to combine technological feasibility with adequate nutritional and palatability requirements.

It is recognized that the existing methods of analysis are, in many cases, inadequate and diverse procedures are employed in different countries for products of these types. It is to be hoped that studies currently underway on methods of analysis will soon be completed in order that they may be used for the necessary determinations as outlined in those specifications.

The first draft of the above specifications was prepared by a Working Party at the FAO International Meeting of Fish Meal, Rome, March 1961. In June 1961, the specifications were reviewed and slightly amended by the WHO/FAO/UNICEF Protein Advisory Group. The specifications were further discussed by the Interim Panel of Experts on Fish Meal and Fish Flour for Human Consumption which was convened by the Director-General of FAO at the end of the FAO Conference on Fish in Nutrition, Washington, September 1961.

The tentative specifications given above are a composite of the views expressed at the above meetings.

Derse Values for VioBin FPC-Cereal Mixtures.—The VioBin Corporation found that when their fish protein concentrate is mixed with cereals, the mixture, when measured by the Derse assay, always gives better results than milk in feeding tests with farm animals. This was true for the defatted nondeodorized as well as for the defatted deodorized product. FPC-rice mixtures produced still better results.

It is the author's opinion that the reason for the good results obtained with the FPC-rice mixtures is the presence of high biological-value proteins in rice, even though the amount of protein is relatively small. Since both FPC and rice possess protein of high biological value, a mixture of them should be highly nutritious.

Table 23 contains Derse assay results of fish flour-rice mixtures.

General Remarks on Fish Protein Concentrate Production

It has been estimated that at least one third of the world's population, or a billion (one thousand million) people, go to bed hungry.

Furthermore, of the total world population of over three billion people, six hundred million, located mostly in Europe and North America, consume most of the world's presently harvested protein. This means that approximately two billion people now lack sufficient protein (U. S. Dept. of Agriculture, Fish and Wildlife Service Report No. 4).

The impact of hunger and malnutrition on the history of the human race is of tremendous proportions. It was the hungry hordes of Asia that

TABLE 23

DERSE ASSAY RESULTS OF VIOBIN FISH FLOUR-RICE MIXTURE

Group	Source of Protein	Average Gm. Gain	P.E.R.
	4 Weeks Assay No. 345		
1	Standard Casein	71.1	2.63
2	Fish Flour	59.7	2.43
3	Fish Flour + Rice/10 + 90 parts	119.3	3.42
4	Fish Flour	67.6	2.81
5	Fish Flour + Rice/10 + 90 parts	111.6	3.31
6	Fish Flour	63.9	2.58
7	Fish Flour + Rice/10 + 90 parts	128.7	3.58
	$3^1/_2$ Weeks Assay No. 346		
1	Standard Casein	75.5	2.77
2	Fish Flour	71.6	2.68
3	Fish Flour + Rice/10 + 90 parts	136.4	3.38
4	Fish Flour	65.7	2.57
5	Fish Flour + Rice/10 + 90 parts	129.4	3.37
6	Fish Flour	51.4	2.21
7	Fish Flour + Rice/10 + 90 parts	137.1	3.46

Courtesy of the VioBin Corp., Monticello, Ill.

wiped out the once mighty Roman Empire. Hunger has been one of the main underlying causes of the many revolutions of the first half of the twentieth century that resulted in the downfall of many empires.

Every effort should, therefore, be made to prevent recurrences of sieges of hunger in any part of the world. We are "our brothers' keepers." In this jet age, the well-being of our antipodes is almost as important to us as the well-being of our next door neighbors.

It is with such benevolent thoughts in mind that most of the countries, the world over, have seen fit to establish the three important organizations: the United Nations Children's Fund; the Food and Agriculture Organization; and the World Health Organization. A discussion on fish protein concentrate, would, therefore be incomplete without mentioning the vital role that these three international organizations are playing and the important contributions that they are making in solving this global problem.

These organizations, the names of which are abbreviated as UNICEF, FAO, and WHO, respectively, have "joined hands" with the U. S. Department of the Interior, Fish and Wildlife Service, in an all-out effort to solve the various problems involved in the perfection of fish protein concentrate manufacture on a worldwide scale. With such powerful teamwork we may expect that this vital world problem will be solved in a manner that will satisfy even the most stringent food manufacturing regulations. With a well-fed and well-nourished world population, many national and international differences could be amicably resolved at the conference table.

CONCLUDING REMARKS

Much progress has been made in the development of processes for the manufacture of the various fishery by-products described in this text, but much remains to be done. The raw material for these products is plentiful and the demand for the finished products is constantly increasing with the expanding world population. Universities, government laboratories, and experienced individual researchers are ready to help explore, perfect, and exploit this important phase of the bounties of the sea. There is, however, one essential element missing in the effort to carry out these vital programs, namely, decisive guiding action.

BIBLIOGRAPHY

ALLISON, H. C. 1962. Protein from the sea. Bull. Atomic Scientist 18, 42–43.

BARTON-WRIGHT, E. C. 1952. The Microbiological Assay of the Vitamin B Complex and Amino Acids. 1st Edition. Pitman Publishing Corp., New York.

BENDER, A. E., and HAIZELDEN, S. 1957. Biological value of proteins of a variety of fish meals. Brit. J. Nutr. 11, 42.

BEVERIDGE, J. M. R. 1948. The nutritive value of marine products. XVI. The biological value of fish flesh proteins. J. Fisheries Res. Board Can. 7, No. 1, 35–49.

BUREAU OF COMMERCIAL FISHERIES. 1960. Fish flour is primarily a protein concentrate—not a substitute for grain flour. Com. Fisheries Rev. 22, No. 6, 13–14.

DOUGLAS, P. 1962A. Fish protein concentrate. Congressional Record 1664–1665.

DOUGLAS, P. 1962B. Fish protein concentrate. Congressional Record 8752.

DREOSTI, G. M., and VAN DER MERWE, R. P. 1956. Factors influencing rate of extraction. Tenth Annual Report of the Fishing Industry Research Institute, Cape Town, South Africa, 34–36.

EVANS, R. J., CARVER, J. S., and DRAPER, C. I. 1944. A comparison of the chemical protein quality index with the gross protein value of fish protein concentrates. Washington Agr. Expt. Sta. Pullman. Arch. Biochem. 3, No. 3, 337–343.

FINN, D. B. 1954. The sea and world food supplies. Nutr. Abstr. and Rev. 24, 487.

FOOD and AGR. ORGAN. OF THE U. N. 1954. FAO's work on the utilization of fish meal in human diet. Fisheries Bull. 7, No. 3, 120–122.

FOOD and AGR. ORGAN. OF THE U. N. NUTR. DIV. 1958. The use of fish flours as human food. Proc. Nutrition Soc. 17, No. 2.

FOOD AND AGR. ORGAN. OF THE U. N. 1961. Tentative specifications for fish protein concentrates. Proceedings of FAO International Conference on Fish in Nutrition. September, Washington, D. C.

FOUGERE, H. 1961. Fish flour-technological developments in Canada. Proceedings of FAO International Conference on Fish in Nutrition. Washington, D. C.

GOMEZ, F. RAMOS–GALVAN, R., CRAVIOTO, J., FRANK, S., and LABARDINI I. 1958. Studies on the use of deodorized fish flour in malnutrition. Boletín Médico del Hospital Infantil. *15*, 485–494.

GRAHAM, G. G., BAERTL, J. M., and CORDANO, A. 1962. Evaluation of fish flour in the treatment of infantile malnutrition. Fish in Nutrition: Protein 271–274.

GRUENING, E. L. 1962. A positive program for fish protein concentrate research and development. Congressional Record. 15033–15034.

GUTTMAN, A., and VANDENHEUVEL, F. A. 1957. Production of edible fish protein (fish flour) from cod and haddock. Fisheries Res. Board Can., Technol. Sta. Progr. Rept. Atlantic Coast Sta. No. *67*, 29–31, Halifax, N. S.

HANNESSON, G. 1961. Fish flour–technological developments in Iceland. Proceedings of FAO International Conference on Fish in Nutrition. Washington, D. C.

HARRIS, R. S. 1964. Personal communication. Cambridge, Mass.

HINNERS, S. W., and SCOTT, H. M. 1960. A bio-assay for determining the nutritional adequacy of protein supplements for chick growth. Poultry Sci. *39*, 176–183.

INDO-PACIFIC FISHERIES COUNCIL, FAO. 1957. South Africa fish flour used for the enrichment of bread. Current Affairs Bull. No. *19*, 11.

IRVING, J. T., SMUTS, D. B., and SOHN, E. G. 1952. The biological value and true digestibility of the proteins contained in whitefish flour, the standard loaf and standard loaf supplemented by whitefish. South African Med. J. *26*, 206–207.

KEITH, H. 1961A. Fish flour. Congressional Record, May 18, A4542–A4543.

KEITH, H. 1961B. Fish and nutrition. Congressional Record, Sept. 23, A7701–A7703.

KEITH, H. 1961C. U. S. Studies fish flour use to aid undernourished. Congressional Record, Sept. 26, A7787–A7788.

LANHAM, W. B., JR., and LEMON, M. M. 1938. Nutritive value for growth of some proteins of fishery products. Food Res. *3*, No. 5, 549–553.

LEVIN, E. 1959. Fish flour and fish meal by azeotropic solvent processing. Food Technol. *13*, No. 2, 132–135.

LEVIN, E. 1961. Brief on fish flour with references. VioBin Corp., Monticello, Ill. 21 p.

LEVIN, E. 1963. Personal communication. VioBin Corp., Monticello, Ill.

LEVIN, E. 1964. Personal communication. Monticello, Ill.

LEVIN, E., and FINN, R. K. 1955. Process for dehydrating and defatting tissues at low temperature. Chem. Eng. Progr. *51*, No. 5, 223–225.

McINTYRE, T. M. 1957. Variability in the nutritive value of fish meals for growing chickens. Can. J. Animal Sci., *37*, 58.

MOHANTY, G. B., and ROY, A. B. 1955. Hydrolyzed fish protein from the flesh of waste fish. Science *121*, 41–42.

MORRISON, A. B., SABRY, Z. I., and MIDDLETON, E. J. 1962. Factors influencing the nutritional value of fish flour; effects of extraction with chloroform or ethylene dichloride. J. Nutr. *77*, 97–104.

NATIONAL ACADEMY OF SCIENCES, NATIONAL RESEARCH COUNCIL. 1962. Report of temporary committee on questions submitted by Secretary of Interior concerning fish protein concentrate.

NEILANDS, J. B., and ELVEHJEM, C. A.   1950.   What is the nutritive value of fish.   Food Can. *10*, No. 5, 32–36.

OLDEN, J. H.   1960.   Fish flour for human consumption.   Com. Fisheries Rev. *22*, No. 1, 12–18.

PARISER, E. R.   1961.   Fish flour—technological developments in the U. S. A. Proceedings of FAO International Conference on Fish in Nutrition.   Washington, D. C.

PARISER, E. R.   1962.   Fish protein concentrate—a high quality animal protein. Com. Fisheries Rev. *24*, No. 5, 1–5.

PARISER, E. R.   1963.   History and present status of fish protein concentrate manufacture.   Proceedings of the Meeting of the Scientific Advisory Group, National Academy of Sciences, May.   Washington, D. C.

PARISER, E. R., and ODLAND, E.   1963.   M.I.T.-Unicef studies on the production of fish protein concentrate for human consumption.   Com. Fisheries Rev. *25*, No. 10, 6–13.

PIKE, O.   1961.   The answer to a great dietary need.   Congressional Record A7630.

PRETORIUS, R. J., and WEHMEYER, A. S.   1964.   An assessment of nutritive value of fish flour in the treatment of convalescent kwashiorkor patients.   Am. J. Clin. Nutr. *14*, No. 3, 147–155.

PRITCHARD, H., McLARNON, J., and McGILLIVRAY, R.   1964.   The available lysine content of animal protein concentrate as determined by reaction with fluorodinitrobenzene.   J. Sci. Food and Agr. *15*, 690–695.

RAND, N. T., and ASSOCIATES.   1958.   Biological evaluation of fish products for protein quality.   Proceedings of 47th annual meeting of the Poultry Science Assn., Ithaca, New York.

RAND, N. T., COLLINS, V. K., VARNER, D. S., and MOSSER, J. D.   1958.   Studies with unidentified growth factors in fish products.   Poultry Sci. *37*, 1236.

SALTONSTALL, L.   1961A.   Fish flour fills need.   Congressional Record 7753.

SALTONSTALL, L.   1961B.   Fish flour.   Congressional Record.   14447.   Contains summary and conclusions of three food scientists at the University of Illinois.

SALTONSTALL, L.   1961C.   The potential importance of fish flour.   Congressional Record.   19717–19718.

SCHIMKAT, U.   1955.   Dry protein from cheap small fish.   Deutsche Fischerei Zeitung *2*, 50.

SCRIMSHAW, N. S., and BRESSANI, R.   1960.   Vegetable protein mixtures for human consumption.   Proceedings Fifth Internat. Cong. on Nutr., Panel II, Washington, D. C.

SHENSTONE, F. S.   1953.   Egg white and yolk substitutes: Wiking Eiweiss Food Preserv. Quart. *13*, No. 3, 45–50.

SMALL, W. E.   1962.   More protein from the sea.   Sci. News Let. *82*, 87.

SMITH, B.   1961.   Fish flour.   Congressional Record.   7753–7754.

SURE, B.   1957.   The addition of small amounts of defatted fish flour to milled wheat flour, corn meal and rice.   J. Nutr. *61*, No. 4, 547–554.

SURE, B.   1958.   The addition of small amounts of defatted fish flour to whole yellow corn, whole wheat, whole and milled rye, grain sorghum and millet.   J. Nutr. *63*, No. 3, 409–416.

U. S. DEPT. OF THE INTERIOR, FISH AND WILDLIFE SERVICE.   1962.   Fish Protein Concentrate.   Report No. 1:   Past and present developments.

U. S. DEPT. OF THE INTERIOR, FISH AND WILDLIFE SERVICE. 1962. Fish Protein Concentrate. Report No. 2: The Resource.

U. S. DEPT. OF THE INTERIOR, FISH AND WILDLIFE SERVICE. 1962. Fish Protein Concentrate, Report No. 3: Hunger, Man and the Sea.

U. S. DEPT. OF THE INTERIOR, FISH AND WILDLIFE SERVICE. 1962. Fish Protein Concentrate. Report No. 4: Action Now . . . Operation Lifeline.

U. S. DEPT. OF THE INTERIOR, FISH AND WILDLIFE SERVICE. 1962. Fish Protein Concentrate. Report No. 5: Summary Lifeline of the Future.

VILLADOLID, D. V., and PIDLAOAN, N. A. 1954. Fish flour; cheap protein food for the masses. Manilla Bur. Fisheries.

VIOBIN CORPORATION. 1956. Fish flour-a review of progress. VioBin Corp., Monticello, Ill.

WILLIAMS, J. P., and MORRISON, F. B. 1944. Protein and vitamin supplements for growing and fattening pigs. Cornell Univ. Agr. Expt. Sta. Bull. No. 730, New York.

WILLIAMS, R. T. Editor. 1952. The biochemistry of fish. Biochem. Soc. Symposia No. 6. Cambridge University Press, New York City.

WILLMER, J. S. 1955. Evaluation of a sample of edible fish flour. Eighth Annual Report of the Fishing Industry Research Institute, Cape Town, South Africa, Apr. 1, 1954 to Mar. 31, 1955, 36.

WORSHAM, E. M., and LEVIN, E. 1950. Simultaneous defatting and dehydrating of fatty substances. U. S. Pat. 2,503,312. Apr. 11.

YOUNG, S. 1962. Fish protein concentrate. Congressional Record. 2900–2901.

Index

Sperm cells, fish, 110, 111
Squalene, occurrence, 80, 81
   structural formula, 81
   uses of, 81
Stearin, definition of, 181
Stickwater, definition of, 127
   treatment of, 131, 173
Strepogenin, 111
Swine feed, 201
Synergism among antioxidants, 157

T

Teleostomi or Teleost fishes, examples of,
   147
Thiaminase, effect on mink, 201
Tocopherols, 73, 158
Top dressings, 206
Trash fish, definition of, 198
Trypsin, activity of, 117
Tyrosine and its esters, 160

U

"Unknown growth factors," in fish meal,
   120
Unsaponifiable components of fish oils,
   69–81
Urea conversion into yeast, 202

V

Vacuum-steam distillation, 180
Vertical mill for grinding fish, 127, 128
Vibratory screen, 127
VioBin's fish protein concentrate, advantages of, 213, 214
   analysis of whole fish flour, 214
   cereal mixtures, Derse values, 221, 222
   compared to dried skim milk, 215
   nutritional evaluation, 214
   process of, 212–215

Vitamin A, antioxidants for, 73, *see also*
   Vitamin A_1, Vitamin A_2, and Vitamins A and D
   concentrate, recent developments, 87
   distribution of in a soupfin shark liver,
   60–61
   from fish liver oils, 47
   occurrence, 70, 71
   potency loss of, 155
   properties of, chemical and physical,
   72–74
     physiological, 69–72
   structural formula, 72
   synthetic, 47
Vitamin A_1, 72, *see also* Vitamin A
Vitamin A_2, 72
Vitamin B complex, from fish liver residue, 47
   in fish meal, 138
   production of concentrate, fish press-liquor, 87–89
   proteinaceous residue of fish levers, 89,
   90
   uses as food or feed, 88
Vitamin D, from fish liver oils, 47
   occurrence, 76
   produced by, 74
   properties of, chemical and physical, 75
     physiological, 74
Vitamins A and D, concentrates, 87
   preparation by adsorption, 86–87
   saponification, 86
   short-path distillation, 86
   stabilization, on dry carriers, 184
   in water dispersions, 184

W

Wet-reduction process, 127, 133, 165
   advantages and disadvantages, 135
     description in detail, 129–131
   for fish meal production, 127
World population, statistics of, 211